Imperial Creatures

Imperial Creatures

Humans and Other Animals in Colonial Singapore, 1819–1942

by

Timothy P. Barnard

NUS PRESS
SINGAPORE

© 2019 Timothy P. Barnard

Published by:

NUS Press
National University of Singapore
AS3-01-02, 3 Arts Link
Singapore 117569

Fax: (65) 6774-0652
E-mail: nusbooks@nus.edu.sg
Website: http://nuspress.nus.edu.sg

ISBN 978-981-3250-87-1 (paper)

National Library Board, Singapore Cataloguing in Publication Data

Name: Barnard, Timothy P., 1963–
Title: Imperial creatures: humans and other animals in colonial Singapore,
    1819–1942/by Timothy P. Barnard.
Description: Singapore: NUS Press, [2019] | Includes bibliographical references
    and index.
Identifier(s): OCN 1104119879 | ISBN 978-981-32-5087-1 (paperback)
Subject(s): LCSH: Human ecology--Singapore--History. | Singapore--History--
    Environmental aspects.
Classification: DDC 304.2095957--dc23

Cover image courtesy of the State Library of Victoria.

Printed by: Markono Print Media Pte Ltd

For the teachers and mentors
who have guided me:

William H. Frederick, Leonard Andaya,
David Hanlon, Tenas Effendy,
Henk Maier, O.W. Wolters,
and especially Barbara Watson Andaya.

Contents

List of Images   ix

Chapter 1:   Animals, Empire and Singaporean History   1

Chapter 2:   Taming an Island   16

Chapter 3:   Fauna in a Colonial Landscape   52

Chapter 4:   Defining Cruelty   103

Chapter 5:   Domestication, Regulation and Control of Dogs,   148
             and Other Animals

Chapter 6:   Markets, Proteins and the Public Abattoirs   192

Epilogue: The White Monkey   236

Acknowledgements   242

Bibliography   244

Index   259

List of Images

Front Cover: Australian troops in Singapore: Australian soldier
with a pet monkey on his shoulder, 1941.
Courtesy of the State Library of Victoria.

Back Cover: Detail from "A Menagerie Race in Singapore."
By John Charles Dollman. *The Graphic*, August 1881.
Courtesy of the National Archives of Singapore.

Map of Singapore   xii

Detail map of Singapore town   xiii

1.1:   Singapore as seen from the deck of British vessels soon   6
after East India Company officials first arrived to
establish a settlement. Sketch of the Land Round
Singapore Harbour 7 Feb 1819 (ADM 344/1307),
courtesy of the National Archives of Great Britain.

2.1:   White hunter with his assistants in front of Bukit Timah   33
Church, 1880. Photograph by John Edmund Taylor.
Courtesy of the Wellcome Collection.

2.2:   Illustration of a European visiting the Singapore Botanic   47
Gardens with domesticated dogs. Illustration by John
Edmund Taylor. Courtesy of the Wellcome Collection.

3.1:   Two race-going celebrities talk as a race horse is ridden   55
       past them, 1881. Illustration by John Edmund Taylor.
       Courtesy of the Wellcome Collection.

3.2:   A Singaporean family in the Singapore Botanic Gardens.   57
       Image from Lee Brothers Studio, courtesy of National
       Archives of Singapore.

3.3:   Malay bird seller. Illustrated London News Collection,   64
       courtesy of National Archives of Singapore.

3.4:   "The well-known dancing monkey, Singapore." Postcard   68
       from the early 20th century, courtesy of National
       Archives Singapore.

3.5:   Portrait of a modern Chinese woman, with her favorite   70
       pet, c. 1920. Image from Lee Brothers Studio, courtesy
       of National Archives of Singapore.

3.6:   Anna Brassey with a pangolin. Brassey, *A Voyage in the*   73
       "Sunbeam", p. 393.

3.7:   "A Menagerie Race at Singapore." By John Charles   80
       Dollman. *The Graphic*, August 1881. Courtesy of the
       National Archives of Singapore.

3.8:   Deformed hog fish, *Synanceia grossa*, Singapore.   86
       Illustration from Hardwicke and Gray, *Illustrations*
       of Indian Zoology. Courtesy of the New York Public
       Library.

3.9:   Inside the Raffles Museum, 1920s. Courtesy of National   92
       Archives of Singapore.

3.10: William Basapa with Apay. Image from Roland Braddell,   100
       The Lights of Singapore.

4.1:   Horse Gharry in late 19th-century Singapore. Courtesy   108
       of the Rijksmuseum, Amsterdam.

4.2:   Draught bullock, 1881. From the John Edmund Taylor   113
        Collection. Courtesy of the Wellcome Collection.

4.3:   Malay bullock cart. Courtesy of the New York Public   130
        Library.
4.4:   Map of the municipal boundaries, 1924. Courtesy of   134
        National Archives of Singapore.

4.5:   One of the last remaining horse gharries in Singapore,   144
        1930s. Courtesy of Cambridge University Digital
        Library.

5.1:   Dog killing notice from the *Government Gazette*,   155
        14 August 1884. CO276/15: "Government
        Notification, No. 345," p. 871.

6.1:   Market scene, 1890s. Courtesy of National Archives   196
        of Singapore.

6.2:   Poultry in baskets. Courtesy of the New York Public   198
        Library.

6.3:   The abattoir at Jalan Besar. Arshauk C. Galstaun   214
        Collection, courtesy of National Archives of Singapore.

7.1:   E.J.H. Corner with one of his botanical monkeys.   239
        Courtesy of the Cambridge University Digital Library.

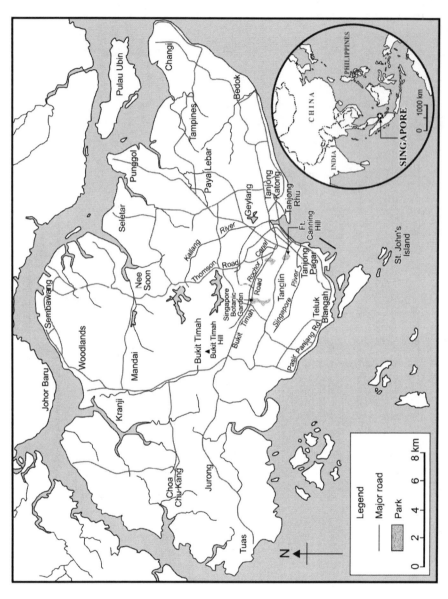

Map of Singapore

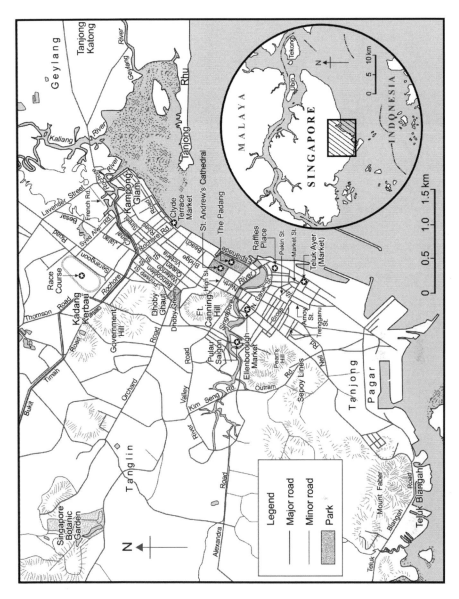

Detail map of Singapore town

CHAPTER ONE

Animals, Empire and Singaporean History

Sometime in the 14th century, according to tales passed down over generations, schools of swordfish (*Xiphias gladius*) attacked the residents of Singapore. One of the most remarkable aspects of this assault was that no one on land was safe. These aquatic animals hurled themselves on shore and speared those unlucky enough to have ventured near the sea. Many died; chaos reigned. According to the *Sulalat al-Salatin*, a canonical text from the region better known as the *Sejarah Melayu* or Malay Annals, "So great was the number of those killed by the swordfish that there was a panic and people ran hither and thither crying."[1]

The swordfish attack, according to the text, was a consequence of a suspicious leader who showed little concern for the populace (*rakyat*), a sign of potential problems in the trading enclave. Singapore was a prosperous port at the time, and it attracted an array of merchants and travelers. Among these visitors was a wandering religious scholar, named Tun Jana Khatib, who tried to gain the attention of the royal concubine. The ruler had the visitor executed for such behavior. This jealous and vengeful decision resulted in a curse being placed upon the island, which led to the extraordinary assault on Singaporeans. Witnessing the chaos that the swordfish had wrought, and fearing

---

[1] C.C. Brown (trans.), *Sejarah Melayu or Malay Annals* (Singapore: Oxford University Press, 1970), p. 40.

1

for his own well-being, the ruler ordered his followers to stand near the water to act as a barrier to protect the royal family. These people soon became further sacrificial victims. Realizing the folly of such an approach, a young boy offered an alternative. He suggested that banana trunks be used to line the shore. During the next attack, the piscine invaders speared themselves on the herbaceous plants, and residents then proceeded to club the fish to death. Singapore had been saved with an innovative solution to a problem. The young boy, however, now represented a potential challenge to the elite. He was too clever. Following the advice of his counselors, the ruler ordered the death of the person who had saved the society. "When the boy was executed the guilt of his blood laid on Singapore."[2]

This fable is one of the earliest accounts of Singapore. Originally existing as an oral tale, it was written down by at least the early 17th century, when it became an allegory to explain how a community of traders in the Straits of Melaka ultimately failed some two centuries earlier. It is part of a larger manuscript that emphasizes a core tenet of the trading culture that dominated the region for over a millennium: openness to outsiders. While the origins of the society lay with a mythically powerful ruler from Sumatra, known as Parameswara in some tales and Sang Nila Utama in others, prosperity came from its port, which was a vital link in the cosmopolitan trade that flowed through the region in the early 14th century. The society thrived for several generations, until the rulers began focusing on protecting their own interests by insulating themselves from outsiders and the knowledge they could bring to the community. Ancient Singapore was doomed, and the swordfish attack prophesied further troubles. Soon afterwards, the ruler and his *rakyat*, facing the attack of a Javanese fleet, fled up the coast of the Malay Peninsula and founded a new trade port in Melaka, and the tale of attacking fish became a metaphor employed to express local understandings of the political and social conditions that had presaged this migration.[3]

The legend best known as *Singapura Dilanggar Todak* (The Swordfish Attack on Singapore) represents some of the basic issues surrounding the recording of history in Southeast Asia, particularly in

---

[2] Brown (trans.), *Sejarah Melayu*, p. 40.
[3] Sophie Sim, "Fishy Tales: *Singapura Dilanggar Todak* as Myth and History in Singapore's Past," unpublished Master's Thesis, Department of History, National University of Singapore, 2005.

the era prior to colonial rule. Remembering the past was a process that wove together compelling narratives, facts, and the basic tenets of the society. The use of parables, a storytelling device much like ancient floods or epic battles have played in other traditions, allowed historians of the region to communicate information to a receptive audience in a manner in which the lessons would be remembered, becoming embedded in the collective conscious.[4] While exaggerations did occur, and details were forgotten, the key factor is that the tale was retold, and in the process core principles and lessons from the past were remembered.[5] It was an approach that made history in the region vibrant, and it involved the use of animals as a device to better understand Southeast Asia, and particularly ancient Singapore.

An Island in History

Although Singapore is over 700 square kilometers today, it was around 500 square kilometers historically. The island is a typical landmass in the larger Malay (or Indonesian) Archipelago, with the highest peak being a modest 130 meters above sea level, and its most remarkable bygone feature being a relatively small rock outcrop that was labeled the Dragon's Tooth, which enabled passing seafarers to orient themselves. Mangrove swamps lined most of its shores while further inland dense forest covered rolling hills for much of its history, particularly before the 19th century and the arrival of Western imperialism. This forest was one in which animals roamed, found shelter and food, lived and died.

Humans have been in Singapore alongside these animals for millennia. Living at the southern reaches of the Melaka Straits, a key trade route, these early residents began inhabiting the island as early as the Stone Age, as implements dating some 4,000 years have been

---

[4] Did swordfish attack Singapore? They most likely did not hurl themselves in a wave of mass suicide, although occasionally a report will appear in modern newspapers regarding a fish inadvertently propelling itself into the air and hitting a boat or unlucky fisherman. Anonymous, "Fisherman Struck by Swordfish," *New Straits Times*, 18 Feb. 2013, p. 31.

[5] This particular saga, with its allegorical lessons, continues to resonate in Singapore, where it is the subject of children's tales and theater productions. Sim, "Fishy Tales"; Henri Chambert-Loir, "The *Sulalat al-Salatin* as a Political Myth," *Indonesia*, 79 (2005): 131–60; Henk Maier, *We Are Playing Relatives: A Survey of Malay Writing* (Leiden: KITLV, 2004).

found on its shores.[6] Most scholars, nevertheless, posit the beginning of history in Singapore to the early 14th century, when it reached its precolonial peak of influence as a trade port with extensive connections to merchants and sailors from throughout the region. The dynamic and cosmopolitan nature of the community at that time has been proven through extensive archaeological discoveries as well as corroboration in Chinese traveler accounts and tales such as those of attacking swordfish.[7] After the inhabitants fled into the Straits and founded a new settlement at Melaka and subsequently Johor, Singapore continued to function as an important harbor serving this larger community. After an Acehnese raid in in the early 17th century destroyed the settlement, Singapore became a bit of a backwater. It was a place where legends, such as *Singapura Dilanggar Todak*, took place or the small remaining community reportedly raided ships. Occasionally, a Western trade company official would note its existence and even propose a fortification be placed there.[8]

While little remained of its glorious past as an ancient trade port by the 18th century, Singapore was located in the center of a dynamic region in a period of disruption preceding the imposition of colonial rule. It is during this long century that residents of communities in eastern Sumatra rose in rebellion against the state of Johor, which exercised sovereignty over Singapore, while new migrants from throughout the archipelago established communities in the immediate environs. Amidst this upheaval, despite sporadic mentions in records, Singapore remained mostly a forgotten place, a site of fables from the past. By the end of the century, Ilanun raiders from the Sulu Sea further disrupted the societies in the region with devastating raids, leaving the area ripe for expanding European powers fueled by the nascent Industrial Revolution. In the aftermath of this chaos, Singapore hosted a small community of plantation workers. Under the sovereignty of the Temenggong, a high official of the nearby Riau-Johor state that had

---

[6] M.W.F. Tweedie, "The Stone Age in Malaya," *Journal of the Malayan Branch of the Royal Asiatic Society* [hereafter JMBRAS] 26, 2 (1953): 69–70.

[7] John N. Miksic, *Singapore and the Silk Road of the Sea, 1300–1800* (Singapore: NUS Press, 2013).

[8] Peter Borschberg, *The Singapore and Melaka Straits: Violence, Security and Diplomacy in the 17th Century* (Singapore: NUS Press, 2010); Kwa Chong Guan and Peter Borschberg (eds.), *Studying Singapore Before 1800* (Singapore: NUS Press, 2018); Miksic, *Singapore and the Silk Road of the Sea*, pp. 204–8.

become a regional power during this turmoil, several hundred people began cultivating pepper and gambier by 1800. When Thomas Stamford Raffles landed on the banks of the Singapore River in January 1819, he met this community and a new era began. Imperialism, and its creatures, had arrived. These were forces that would completely transform a tropical island economically, socially and physically.[9]

The status of Singapore as the epicenter of the British imperial presence, as well as its relatively small size, makes it an interesting site for the study of imperialism, as well as the administration and maintenance of the space, which is essentially colonialism.[10] The intense focus that East India Company officials and later colonial government administrators placed on transforming the island meant it was a model for the hopes and desires they had for imperial rule. Accounts of this can be found in archival records stored in the United Kingdom and other countries, which exist alongside travelers' reports and literature that describe and detail developments on the island throughout the entire period. This is further supported by an active local newspaper industry that was also the locus of modern communication and technology in the port, all resulting in a range of sources that provide a fairly thorough description of the perspectives and goals of an outside economic and political force that took control over a Southeast Asian

---

[9] Timothy P. Barnard, *Multiple Centres of Authority: Society and Environment in Siak and Eastern Sumatra, 1674–1827* (Leiden: KITLV, 2003); Timothy P. Barnard, "Celates, Rayat-Laut, Pirates: The Orang Laut and their Decline in History," *Journal of the Malaysian Branch of the Royal Asiatic Society* 80, 2 (2007): 33–49; Koh Keng We, "Familiar Strangers and Stranger-Kings: Mobility, Diasporas, and the Foreign in the Eighteenth-Century Malay World," *Journal of Southeast Asian Studies* 48, 3 (2017): 390–413; James Francis Warren, *The Sulu Zone, 1768–1898: The Dynamics of External Trade, Slavery and Ethnicity in the Transformation of a Southeast Asian Maritime State* (Singapore: Singapore University Press, 1981); Marcus Langdon and Kwa Chong Guan, "Notes on 'Sketch of the Land Round Singapore Harbour, 7 February 1819'," *Journal of the Malaysian Branch of the Royal Asiatic Society* 83, 1 (2010): 1–7.

[10] Sean Kheraj emphasizes the role that the boundaries of a relatively "multi-species habitat" can play in providing a focus for material and research, with his own study of the urban space of Winnipeg, Canada in environmental history during a similar time period as this study. Sean Kheraj, "Animals and Urban Environments: Managing Domestic Animals in Nineteenth-Century Winnipeg," in *Eco-Cultural Networks and the British Empire: New Views on Environmental History*, ed. James Beattie, Edward Melillo and Emily O'Gorman (London: Bloomsbury, 2015), pp. 263–88.

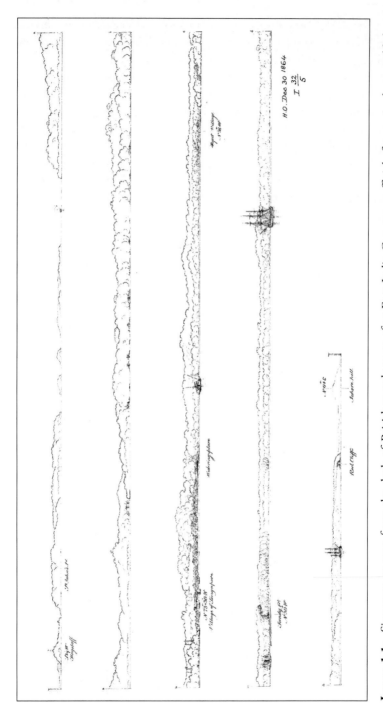

Image 1.1: Singapore as seen from the deck of British vessels soon after East India Company officials first arrived to establish a settlement. Sketch of the Land Round Singapore Harbour 7 Feb 1819 (ADM 344/1307), courtesy of the National Archives of Great Britain.

island. Ultimately, Singapore is a site of tales in which the reader can gain greater insight into numerous developments in the past, particularly during the era of imperialism.

The arrival of Western trade companies and governments also introduced new approaches to the recording of history in Southeast Asia. While Singapore had a precolonial past, the imperial transformation was so revolutionary—moving from a jungle-covered island of less than 1,000 inhabitants in 1819 to a deforested, vibrant commercial port of 800,000 by 1942—that any history prior to the 19th century was considered irrelevant, or at least difficult to incorporate into the master narrative as it seemed to have little importance for a modern, colonial emporium and its understanding of society. Imperialism had created a blank slate on which the goals and desires of the new inhabitants were recorded. Singapore's history now became one in which facts were found in archival records of foreign governments or corporations stored in distant capitals, not in legends that master storytellers passed down orally.[11]

The influence of imperialism on the development of historiography, and a general historical understanding of the past, in Singapore has resulted in a focus on the administrative decisions of great men, an approach that is framed rather rigidly by those in power, whether it be the merchants of a trade company, colonial administrators or even the post-independence national government. The actions and decisions of these great men thus become the key element for understanding the past and what is considered to be germane. This would be an apt description of much of the written history of Singapore, a place in which empire and nation are often intertwined and retold in increasingly involute detail and research becomes an expedition into factuality instead of intent and result. The most conspicuous example of the focus on empirical, positivist history of the island is C.M. Turnbull's *A History of Singapore*, which has gone through numerous editions and has even

---

[11] While it was the focus of a short debate in the 1980s, most historians of Singapore simply continued to use these sources in a fairly rigid manner to follow the traditional, empiricist narrative, particularly for the colonial era. Anthony Milner, "Colonial Records History: British Malaya," *Kajian Malaysia* 4, 2 (1986): 1–18; Yeoh Kim Wah, "The Milner Version of British Malayan History: A Rejoinder," *Kajian Malaysia* 5, 1 (1987): 1–28 Karl Hack, "Framing Singapore's History," in *Studying Singapore's Past: C.M. Turnbull and the History of Modern Singapore*, ed. Nicholas Tarling (Singapore: NUS Press, 2012), pp. 17–49; Miksic, *Singapore and the Silk Road of the Sea*; Timothy P. Barnard, *Raja Kecil dan Mitos Pengabsahanya* (Pekanbaru: Pusat Pengajian Melayu, Universitas Islam, 1994).

merited a separate study that discusses its impact on historiographical trends in the modern nation state. While not all scholarship of the society fits the rigid, political approach that Turnbull represents, with the work of Jim Warren on the social lives of rickshaw coolies and prostitutes being the most prominent exception, most studies of the Singaporean past simply fit into an imperial framework that mines trivia to recount the political and economic expansion of Western powers and ultimately an independent national government.[12]

Outside of traditional Singaporean historiography, however, numerous scholars throughout the world have been employing multi-disciplinary frameworks over the past few decades to the study of history. Much of this began in the 1960s and 1970s when historians began to provide new perspectives of the past as they asked different questions from archival materials, as well as employed non-archival sources, to move beyond a rigid consideration of politics, economics and military endeavors when seeking to understand the multilayered influences that have played in the development of societies throughout the world. These historians, loosely grouped under the rubric of "new cultural history," soon came to influence the study of histories outside the nation state. While this "imperial turn," as Durba Ghosh has pointed out, may have become a many-headed monster that many believe is exasperating, others employed such approaches to take the study of the past in a variety of interesting directions, as it allowed for diverse and insightful studies on a wide range of subjects and perspectives.[13] In Singaporean historiography such an approach is relatively unexplored, although it has resulted in some interesting studies of topics such as the colonial prison system or the role that underclass migrants have played in the development of the society.[14]

---

[12] C.M. Turnbull, *A History of Modern Singapore, 1819–2005* (Singapore: NUS Press, 2008); Nicholas Tarling (ed.), *Studying Singapore's Past: C.M. Turnbull and the History of Modern Singapore* (Singapore NUS Press, 2012); James Francis Warren, *Rickshaw Coolie: A People's History of Singapore, 1880–1940* (Singapore: NUS Press, 2003); James Francis Warren, *Ah Ku and Karayuki-san: Prostitution in Singapore, 1870–1940* (Singapore: NUS Press, 2003).

[13] Durba Ghosh, "Another Set of Imperial Turns?," *American Historical Review* 117, 3 (2012): 772–93; Lynn Hunt, *The New Cultural History* (Berkeley, CA: University of California Press, 1989).

[14] Anoma Pieris, *Hidden Hands and Divided Landscapes: A Penal History of Singapore's Plural Society* (Honolulu: University of Hawai'i Press, 2009); John Solomon, *A Subaltern History of the Indian Diaspora in Singapore: Gradual Disappearance of Untouchability, 1872–1965* (New York, NY: Routledge, 2016).

This work is an attempt to apply these new perspectives to explore the history of animals in Singapore to better understand how the imposition of colonial rule transformed an island. Such an approach with unique subject matter allows for a reconsideration of the imperial past in Southeast Asia, and particularly Malaya and Singapore, that incorporates a variety of multidisciplinary approaches ranging from zoology to cultural studies. The fauna of Singapore, and how they were perceived, regulated, domesticated and even slaughtered, thus become a vehicle to better understand the expansion of imperialism on the island, which allows for greater insight into issues of governance, economics, the environment and society during a period in which external, transformative ideologies of control were imposed. While the usual sources—archival reports, newspaper accounts, and traveler's tales—from the period are employed, such an approach allows for a deeper consideration of the material. Much like the swordfish that attacked ancient Singaporeans, animals and their relationship to humans can act as a metaphor for how we can interpret the past on a small island, and the forces of imperialism that shaped the society on it.

Animals and Empire

The interaction of humans and animals is one of the key experiences in history.[15] The domestication of animals and the harnessing of their power for cultivation of the land and the provision of steady supplies of food created civilizations, while the development and reinforcement of control and differences helped separate the civilized from the savage. As humans moved into new lands for discovery and conquest, animals accompanied them. Pigs rapidly populated islands, providing protein for the new settlers; horses and cattle altered agriculture, travel and landscapes; rats carried disease. These are just a few of the numerous

---

[15] It needs to be clarified that while humans are a type of animal, non-humans will be referred to in this work as animals for the sake of clarity and simplicity. There are numerous works that discuss the implications of this decision, although Harriet Ritvo and Joyce Chaplin—as well as a series of articles in the December 2013 issue of the journal *History and Theory*—provide good summaries of the arguments. Harriet Ritvo, "On the Animal Turn," *Dædalus*, 136 (2007): 118–22; Joyce E. Chaplin, "Can the Nonhuman Speak?: Breaking the Chain of Being in the Anthropocene," *Journal of the History of Ideas* 78, 4 (2017): 509–29; Erica Fudge, "Milking Other Men's Beasts," *History and Theory* 52, 4 (2013): 13–28.

species that moved alongside humans, transforming societies and continents, and creating histories.[16]

The study of the historical relationship between humans and animals in academic discourse—often referred to as human-animal studies or animal studies—is relatively young, much like new cultural history, having only become a focus of scholarship in the late 20th century. In this regard it is part of larger trends in which traditional disciplines have used a broader range of tools and approaches to understand the development of societies and how we understand them. The earliest contributions to the subfield reflected how illuminating such an approach could be, providing new insights into a variety of issues, with the work of Alfred Crosby on the environmental factors assisting the expansion of Europe in the previous millennium and the role that animals played in the Victorian Age in Britain by Harriet Ritvo leading the way.[17] These pioneering studies promoted the use of a host of multidisciplinary material from zoology to philosophy in an innovative manner to ask unconventional questions while interpreting a range of historical sources. The result has been a wide variety of publications that focus on topics ranging from how the extinction of native species in America led to racial anxieties and conservation to the development of zoological gardens.[18] In each case, animals provide a focus for the consideration of the material.[19]

---

[16] Alfred Crosby, *Ecological Imperialism: The Biological Expansion of Europe, 900–1900* (Cambridge: Cambridge University Press, 1986); Virginia DeJohn Anderson, *Creatures of Empire: How Domestic Animals Transformed Early America* (Oxford: Oxford University Press, 2004).

[17] Crosby, *Ecological Imperialism*; Harriet Ritvo, *The Animal Estate: The English and Other Creatures in the Victorian Age* (Cambridge, Mass: Harvard University Press, 1987); Aaron Skabelund, "Animals and Imperialism: Recent Historiographical Trends," *History Compass* 11, 10 (2013): 801–7.

[18] Miles A. Powell, *Vanishing America: Species Extinction, Racial Peril, and the Origins of Conservation* (Cambridge, MA: Harvard University Press, 2016); Nigel Rothfels, *Savages and Beasts: The Birth of the Modern Zoo* (Baltimore, MD: Johns Hopkins University Press, 2002); Susan Nance, "Introduction," in *The Historical Animal*, ed. Susan Nance (Syracuse, NY: Syracuse University Press, 2015), p. 3.

[19] When focusing on the relationship between humans and animals in the humanities, one of the key considerations is whether animals can be self-contained objects of study. Do they have their own history, or are they simply vehicles for understanding the human condition? It is my conclusion that while discussions and descriptions can focus on behavior and biological similarities of animals, humans ultimately observe and mediate this process. Animals thus are not

The study of human-animal history has primarily concentrated on developments in North America and Europe, although it has slowly become the subject of studies in other regions of the world.[20] In Southeast Asia, Peter Boomgaard and Greg Bankoff initiated such research by focusing on individual animals in Indonesia and the Philippines respectively, while encouraging others to consider the application of the approach across the region. Robert Cribb has also led a team that focused on how perceptions of orangutans in society have shaped their treatment and presentation in Southeast Asia and globally. Boomgaard has been particularly influential as the author of a monograph exploring the role that tigers have played in the archipelago, as well as the leader of a research group based in Leiden, the Netherlands that focused on the environmental history of island Southeast Asia. Other works, such as that of Jonathan Saha on elephants in Burma and my own interest in the Singaporean past and Komodo dragons, have recently contributed to a growing interest in animal history in the region.[21]

---

given their own autonomy in this work. While this can be perceived as "human supremacism" or exceptionalism, this decision has been made in light of the fact that humans are the arbitrators and interpreters of the past portrayed in this work. Brett L. Walker, "Animals and the Intimacy of History," *History and Theory* 52, 4 (2013): 45–67; Susan J. Pearson and Mary Weismantel, "Does 'The Animal' Exist?: Towards a Theory of Social Life with Animals," in *Beastly Natures: Animals, Humans, and the Study of History*, ed. Dorothee Brantz (Charlottesville, VA: University of Virginia Press, 2010), pp. 17–37; Nance, "Introduction"; Chaplin, "Can the Nonhuman Speak?"; Harriet Ritvo, "Animal Planet," *Environmental History* 9, 2 (2004): 204–20; Erica Fudge, "A Left-Handed Blow: Writing the History of Animals," in *Representing Animals*, ed. Nigel Rothfels (Bloomington, IN: Indiana University Press, 2002), pp. 3–18.

[20] Recent exceptions from Asia include Ian Jared Miller, *The Nature of Beasts: Empire and Exhibition at the Tokyo Imperial Zoo* (Berkeley, CA: University of California Press, 2013); Julie E. Hughes, *Animal Kingdoms: Hunting, the Environment, and Power in Indian Princely States* (Cambridge, MA: Harvard University Press, 2013).

[21] Peter Boomgaard, *Frontiers of Fear: Tigers and People in the Malay World, 1600–1950* (New Haven, Conn.: Yale University Press, 2001); Peter Boomgaard, Freek Colombijn, and David Henley (ed), *Paper Landscapes: Explorations in the Environmental History of Indonesia* (Leiden: KITLV Press, 1997); Greg Bankoff, "*Bestia Incognita*: The Horse and Its History in the Philippines, 1880–1930." *Anthrozoös*, 17, 1, 2004: 3–25; Greg Bankoff and Sandra Swart (ed.), *Breeds of Empire: The "Invention" of the Horse in Southeast Asia and Africa, 1500–1950* (Copenhagen: NIAS Press, 2007); Robert Cribb, Helen Gilbert and Helen Tiffin, *Wild Man of Borneo: A Cultural History of the Orangutan* (Honolulu, HI: University of

Much of the work at the intersection of human-animal studies in Southeast Asia has focused on charismatic megafauna, such as elephants, tigers, or orangutans. The celebrated status of these animals even plays an important role in the ability of researchers to study them, as the mere sighting of one deserved a report or comment in the records, while their conservation also became an issue for consideration.[22] In contrast, this work focuses on a wide variety of relatively uncharismatic and common animals, with considerable attention given to dogs, cattle and horses. As these creatures rarely appeared in reports when they were simply sighted, their presence in accounts usually occurred following an act of violence. After all, this work began with the spearing of many humans along a shore, and it will end with the death of a single animal in a cage. The nature of such activity is usually why animals appear within the records, as such a spasm of violence merited a note. The role of violence not only exposes some of the basic elements in this human-animal relationship but also that of imperialism.

The ability of an outside entity, whether a company or government, to enforce its power over a land and its inhabitants is an activity that is inherently violent. The tremendous transformation of global societies that took place during the era of high imperialism, in the 19th and early 20th centuries, involved the development of new forms of economic, political and military power. These were rooted in European (and for Singapore, mainly British) understandings of how societies should be managed and administered, resulting in the replacement of systems of governance, economy and social interaction in a process that involved coaxing, regulating and controlling, as well as occasionally outright force. Imperialism was a series of power relationships. The imposition of these relationships was a process that was often complex and messy, and it led to the creation of new communities throughout the world, one of which was the colonial port city of Singapore. The forms of control that allowed this to occur were exerted

---

Hawai'i Press, 2014); Jonathan Saha, "Among the Beasts of Burma: Animals and the Politics of Colonial Sensibilities, c. 1840–1940," *Journal of Social History* 48, 4 (2015): 910–32; Timothy P. Barnard (ed.) *Nature Contained: Environmental Histories of Singapore* (Singapore: NUS Press, 2014); "Protecting the Dragon: Dutch Attempts to Limit Access to Komodo Lizards in the 1920s and 1930s," *Indonesia* 92 (2011): 97–123; Skabelund, "Animals and Imperialism," p. 804.

[22] Robert Cribb, "Conservation in Colonial Indonesia," *Interventions* 9, 1 (2007): 49–61.

over not only human populations but also all animals in these newly developing realms. Through an examination of animals, and how they were cherished, slaughtered, monitored and employed, greater insights into how imperial rule was imposed on a society can be achieved. In this manner fauna continue to be useful tools for understanding our past, as they allow for greater insight into how the society developed, and the institutions that helped govern it.[23] All animals, including humans, have been creatures of imperialism in Singapore. Their tales teach us lessons about the structures, the frameworks, which upheld such a society.

Structures

The chapters that follow will explore the interaction of humans and other animals in Singapore society during the period of high imperialism on the island, from 1819 until 1942. The chronology of the discussions often overlaps, like a story, as the relationships and connections are complex. Each chapter, however, does survey an aspect of colonial rule in Singapore in which animals were monitored, regulated, and often killed as human settlers took control over a tropical island in Southeast Asia.

This study will begin with an exploration of what imperialism meant for the natural landscape of Singapore. As the island fell under colonial rule, so did all of the creatures that lived on it. The imposition of new perspectives and understandings of the human-animal relationship with regard to empire and global commerce resulted in a massive decline in biodiversity as the tropical forest came under the axe, mainly for the development of plantations that cultivated pepper and gambier. The fauna that had lived in this forest then faced firearms, clubs and traps to limit, or even eliminate, their presence, a practice that was translated into the programs to rid the town of pariah curs that roamed the streets. The result was an imperial settlement in which native fauna were either brought under the control of humans or eliminated.

Although the imposition of imperial rule meant a reduction in native fauna, colonial Singapore was filled with animals, and this is the focus of Chapter Three. The vast majority of these animals were

---

[23] William Beinart and Lotte Hughes, *Environment and Empire* (Oxford: Oxford University Press, 2007), p. 4.

imported, having arrived via the expanding port. Once they entered the imperial society they became objects of commerce and consumption while also providing companionship, entertainment and insight into a growing knowledge of nature in the region. In this manner, animals were selected and presented alongside humans, becoming an integral part of colonial society. They reflected the ability of an imperial government to shape the landscape so that it served its cultural, political and social needs.

A consideration of how these animals were understood in this shifting milieu in which their relationship with humans would be determined by values originating from the imperial power of Britain is the focus of the subsequent chapter. Animals provided the energy that moved goods and people over the island in the 19th century. The treatment of these beasts became the focus of the ever-shifting concept of cruelty with regard to the human-animal relationship and the creation of organizations to prevent it in the imperial port. This began with concerned British residents founding a social organization, which was incorporated slowly into the government bureaucracy as imperial mores and foreign understandings were increasingly promoted in the port to protect fauna that were deemed important, in this case mainly animals that provided labor. Through such an examination, a more in-depth understanding of how foreign concepts related to governance and administration were imposed in new lands, and how the types of animals that should be monitored expanded to domestic pets as the labor of animals became increasingly irrelevant in a coming age of mechanized vehicles, will be gained.

This perception of domestic pets, and the ability of residents to control and regulate their relationship with humans, was tested in the late 19th century when rabies became endemic in Singapore in the 1880s. The treatment of this issue is the focus of Chapter Five. The appearance of the terrifying disease resulted in a clash between how the elite, mainly British in origin, of society viewed mutts in the port in contrast to the imported, high-bred canines that they used as symbols of their status in society. Efforts to limit disease, and local pariah dogs, exposed not only rifts in how the society was governed, but also new approaches to how the creatures within it could be monitored so that they were acceptable to the society. The ability of the imperial society the British created in Singapore to surveil and regulate animals was further tested when it came to the need to provide protein. Chapter Six will examine how animals, mainly cattle, pigs and fish, were imported to sustain the human populace. The development of a system of modern markets and slaughterhouses led to the creation of a system that examined and processed animals for slaughter that was considered a model of modern imperial rule and sanitation, with over 300,000 animals passing through the abattoirs every year by the end of the time period under consideration.

The result of this human-animal relationship was the development of imperial rule in Singapore in which all of its creatures inhabited a landscape that was under the control of humans from a distant land that imposed its own understanding of how the society should function and interact. While one era of rule over the island ended with an attack of swordfish, the next one begins with an infestation of rats. The reaction of humans in Singapore to these animals is the story of the creation of an imperial society, one in which all creatures played a part.

CHAPTER TWO

Taming an Island

One of the most important accounts of early colonial Singapore is the autobiography of a Tamil resident who worked as a translator and teacher of the Malay language. His name was Abdullah bin Abdul Kadir, but he is better known as Munshi (or "Language Master") Abdullah and his best-known work is *Hikayat Abdullah* (The Story of Abdullah). Originally written in Malay, *Hikayat Abdullah* describes life in Melaka and Singapore in the first half of the 19th century. The text provides numerous anecdotes about the early colonial residents of the ports, and reflects the concerns of the author with regard to changing cultures and attitudes, and his desire that the Malay community embrace many of the aspects of foreign rule. His promotion of more personal perspectives and a questioning of conventions, which are contrary to traditional approaches within Malay literature, have made Abdullah a controversial character and the subject of much debate among scholars. He was a transitional figure, freely moving between ancient tales and modern reporting while often mixing genres and approaches. Reflecting his continuing adherence to common tropes in traditional Malay literature, Abdullah employed metaphors of animals to provide insight into the milieu of expanding British control over a port in Southeast Asia. In one of his most famous anecdotes regarding early colonial rule in Singapore, he describes problems the residents were having with rats.[1]

---

[1] Abdullah bin Abdul Kadir, "The Hikayat Abdullah, An Annotated Translation by A.H. Hill", *Journal of the Malayan Branch of the Royal Asiatic Society*, 28, 3 (1955): 131–2; Amin Sweeney, "Abdullah bin Abdul Kadir Munshi: A Man of Bananas and Thorns," *Indonesia and the Malay World* 34, 100 (2007): 223–45.

There were "few animals, wild or tame on the Island of Singapore" in the first few years of colonial rule, according to Abdullah, with the exception being rodents that inundated the small settlement situated near the mouth of the Singapore River. "There were thousands of rats all over the district, some were almost as large as cats. They were so big that they used to attack us if we went out walking at night and many people were knocked over." The rodents were so fierce and omnipresent, they even terrorized the cat Abdullah kept in his house. One night, six or seven rats cornered and attacked the feline, which cowered in fear, mewing for help. A housemate of Abdullah awoke, grabbed a stick, and began swinging it in an attempt to push the attackers away from the defenseless animal. The stick hit its mark. Two rats were killed, and the remaining ones—who were gnawing on the ears of the cat— retreated. Sensing an opportunity, the cat pounced on one of the rats and killed it while the human savior proceeded to kill another. The surviving rodents fled, while the gathering crowd of spectators gawked at a cat suffering from a severely lacerated face and nose that was bleeding. "This was the state of affairs in all houses, which were full of rats. They could hardly be kept under control."[2]

The ability to keep animals under control, taming them, is one of the key markers of civilization. Thomas Stamford Raffles used the metaphor of taming the wild to describe his hopes for the island in letters he wrote to the Governor General of India in the early years of the British presence. In one letter Raffles wrote in October 1820, he proclaimed, "After having drawn together all the wild animals of the Forest ... collected the rich plants of the mountains I am now endeavouring to tame the one and cultivate the other and have under-taken the arduous task of converting a wilderness into a garden."[3] The metaphor of taming, or domestication, is one that can be applied to both nature and society. To domesticate a society was to develop rules and boundaries that would channel the energy of all of the species present for the benefit of humans. Such rules were the basis of empire.

This taming of the island began with the arrival of East India Company officials in 1819. The previous year, the Company had

---

[2] Abdullah bin Abdul Kadir, "The Hikayat Abdullah," p. 131.

[3] While Raffles wrote this letter in Bengkulu, it reflects his desires for all of the territories in which he had influence. John Bastin (ed.), *Raffles and Hastings: Private Exchanges behind the Founding of Singapore* (Singapore: Marshall Cavendish and National Library Board, Singapore, 2014), p. 120.

returned the administration of Melaka to the Netherlands, following the end of the Napoleonic Wars in Europe. In response to these developments, Raffles and William Farquhar—the Resident and Commandant of Melaka from 1813 until 1818—searched for an alternative site for a British trade port in the southern region of the Melaka Straits. When Raffles arrived on the island of Singapore in January 1819, he found a small community of pepper and gambier cultivators and signed an agreement to establish a warehouse, known as a "factory," with two disgruntled traditional leaders from the nearby polity of Riau-Johor. Raffles departed for the minor British pepper station of Bengkulu on Sumatra shortly after signing the treaty, leaving Farquhar in charge as the Chief Resident. This was the beginning of imperial rule in Singapore.

Farquhar was tasked with initiating the development of a colonial outpost on an island in Southeast Asia. He began by clearing the flat ground that lay to the northeast of the river. In this area, he oversaw the construction of buildings for Company officials while trade began flowing through the port. In these new environs, in which the British were actively taming the space, the house where Farquhar stayed also was overrun with rats in the extended allegory that Abdullah uses for the early years of colonial rule. Exasperated, Farquhar offered a bounty of one *wang* (or one dollar) for every rat that was killed and brought to him.[4] "When people heard of this they devised all manner of instruments for killing rats. Some made spring-traps, some pincer-traps, some cage-traps, some traps with running nooses, some traps with closing doors, others laid down poison or put down lime." These rat catchers brought thousands of carcasses to Farquhar, who "paid out according to his promise." These efforts, however, did little to alleviate the problem. The rats were proliferating. The Resident began offering $5 for each rat caught. This resulted in so many being brought in that Farquhar ordered the digging of a "very deep trench," where they could be buried. Eventually, the number of rats caught began to dwindle; the infestation subsided.[5]

---

[4] Although the official currency changed over time—for example, it was the Indian rupee from 1837 until 1867—the Spanish dollar was the dominant form of currency in 19th-century Singapore and the Straits Settlements, and the one referred to in most accounts. The exchange rate for Spanish dollars was $4.7 for £1. By the late colonial era the set rate was 8.57 Straits Settlements Dollars for £1.

[5] Abdullah, *Hikayat Abdullah*, pp. 131–2. There is a record of another massive rat infestation in Singapore that occurred in 1845. This time it was at Kampong

An interesting aspect of the account of rat infestations is that Abdullah repeated the story in the paragraph that followed in his memoir. This time the infestation involved centipedes. They overran homes, and created such havoc that Farquhar offered $1 for their destruction. Just like the rats, the campaign resulted in ingenious methods for capturing the multi-limbed creatures, eventually resulting in their decline and the suspension of the campaign against the insects. The repetition of animal tropes is a cornerstone of Malay literature, and reflects the continuing use of metaphor in explicating events. This does not mean the rat and centipede infestation is fictional. It does, however, reflect the multilayered and complex history of events on the island, how they have been depicted, and how we can understand them.[6]

Such interactions were part of the larger metaphor of expanding colonial rule. Humans were taking over a space, imposing their will upon it, and determining who and what could live there. Rats, and perhaps even centipedes, simply represented the many animals that humans encountered in colonial Singapore that needed to be eliminated, or at least brought under the control of the new power present on the island.[7] The tools to tame all imperial creatures were traps, rewards, violence and eventually rules and regulations. It was part of the imperial process.

Glam Beach, and merchants' houses were overrun. Charles Burton Buckley, *An Anecdotal History of Old Times in Singapore: From the Foundation of the Settlement under the Honourable East India Company on February 6th, 1819 to the Transfer to the Colonial Office as Part of the Colonial Possessions of the Crown on April 1st, 1867* (Singapore: Fraser and Neave, 1902), p. 53.

[6] Abdullah, *Hikayat Abdullah*, p. 132; Sweeney, "Abdullah bin Abdul Kadir Munshi," pp. 239–40.

[7] The interaction between many animals and humans is commensal, a term used in ecology and biology to refer to a relationship between two organisms in which one benefits from another without unduly affecting the other. In the study of animal-human relations, archaeologist Terry O'Connor uses it to better understand the origins of human-animal relations and how they have adapted to each other. In this regard, the use of the term reflects the close associations that humans have had with the animal world, even if we may not want—for a variety of reasons—to associate with certain animals. Many animals have evolved to thrive and fit into the human-created environment. When they did not evolve these characteristics, they were often exterminated, or they became invisible within the human-created environment. This is the case with rats. After all, they still exist in Singapore, where they are occasionally seen scampering in drains or near hawker centers. Terry O'Connor, *Animals as Neighbors: The Past and Present in Commensal Animals* (East Lansing, MI: Michigan State University Press, 2014), pp. 1–12.

Between 1819 and 1867 Singapore was a peripheral port on the edge of an expanding British Empire. It was under the control of a quasi-governmental trading entity, the East India Company, which sent officials from its Asian headquarters in Calcutta to oversee an important node in its valuable India to China trade while also accessing the wonders of Southeast Asia. It was a merchant colony, and part of a larger empire. In the first few decades following the landing of Company officials, the island was one on which humans developed infrastructures to help them access the trade riches of Asia, as well as govern an island. Roads were laid. Buildings constructed. A port developed. Singapore became a domesticated space in which a British vision of civilization could be imposed.

Developing a colonial port essentially meant transforming, in biological terms, a "multi-species habitat" into a more simplified landscape that would fulfill the needs of a Western trade company and the humans that served it. With the creation of this habitat, a small island in Southeast Asia was brought under the control of a European power and the market forces that motivated the presence of new residents of the island. Singapore was to be colonized, and animals were part of this process. Those animals that were present to serve and accompany humans for work, companionship and food were regulated and domesticated; all other animals were to be controlled or eliminated, or at least not seen. To mold a land and the animals within it in such a manner was to tame it.[8]

There was a diverse array of fauna in this new imperial environment, although they were often overlooked in colonial records and accounts. The most memorable animals, according to colonial engineer John Turnbull Thomson, were those that "often detract from the comforts of life." He was referring to insects and reptiles, which ranged from cockroaches and termites (also known as "white ants"), which would eat through the beams that supported houses, to scorpions and centipedes, which would cause temporary discomfort with their bites. Isabella Bird complained, "heat-loving insects riot" in the tropical climate of Singapore. "Ants," she commented, "are a pest of the second magnitude, mosquitoes being the first." Another colonial observer, James Low, supported Bird when he wrote, "mosquitoes are rather

---

[8] Kheraj, "Animals and Urban Environments," pp. 263–6.

numerous at times," although they could be "kept off by gauze curtains at night, when they are troublesome." As for reptiles, small lizards were found in every abode while snakes would "infest the bath-rooms and foundations of houses; and, in wet weather, they ascend into the upper rooms."[9] Attempts to control and limit the presence of these animals came through traps, salves and resigned tolerance, or the occasional whack of a hand. Such efforts would take on wider consequences when they expanded into the forested interior with its rich biodiversity.

Biodiversity and the Effects of Cultivation

As was true throughout Southeast Asia, the biodiversity of Singapore dwarfed that found in Europe. As the British presence grew, the island came to be seen as a microcosm of the larger regional environment, leading one chronicler to mention that it was as rich in flora and fauna "as the neighboring continent." Within its limited boundaries, Singapore became a model for the goals of the expanding trade company that gained control over it, and how nature would be treated under British imperial rule. It was a space to be studied and ultimately dominated.[10]

Raffles was profoundly interested in the natural world of the archipelago. He collected examples of plants and animals at every post to which he was assigned, and supported other naturalists in their investigation of the bounty of nature.[11] While much of this was rooted

---

[9] J.T. Thomson, *Some Glimpses into Life in the Far East* (London: Richardson and Company, 1864), pp. 150–2; Low, "Extracts from an Unpublished Journal of a Residence at Singapore during Part of 1840 & 41," *The Singapore Free Press and Mercantile Advertiser* [hereafter, *SFP*], 16 Dec. 1841, p. 3; Isabella L. Bird, *The Golden Chersonese and the Way Thither* (New York, NY: G.P. Putnam's Sons, 1883), p. 144.

[10] Victor R. Savage, *Western Impressions of Nature and Landscape in Southeast Asia* (Singapore: Singapore University Press, 1984); Crawfurd, *A Descriptive Dictionary*, p. 397; Richard Grove, *Green Imperialism: Colonial Expansion, Tropical Edens, and the Origins of Environmentalism, 1600–1860* (New York: Cambridge University Press, 1995).

[11] John Bastin, "Sir Stamford Raffles and the Study of Natural History in Penang, Singapore and Indonesia," *JMBRAS* 63, 2 (1990): 1–25; Timothy P. Barnard, "The Rafflesia in the Natural and Imperial Imagination of the East India Company in Southeast Asia", in *The East India Company and the Natural World*, ed. Vinita Damoradaran, Anna Winterbottom, and Alan Lester (London: Palgrave Macmillan, 2015), pp. 147–66.

in an Enlightenment-era curiosity, there were also financial considerations. As the riches of Asia lay in unique environmental products, such as cloves and nutmeg, it was a subject that could not be ignored. This led to a tremendous amount of energy being directed toward the documentation of the flora and fauna of Singapore, thus bringing it under the purview of the colonizer. During his visit to Singapore in 1823, according to Abdullah, Raffles collected "thousands of different creatures" including "two or three chests filled with many kinds of birds" as well as "hundreds of bottles, large and small, tall and short, filled with snakes, centipedes, scorpions, worms and so on." He "prized all these specimens very highly, more than gold and diamonds." Unfortunately, this collection was lost when *The Fame*, a ship transporting all of his possessions back to England, caught fire and sank. The only physical remains of that collection are the numerous illustrations of birds and other animals that he commissioned during this period, documenting the wildlife of Sumatra and the Malay Peninsula.[12]

Raffles was not alone in his interest in the flora and fauna of Singapore, as many early administrators and officials were enthralled with the biodiversity of the island as well as the nearby Malay Peninsula. They filled diaries, short essays and official reports with numerous references to animals that were quite exotic to the European eye. This can still be seen in the illustrations that officials such as Farquhar commissioned and maintained when he led the settlements of Melaka and Singapore.[13] In addition, while in Singapore, Farquhar collected "unusual jungle animals" and donated specimens to the Asiatic Society of Bengal for further classification. This fascination continued with John Crawfurd, the second Resident of Singapore, as well as many other officials. Thomas Oxley, a surgeon who lived in Singapore in the 1840s and 1850s, even wrote an extensive survey of the fauna of Singapore in 1843, although he focused on only a "few genera of

---

[12] Abdullah, *Hikayat Abdullah*, p. 170; H.J. Noltie, *Raffles' Ark Redrawn: Natural History Drawings from the Collection of Sir Thomas Stamford Raffles* (London: The British Library and Royal Botanic Gardens Edinburgh, 2009); Bastin, "Sir Stamford Raffles and the Study of Natural History," pp. 18–19.

[13] Anonymous, *Natural History Drawings: The Complete William Farquhar Collection* (Singapore: Editions Didier Millet, 2010).

quadrupeds," birds, reptiles and fish, as any attempt to describe the plethora of animals seemed too great a task.[14]

Reports from these various colonial officials emphasized the wide array of fauna that was seen once residents ventured outside the port. Thomson, for example, reported that "the encountering of snakes is of daily occurrence" in rural areas, while Low mentioned sightings of "tigers; also elk, small deer, the plandok, or deer about the size of a hare—monkeys, wild cats, beautifully striped civet cats, lemurs, flying foxes, small squirrels, &c." Oxley added to this list when he noted the presence of *rimau dahan* [clouded leopard (*Neofelis nebulosa*)], otters, wild boar, and flying squirrels as well as five species of deer and three species of monkey. The biodiversity of Singapore, particularly for 19th-century visitors, seemed endless and painted a picture of a fertile island.[15]

Within this tropical green landscape particular interest was directed toward the bird life, making the rich avian biodiversity of the island one of the major obsessions of early European residents. There were snipes, quails, and pheasants as well as several species of wild pigeon. Among smaller songbirds there was the Java sparrow (*Lonchura oryzivora*) and wagtails, "a pretty little bird with an agreeable note of the genus Motacilla." Owls and falcons were also found on the island, "which although not much larger than a sparrow will kill and carry off a bird the size of a thrush." Supplementing this splendor were migratory birds, particularly plovers and starlings, which would appear from October to March. Finally, there were reports of flocks of green parakeets in the interior forests, "although they keep to the highest trees and rarely come within shot."[16]

---

[14] Crawfurd, *A Descriptive Dictionary*, p. 396; T. Oxley, "The Zoology of Singapore," *Journal of the Indian Archipelago and Eastern Asia*, 3 (1849): 594–7; John Bastin, "William Farquhar: First Resident and Commandant of Singapore," in *Natural History Drawings: The Complete William Farquhar Collection* (Singapore: Editions Didier Millet, 2010), p. 31.

[15] Low, "Extracts from an Unpublished Journal of a Residence at Singapore during Part of 1840 & 41," *SFP*, 16 Dec. 1841, p. 3; Thomson, *Some Glimpses into Life in the Far East*, p. 151; Oxley, "The Zoology of Singapore," p. 594.

[16] Buckley, *An Anecdotal History of Singapore*, Vol. 1, p. 364; Low, "Extracts from an Unpublished," *SFP*, 16 Dec. 1841, p. 3.

John Cameron, another early chronicler of colonial life in the British ports of the region, looked beyond the massive variety of birds in his own vivid account of the wildlife in Singapore when he focused on animals that were beginning to intrude into the human settlement:

> The wild hogs, which crowd all the swampy parts of the jungle, are precisely the same animal as is to be seen all over the world, but are usually black, and much smaller and more wiry than the common pig of Europe. There are two kinds of deer; both are found in considerable numbers, and supply the natives with food. Alligators and boa-constrictors are likewise frequently to be met with; the latter are harmless to man, but destructive to poultry, and are discovered near the henroosts of houses close to the jungle, either unable or indisposed to move after having gorged four or five fowls. Otters have also been captured in the creeks and rivers.[17]

In this instance, the significance of this account is that it not only mentions the rich biodiversity found on the island, but also how animals were beginning to be perceived as encroaching on an expanding landscape that humans controlled as they pushed into the interior.

Encounters with wildlife, and considering them as an obstacle or menace, were part of the process of taming the island. While officials were fascinated with the flora and fauna of Singapore, their ultimate goal—in the words of Raffles—was to cultivate one and tame the other in order to civilize the space. This meant that much of the flora and fauna of the island was to be documented, while also coming under the axe. Within decades after 1819, plantations expanded to encompass much of Singapore in an attempt to cultivate the products a trading company greatly desired. The extent and rapidity of deforestation in the early decades of colonial rule over Singapore was remarkable, and is one of the most important developments on the island in the 19th century. A survey conducted in the 1880s, following several cycles of plantation growth and contraction, estimated that 92 percent of the original forest cover in Singapore had been lost, making it one of the first legacies of imperialism on the island. Essentially, an island

---

[17] John Cameron, *Our Tropical Possessions in Malayan India: Being a Descriptive Account of Singapore, Penang, Province Wellesley, and Malacca; Their Peoples, Products, Commerce, and Government* (London: Smith, Elder and Co, 1865), p. 90.

under British colonial rule that had been mostly covered in forest was devastated biologically.[18]

Tony O'Dempsey has recounted how this was possible due to the cultivation of spices that required huge amounts of timber, mainly as firewood for processing after harvest. The chief export product during this period was pepper and gambier, which has a life cycle of approximately 20 years, resulting in much of the soil in Singapore becoming bare and exhausted by the mid-nineteenth century. As James Low related, the cultivators "have no attachment to the soil. Their sole object is to scourge the land for a given time—and when worn out to leave it a desert." This resulted in large swathes of the interior being covered in *lalang* grass (*Imperata cylindrica*) until it encompassed at least a third of the island (45,000 acres, or 182 square kilometers).[19]

The deforestation that accompanied the spread of British imperialism in Singapore quickly reduced biodiversity, which was particularly evident on such a small island. This was a result of domestication and taming. To domesticate a space biologically is to simplify its contents and direct it toward a benefit for the human community. Thus, for example, by removing much of the floral diversity of the island and replacing it with pepper and gambier, early agriculturalists were reducing the number of species found within a designated space. This not only meant a reduction in plant variety, but also that of animals, including green parakeets.[20]

It is difficult to account in any exact manner the number of animal species that became extinct due to colonial rule in Singapore. Biologist Richard T. Corlett has estimated that at least 100 bird species, 20 freshwater fish and several species of mammal were lost.

[18] Nathaniel Cantley, *Report on the Forests of the Straits Settlements* (Singapore: Singapore and Straits Printing Office, 1883), pp. 7–9.

[19] Tony O'Dempsey, "Singapore's Changing Landscape since c. 1800" in *Nature Contained: Environmental Histories of Singapore*, ed. Timothy P. Barnard (Singapore: NUS Press, 2014), pp. 20–8; James Low, "Extracts from an Unpublished Journal of a Residence at Singapore During Part of 1840 & 41," SFP, 2 Dec. 1841, p. 2; Richard T. Corlett, "The Ecological Transformation of Singapore, 1819–1990," *Journal of Biogeography* 19, 4 (1992): 411–20; I.H. Burkill, "The Establishment of the Botanic Gardens, Singapore," *Gardens' Bulletin, Straits Settlements* 2, 2 (1918): 55.

[20] Grove, *Green Imperialism*; Gregory Alan Barton, *Empire Forestry and the Origins of Environmentalism* (Cambridge: University Press, 2002).

Other scientists, including Peter Ng and Navjot Sodhi of the National University of Singapore, have labeled the loss as "catastrophic," with extinctions being particularly high among butterflies, freshwater fish, birds and mammals. As Singapore is a small island in a diverse region, some of the loss meant these animals were simply no longer present on the island, while other—truly unique—species were lost forever. These same scientists, however, estimate that the total local extinction rate was as high as 73 percent for all species, with much of it occurring during the intense period of deforestation in the 19th century.[21]

While the number of species lost is uncertain, as early scientific records can be spotty, a decline in the diversity of the faunal population following the cultivation of the island clearly occurred. By another estimate there were 383 species of birds recorded in early Singapore. Among these animals, 106 are now considered extinct on the island with 87 of them being forest dwellers, thus reflecting the level of ecological change that colonial rule and deforestation wrought.[22] This was apparent to residents of Singapore during the colonial era. As G.P. Owen described the situation in the early 20th century, "before the introduction of cultivation there were many miles of virgin forest, providing shelter, food, and quiet places for bird and beast to breed. All the forest, original and secondary, has given place to ... plantation, mostly clean weeded, alike destitute of edible seeds and fruit, and of insects."[23]

An example of the reduction in faunal diversity in Singapore due to the arrival of imperialism can be found in a footnote Oxley devoted to the *kalong*, or the large flying fox (*Pteropus vampyrus*). A colony of the animal was originally located at the head of the Johor River estuary. As he described:

---

[21] Corlett, "The Ecological Transformation of Singapore," p. 416; Barry W. Brook, Navjot S. Sodhi and Peter K.L. Ng, "Catastrophic Extinctions Follow Deforestation in Singapore," *Nature*, 424 (24 Jul 2003): 420–3.

[22] Christopher Hails, *Birds of Singapore* (Singapore: Times Editions, 1987).

[23] G.P. Owen, "Shikar," in *One Hundred Years of Singapore, Being an Account of the Capital of the Straits Settlements from its Foundation by Sir Stamford Raffles on the 6th February 1819 to the 6th February 1919*, vol. II, ed. Walter Makepeace, Gilbert E. Brooke, and Roland St. J. Braddell (London: John Murray, 1921), pp. 367–8.

In the day they are seen asleep hanging in the millions from the branches of the mangrove. At sunset they begin to stir, and presently they ascend into the air and winger their way to the south-east in one vast uninterrupted cloud. They pass the whole night in the jungle and plantations devouring fruit, and as soon as dawn begins to appear, they mount the air again and return to their roosting-place at the head of the estuary.

Oxley took note of their existence as they could be "most destructive" to fruit plantations, while Crawfurd argued that these vast flocks of bats were "the locust of the country."[24] The elimination of their food source, following the abandonment of the plantations, over a couple of decades led to a tremendous reduction in their numbers. Fruit bats are rarely found in Singapore and the southern Malay Peninsula today, particularly not "in one vast uninterrupted cloud" that would darken the sky, thus making them an example of the reduced biodiversity that resulted from the introduction of colonial rule in Singapore.[25]

While many native species were lost due to the spread of deforestation and the spread of cultivation, the transformation of the environment in Singapore also led to new animals moving into the ecosystem. Humans introduced some of these animals, as occurred with jackals (*Canis aureus*). According to George Windsor Earl, a lawyer living in the Straits Settlements at the time, "a few years after the establishment of the settlement, an individual who arrived from Bengal brought with him a male and female jackal, and thinking perhaps to confer an inestimable benefit on the colony, he turned them into the jungle, where these noisy and troublesome animals have now become

---

[24] Oxley, "The Zoology of Singapore," p. 594; Crawfurd, *A Descriptive Dictionary*, p. 398.

[25] A few native species thrived in the disturbed ecosystem of Singapore. Alfred Russel Wallace, the accomplished naturalist, found Singapore to be an ideal location for the collection of beetles when he first visited in 1854, in the midst of this deforestation. According to Wallace, due to "the labours of Chinese wood-cutters. They had been at work here for several years had furnished a continual supply of dry and dead and decaying leaves and bark." Alfred Russel Wallace, *The Malay Archipelago: The Land of the Orang-Utan, and the Bird of Paradise. A Narrative of Travel, with Studies of Man and Nature*, vol. 1 (London: Macmillan and Co., 1869), p. 38; John van Wyhe, "Wallace in Singapore," in *Nature Contained: Environmental Histories of Singapore*, ed. Timothy P. Barnard (Singapore: NUS Press, 2014), pp. 85–109.

numerous." When they began raiding poultry yards, humans hunted them to extinction in Singapore by the early 1840s.[26]

The most famous arrival to Singapore as a result of the imperial transformation of the island, nevertheless, was not the jackal. It was the tiger, an "animal unknown on the island in the earlier years of the British settlement." Tigers began appearing as early as 1831, having reached Singapore after swimming across the narrow Straits of Johor from the Malay Peninsula. Humans first encountered tigers on the island in September of that year, when several woodcutters searching for a missing companion behind a Chinese temple on the edge of the town came across their friend, or at least some of him. At the edge of the forest was his head as well as "part of one leg." Paw prints were found near the remains. Soon thereafter, a tiger killed another human.[27] These were the first two recorded victims of a plague that haunted Singapore for the next three decades, and periodically occurred afterwards until the end of the century.

The arrival of tigers was primarily due to the rapid increase in agricultural cultivation on the island. In general, large mammals do not live in the jungle, as the dense canopy reduces the number of food sources available. Disturbed forest, however, leads to the growth of underbrush, which may contain nutrients that attract animals such as deer and wild pigs. This would also lead to a rise in carnivores seeking prey. In the first few decades of colonial rule, the desire of humans to convert jungle into plantations created a perfect environment for these large carnivores. The entire island was simply a disturbed forest. Trees were cut; plantations arose.[28]

---

[26] George Windsor Earl, *The Eastern Seas, or, Voyages and Adventures in the Indian Archipelago, in 1832–33–34: Comprising a Tour of the Island of Java, Visits to Borneo, The Malay Peninsula, Siam and &c.; Also an Account of the Present State of Singapore, with Observations on the Commercial Resources of the Archipelago* (London: Wm. H. Allen and Co, 1837), pp. 358–9; Buckley, *An Anecdotal History of Singapore*, p. 364; Russell Jones, "George Windsor Earl and 'Indonesia'," *Indonesia Circle* 22, 64 (1994): 279–90.

[27] Crawfurd, *A Descriptive Dictionary*, p. 397; Anonymous, "The War at Malacca," *Singapore Chronicle and Commercial Register*, 8 Sep. 1831, p. 3.

[28] Peter Boomgaard, "Hunting and Trapping in the Indonesian Archipelago, 1500–1950," in *Paper Landscapes: Explorations in the Environmental History of Indonesia*, ed. Peter Boomgaard, Freek Colombijn, and David Henley (Leiden: KITLV Press, 1997), pp. 188–9; Timothy P. Barnard and Mark Emmanuel, "Tigers of Colonial Singapore," in *Nature Contained: Environmental Histories of Singapore*, ed. Timothy P. Barnard (Singapore: NUS Press, 2014), pp. 60–3.

The role that deforestation played in the rise of tiger attacks was mentioned as early as 1839 in one account in *The Singapore Free Press and Mercantile Advertiser*. "It is somewhat singular," the author reasoned, that "fatal accidents of this kind should happen just as the island begins to be cleared of jungle, and roads to be carried into the interior in various directions." By 1841 at least 500 pepper and gambier plantations existed in Singapore, and this expanded to 800 by 1850, which led Thomson to comment that the forest had retreated "a considerable distance" from the port. On the edges of this expanding agricultural zone roamed a variety of animals, among them "unfortunately too many tigers."[29]

Within this cleared jungle tigers attacked their prey. Following the initial assault, they would usually drag their victims to a shaded location near water, and would only then proceed to eat it over a few days. The victims comprised numerous other mammals, including humans, living in this area. A report in May 1850 provides an example of the devastation tigers caused with its account of a spate of deaths in the "Bukit Timah district and along Thomson's road" that included goats, pigs, and numerous dogs that were taken from plantation communities. The attacks were so frequent, and so malicious, that one newspaper bemoaned, "It has now become nearly a regular part of our weekly duty to chronicle these melancholy tragedies."[30]

While the primary casualties of the rise in the tiger population were animals in this same biosphere—often pigs or deer—greater emphasis, of course, was placed on human victims. Hundreds of residents of Singapore died from tiger attacks in the 19th century. Based on a survey of contemporary newspaper reports, a team of scholars has

---

[29] Anonymous, "More Tigers," *SFP*, 25 Jul. 1839, p. 3; Boomgaard, *Frontiers of Fear*, pp. 22–6; Oxley, "The Botany of Singapore"; J.T. Thomson, "General Report on the Residency of Singapore, Drawn Principally with a View of Illustrating Its Agricultural Statistics," *Journal of the Indian Archipelago and Eastern Asia*, 4 (1850): 219; Barnard and Emmanuel, "Tigers of Colonial Singapore"; James Low, "Extracts from an Unpublished Journal of a Residence at Singapore during Part of 1840 & 41," *SFP*, 16 Dec. 1841, p. 3; O'Dempsey, "Singapore's Changing Landscape since c. 1800," pp. 29–32; Timothy P. Barnard, *Nature's Colony: Empire, Nation, and Environment in the Singapore Botanic Gardens* (Singapore: NUS Press, 2016), pp. 50–9.

[30] Anonymous, "Local", *SFP*, 17 May 1850, p. 2; Anonymous, "Miscellaneous", *SFP*, 31 Jan. 1839, p. 7; Anonymous, "Tigers again," *SFP*, 6 Aug. 1840, p. 3; Tan et al, "Managing Present Day Large-Carnivores," p. 3113.

recently proclaimed that 211 people died from tiger attacks between 1831 and 1930. This number, even the authors admit, is probably a gross underestimation.[31] Most of the humans that worked on the plantations were poor Chinese laborers, who had fled poverty and persecution, only to experience an often more violent end in Southeast Asia. An accurate number of these victims, however, will never be known, as coverage was irregular given that reporting on such events would hinder the ability of plantation owners to recruit workers as well as a cultural distance between the British record keepers and Chinese agriculturalists.[32]

Although the number of victims of tiger attacks is uncertain, Singapore developed a reputation as a haunt for the beasts. One English sailor visiting the island in 1854 reported in a scattered manner that befits the concern they engendered:

> The tigers have of late been so numerous that it is dangerous to drive any distance into the country and many been lost of late owing to the number that swim from the main land and that the scarcity of deer in the jungle compels them to approach nearer the inhabited part to feed on fat Chinamen between 3 and 400 having fallen into their jaws during the last 12 months.[33]

That same year, in a letter to Company officials in Bengal, Straits Settlements Governor E.A. Blundell tried to address this reputation when he wrote, "the number of human lives destroyed by tigers has been much exaggerated." Despite such protests, he went on to assure his administrative superiors that "all practical measures will continue to be resorted to for exterminating these animals."[34]

---

[31] Cedric Kai Wei Tan et al, "Managing Present Day Large-Carnivores in 'Island Habitats': Lessons in Memoriam Learned from Human-Tiger Interactions in Singapore," *Biodiversity and Conservation* 24, 12 (2015): 3109–24; An Old Resident (W.H. Read), *Play and Politics: Recollections of Malaya* (London: Wells Gardner, Darton and Co., 1901), p. 156.

[32] Miles Alexander Powell, "People in Peril, Environments at Risk: Coolies, Tigers, and Colonial Singapore's Ecology of Poverty," *Environment and History* 22, 3 (2016): 455–82.

[33] Wellcome Collection: MS5958: "Saturday, 17th Feb 1854," *Journal of a Voyage from London to the Far East, and Voyages between Bombay, Singapore and Hong Kong*, p. 50.

[34] Straits Settlements Records [Herafter: SSR]: Governor's Letters from Bengal, S21 (1854), p. 58.

The "practical measures" the government began promoting for the elimination of the savage beasts were varied. Just as Farquhar offered compensation for rat killers in the early years of colonial rule, so would subsequent colonial governors for those who brought about the "destruction of wild animals," with particular emphasis on tigers, panthers, bears, crocodiles and snakes. The amount of the reward shifted over time and depended on the animal and its size. The government, for example, initially offered $20 for each tiger captured, although it quickly rose to $50 and then $100—a considerable amount in a society where the average laborer made less than a dollar a day. Eventually the market stabilized, with full-grown tigers bringing $50 and cubs meriting half that amount, while bears and panthers earned $20.[35] As for snakes, the monetary payouts were based on their length. Those over 14 feet (4 meters) were worth $5, while the scale of payment retracted until a serpent under a foot in length (33 centimeters) merited 25 cents. Pythons were the main targets of these efforts, although at least eight other species also earned compensation for those who claimed rewards.[36]

These rewards appeared to work, particularly for tigers, as can be seen in the tale of an unnamed Chinese squatter who captured at least four of the beasts in 1841, for which he received monetary prizes and was celebrated in the local press. This anonymous squatter, according to newspapers reports, "had apparently discovered a lure for the Tigers." When he learned that one of the savage beasts roamed an area searching for prey, he "makes his observations, digs his pit, effects his other arrangements, and on the morrow has his victim all snug!"[37] This was the most effective approach in capturing the beasts of the forest. Over the next several decades, plantation owners tasked their workers in the digging of large holes—usually four meters deep and about between one- and two-meters square at the mouth—near their plots of land. Laborers would check the pits, which were covered with

---

[35] Barnard and Emmanuel, "Tigers of Colonial Singapore," pp. 69–70; Crawfurd, *A Descriptive Dictionary*, p. 397; SSR: Governor's Letters to and from Resident Councilors, U34 (Jan. 1858), pp. 238–9.

[36] These other species of snake were identified by their local names: "Tedong, Matahari, Katam, Tebu, Kapak Bakau, Kapak Api, Punit Blerang and Selimpat." Colonial Office [hereafter, CO] 276/15: "Government Notification, No. 38," (1884), p. 64.

[37] Anonymous, "Untitled," *SFP*, 4 Nov. 1841, p. 3.

dead branches, grass and ferns, every few days, with the most common animal found inside being wild boars.[38]

To further regularize the capture and destruction of wild animals, the practice eventually was placed under the coordinating purview of the government. During the tenure of Governor William Orfeur Cavenagh, in the 1860s, Thomas Dunman took control over these activities as the first Commissioner of Police as well as the Superintendent of Convicts. In this capacity, Dunman assigned convicts to the task of tiger extirpation. As Cavenagh remembered in his memoirs, "amongst the prisoners … there were several good shots," and:

> It was arranged that two parties, of eight men each, should be furnished with arms and ammunition, and sent out into the jungles, where they would be allowed to remain, merely coming in to attend the monthly muster, so long as they succeeded in destroying a tiger every three months, they being at the same time allowed to receive the Government reward as a stimulus to their exertions.

This program was so successful that the need for two government-supported convict gangs of tiger killers was reduced to one. In the meantime, Dunman expanded his authority to include the investigation of sightings and the establishment of new rules for the construction of pits, requiring the use of ribbons or flags to mark their edge to prevent humans from stumbling into them.[39]

Alongside these government-sponsored efforts, recreational hunters began entering the forests of Singapore. In the early decades of colonial rule, these shikars found "ample amusement in the low lands at the back of the town, which abound in snipes and plovers, or in the creeks on the east side of the harbor, where flocks of pigeons assemble every evening from all parts of the island, to roost on the trees in the little detached islets, where they are free from the attacks of the smaller beasts

---

[38] Newbold, *Political and Statistical Account of the British Settlements*, vol. 2, pp. 190–3; Peter Boomgaard, "'Primitive' Tiger hunting in Indonesia and Malaysia, 1800–1950," in *Wildlife in Asia: Cultural Perspectives*, ed. John Knight (London: RoutledgeCurzon, 2004), pp. 185–206; Barnard and Emmanuel, "Tigers of Colonial Singapore," pp. 70–1.

[39] Orfeur Cavenagh, *Reminiscences of an Indian Official* (London: W.H. Allen and Co., 1884), pp. 272–3; Barnard and Emmanuel, "Tigers of Colonial Singapore," p. 73; J.F.A. McNair, assisted by W.D. Bayliss, *Prisoners Their Own Warders* (London: Archibald Constable and Co., 1899), p. 52.

Image 2.1: White hunter with his assistants in front of Bukit Timah Church, 1880. Photograph by John Edmund Taylor. Courtesy of the Wellcome Collection.

of prey." Eventually, even the opportunity to shoot birds diminished. As James Low complained as early as 1841, "game is scarce, if we except snipe."[40]

This reduction in prospects for those interested in shooting birds in Singapore corresponded with an increased focus on larger game, and an expansion of hunting into the interior of the island. In such an atmosphere, and supported by improving rifle technology, these hunters would seek out boar, deer and the occasional tiger, although these beasts were more "often caught by nooses and pit-falls." Expeditions often employed dogs, which would channel the game into "toils," or traps, where they could be shot or speared. This resulted in Singapore having an active culture of hunting throughout the 19th century. It was a place in which Ida Pfeiffer could, armed with "fowling-pieces,"

---

[40] Low, "Extracts from an Unpublished Journal," *SFP*, 16 Dec. 1841, p. 3; Earl, *The Eastern Seas*, p. 358.

enjoy an excursion in the late 1840s in search of a tiger, although she was also prepared to shoot at "bears, wild boars, and large serpents."[41]

The interior of the island became a place in which all residents sought adventure, not just Westerners who related hunting to notions of masculinity and elite culture.[42] Indians, for example, made a pastime of tracking animals by the mid-1840s, particularly at night or on Sundays when they had no work obligations, with one report describing their pursuit of wild boar on Mount Faber, while Malays had a repu-tation for using "strings of fine nooses, bird-lime, and decoys," which made them "admirable snarers of birds and wild animals." The numbers of Asians tramping in the forest ultimately reached such a point by the beginning of the 20th century that some Westerners complained about "half castes carrying guns who come out on Sundays and holidays and murder everything having fur or feathers." Despite such complaints, hunting continued as a pastime until the Japanese Occupation in 1942.[43]

Whether it was tigers or other animals, all residents of the island —Chinese, Malay, Indian, European and even visitors from afar— participated in activities to contain the fauna of Singapore, to eliminate pests, both in settled areas around the port as well as the quickly cultivating interior. These activities may not have been defined strictly as hunting. They were, however, limiting. Armed with rifles, shovels and clubs, they were motivated by a desire to make Singapore more habitable for its human occupants, which was often channeled through cultures of hunting and domestication. These adventurers cultivated the

---

[41] Ida Pfeiffer, *A Woman's Journey Round the World from Vienna to Brazil, Chili, Tahiti, China, Hindostan, Persia and Asia Minor* (London: Ingram, Cooke, and Co., 1852), p. 122; Barnard and Emmanuel, "Tigers of Colonial Singapore," pp. 73–5; T.J. Newbold, *Political and Statistical Account of the British Settlements in the Straits of Malacca, viz. Pinang, Malacca, and Singapore; with a History of the Malayan States on the Peninsula of Malacca* (London: John Murray, 1839), p. 190.
[42] This is mostly in contrast to developments in other parts of Asia and Africa. John M. MacKenzie, *The Empire of Nature: Hunting, Conservation and British Imperialism* (Manchester: Manchester University Press, 1997).
[43] William Louis Abbott, "Letter to Dr. Miller, 18 Oct. 1903," (Smithsonian Archives: William Louis Abbott Papers, RU7117, Box 1, Folder 6), p. 2; Newbold, *Political and Statistical Account of the British Settlements*, p. 190; Anonymous, "Singapore: Saturday, March 25th," *The Straits Times* [hereafter, *ST*], 25 Mar. 1846, p. 2; Thomson, *Some Glimpses into Life in the Far East*, p. 226; McNair, *Prisoners Their Own Warders*, p. 52; Barnard and Emmanuel, "Tigers of Colonial Singapore."

land and hunted a variety of fauna, thus creating boundaries between civilized and savage, and limiting the space in which non-domesticated animals could be present. Efforts to eradicate tigers, boars, jackals, crocodiles, and even rats reflect a desire among the residents of Singapore to tame the island, creating boundaries for the acceptable interaction of animals and humans, thus reinforcing the commensal relationship.

Despite efforts to kill animals directly, the ultimate tool for eliminating savage beasts in the interior remained deforestation. As John Cameron argued, "If the island could be cleared and kept free of jungle, no doubt the tigers would immediately desert it." And, this is what occurred. As the island of Singapore became increasingly cultivated for pepper and gambier plantations, and then abandoned, an ecosystem that could support a variety of beasts disappeared. This can be seen in a reduction in tiger attacks. After peaking in 1865, the number of human deaths from savage mauling plummeted over the subsequent decades as the landscape in which tigers could thrive also disappeared. This was true for all wild animals. By the early 20th century, renowned hunter G.P. Owen complained, "at the present time game consists of a few wild pig and a half-a-dozen or so of deer." The was a result, he declared, of a "gauntlet of acres of bare or cultivated land" in which animals "would find the fruit trees mostly disappeared and the swamps drained, leaving a desert land for pigeons and snipe. Singapore is no longer the place for the sportsman."[44]

While the reduction in biodiversity due to clear cutting and cultivation was apparent in the interior of Singapore, efforts to control feral animals also included the developed parts of the island. While the forest was being cut, buildings were rising in the port, roads were being laid and a colonial landscape was developing. The construction of the port and town, and the assertion of human dominance for settlement and commerce also included many animals that needed to be tamed

---

[44] Owen, "Shikar," pp. 367–8; Low, "Extracts from an Unpublished Journal," *SFP*, 16 Dec. 1841, p. 3; Tan et al, "Managing Present Day Large-Carnivores," p. 3113; Jeya Kathirithamby-Wells, "Human Impact on Large Animal Populations in Peninsular Malaysia from the Nineteenth to the Mid-Twentieth Century," in *Paper Landscapes: Explorations in the Environmental History of Indonesia*, ed. Peter Boomgaard, Freek Colombijn, and David Henley (Leiden: KITLV Press, 1997), p. 220; Cameron, *Our Tropical Possessions in Malayan India*, pp. 101–2.

in the creation of a symbolic boundary between civilized and savage, between cultured and wild. Violence was often the first tool in creating this boundary, as it often occurred through the swing of an axe or the shot of a rifle. In the settled areas of Singapore, in many respects, the ferocity of the human response began when a crocodile killed one of Farquhar's dogs. According to Abdullah in another of his extended allegories, the Chief Resident had been walking along the Rochor River with a canine, whose curiosity led to its death in the jaws of the reptile. Farquhar "ordered his men who were there to put a dam blocking the river. The crocodile was hemmed in by the obstruction and speared to death." The carcass, which was 15 feet (4.5 meters) in length, was hung from a fig tree along Bras Basah Stream for all to see.[45] Any beast that disturbed humans and their chosen animal companions could expect the same treatment.

While Farquhar's dog may have been the first one of its species to die in this newly established colonial town, it would not be the last. The domestic dog (*Canis lupus familiaris*) was one of the most common animals found in Singapore throughout the colonial era. Initially, however, they were not very tame and their presence was considered an affront among the human residents. This is because most of these dogs were feral, living on the edge of the settlement and their bothersome presence was one of the great concerns of those who lived in the town in the first few decades of colonial rule. Establishing control over these wild animals echoed the growing dominance of humans in the ecosystem of urban Singapore that was taking place at the same time that the interior was being brought under human control.

The Dog Nuisance

Canines have been present in Singapore as long as there have been humans on the island. Dogs most likely roamed in and around the settlement of Temasek, ancient Singapore, although archaeologists have

---

[45] Crocodiles remained a pest throughout the early decades of colonial rule. For example, in 1853, it was reported that they were becoming quite bothersome in the Geylang and Kallang rivers, where they were "snapping at natives sitting in boats, and carrying off many ducks and fowls." Buckley, *An Anecdotal History of Singapore*, p. 574; Abdullah, *Hikayat Abdullah*, p. 149.

yet to find any canine remains in the acidic soil. Dogs were present in Majapahit, however, a society that was a contemporary of Temasek.[46] They were also present in early colonial societies throughout Southeast Asia. As John Crawfurd, the second Resident of Singapore, wrote, "the dog is found in all the islands of the Archipelago in the half-domestic state in which it is seen in every country of the East." He went on to add, "it is the same prick-eared cur as in other Asiatic countries, varying a good deal in colour,—not much in shape and size,—never owned,—never become wild, but always the common scavenger in every town, and village." These dogs were to come under imperial control.[47]

The expansion of efforts to regulate the savage occurred during a period and alongside a process that Aaron Skabelund terms "canine imperialism," in which appearance began to take precedence over function among dogs. This was related to growing class, racial and even national categorizations being impressed upon a species of animal that previously had been largely undefined and unstable, which echoes in the description Crawfurd provided.[48] The only status a dog may have had in England in the 19th century, prior to the development of specific breeds, was due to the owner. In Southeast Asia this is less certain. While some dogs may have had a utilitarian function, such as protecting premises or carrying goods and even people, there was little differentiation afforded the animal. Basically, a dog was a dog. For the most part they had a relatively informal attachment to human

---

[46] I would like to thank John Miksic for this information. Recent DNA analysis has shown that dogs south of the Yangtze River show the greatest genetic diversity in the world, pointing to a high probability of early domestication in southern China, which is ecologically part of Southeast Asia. John Dodson and Guanghui Dong, "What Do We Know about Domestication in Eastern Asia?" *Quaternary International* 426, (2016): 2–9.

[47] Crawfurd, *A Descriptive Dictionary of the Indian Islands and Adjacent Countries*, p. 121; Keith Thomas, *Man and the Natural World: Changing Attitudes in England, 1500–1800* (London: Allen Lane, 1983); Alan Mikhail, "A Dog-Eat-Dog Empire: Violence and Affection on the Streets of Ottoman Cairo," *Comparative Studies of South Asia, Africa and the Middle East* 35, 1 (2015): 87.

[48] Any breeding that did occur prior to the 19th century focused on function over appearance. An example of such breeding was small dogs that could enter lairs or holes in assisting elite hunters. Aaron Herald Skabelund, *Empire of Dogs: Canines, Japan, and the Making of the Modern World* (Ithaca, NY: Cornell University Press, 2011), p. 2.

communities, with most dogs scavenging in packs as they roamed the edges of these settlements. They were not thought of as pets, or trusted companions. Dogs, for the most part, were feral annoyances in urban environments globally, and this was particularly true in newly established colonial centers in Asia.[49]

Most dogs in early colonial Singapore roamed in packs of strays about the town, making them "one of the greatest nuisances in the settlement." The "wretched creatures" would follow the "dust carts" that collected rubbish, or tag along with soldiers that were carrying out their duties. One newspaper report in the 1840s complained that, "Every morning when the guard is relieved at the Court house a swarm of Pariah dogs come out with the soldiers, and attack the passing natives and many times through them down and bite them, and tear their cloths off, and the sepoys appear to injoy it, although he says they take the dogs off when they see them going to extremities."[50] As another account of Singapore summarized the situation, "dogs of most anomalous breeds ... infest the streets both day and night."[51]

The annoyance these dogs created was so great in the first few decades of British imperial rule in Singapore that Company officials decided to take action, which mirrored efforts taken in India during this same period.[52] Magistrates issued a notice in April 1833 that read, "All dogs found running loose about the streets between the 8th and 18th ... will be destroyed." This was the beginning of an approach used to control canines that was exercised throughout the world. With extreme malice, stray dogs were to be killed. Over the next few decades, the Superintendent of the Singapore Police periodically published announcements warning the public about any upcoming exercise aimed at destroying the canine population of the island. By the mid-1830s, the warnings for these culling activities normally read:

---

[49] Jesse S. Palsetia, "Mad Dogs and Parsis: The Bombay Dog Riots of 1832," *Journal of the Royal Asiatic Society* 11, 1 (2001): 14.

[50] Spelling is as in the original. The author goes on to add that the only solution would be the imposition of a $2 dog tax on each animal. Anonymous, "Untitled," *SFP*, 5 Jan 1843, p. 3. Another report mentioned that "about 30 dogs" accompany the sepoys when they change guard, and "are a complete nuisance to the neighborhood." An Observer, "Correspondence," *SFP*, 8 Aug. 1844, p. 2.

[51] Buckley, *An Anecdotal History of Singapore*, p. 365; Low, "Extracts from an Unpublished Journal," *SFP*, 16 Dec. 1841, p. 4.

[52] Palsetia, "Mad Dogs and Parsis."

> Notice is hereby given, that all Dogs found straying about in the Road and Streets, on Monday, Tuesday, and Wednesday next, will be destroyed. Persons desirous of preserving their Dogs are recommended to keep them secured within their premises during that period.

For rest of the era of East India Company rule, and for decades afterwards, curs were publicly destroyed in the streets of Singapore when, "the number of Pariah dogs straying about the town to the no small terror of the inhabitants" reached uncomfortable proportions.[53]

A pattern to the dog culling exercises eventually developed. It normally occurred four times a year, although extra sessions could be announced if needed or with slight variations regarding the justification and rules surrounding the activities. This continued for decades, with the only change in violence and victims occurring in the mid-1840s when culling efforts began to focus on dogs without collars. The use of such chokers was perceived as a symbol of ownership, and a sign of the arrival of domestic pets in the port, although they were not required at the time. In April 1845, for example, the Magistrates issued an order "for the slaughtering of all species of the Canine Race that may be found in the streets without collars." By the next year, a police peon was stationed at the gate of St. Andrew's Cathedral with a fowling piece (an 18th-century shotgun) and ordered to shoot any dog that came within the firing range of the weapon. When a passerby enquired about his task, the peon "leveled his piece at a dog that was passing by and shot him dead."[54]

Such actions, nevertheless, seemed to have little influence over the canine population. As one newspaper in the late 1840s recounted, "Dogs, half starved, roam at large, terrifying Her Majesty's good lieges, and appear to laugh at the orders given for their destruction—two saucy curs, minus collars and good manners, prowl in front of the dwelling

---

[53] Anonymous, "Notice," *Singapore Chronicle and Commercial Advertiser*, 4 Apr. 1833, p. 1; Anonymous, "Notice," *Singapore Chronicle and Commercial Register*, 28 Aug. 1834, p. 3; Anonymous, "Notice," *SFP*, 7 Oct. 1841, p. 1; Anonymous, "Notice," *SFP*, 30 Jul. 1846, p. 1; Anonymous, "Advertisements," *SFP*, 4 Feb. 1847, p. 1; Anonymous, "Notice," *SFP*, 6 May 1847, p. 1; Anonymous, "Calcutta," *ST*, 22 Jul. 1846, p. 2.

[54] H.W., "Correspondence," *ST*, 17 Jan. 1846, p. 3.

of Tan Tock Sing, a Justice of the Peace, and make attempts to bite the passer by." Under such circumstances, "dog killing" transformed into a "necessity" in Singapore for "suppressing the nuisance occasioned by loose dogs being allowed to roam about the streets of the Town," particularly after a stray bit a peon working for the Government Surveyor in 1848, which reinforced fears over the possibility of a rabies outbreak. This resulted in the government investing the Municipal Committee with the power to "kill and destroy all dogs found loose in the streets and not accompanying their owners or some person in charge of them." The official policy of the government now was to eliminate all dogs "at liberty during the day" that were without a collar on the first three days of every month, unless it was a Sunday. In 1849, this strategy resulted in the destruction of 427 dogs and 146 bitches.[55]

Although police officers actively killed dogs as early as the 1830s, the task ultimately was assigned to a group of Indian convicts, who formed a "permanent detachment" that operated in Singapore for several decades. The system of using convicts to kill dogs was due to Singapore being under the East India Company as a merchant colony, where there was very little financial outlay for anything beyond rudimentary services. This resulted in much of the manual labor in service to governmental needs falling to those who could not refuse, Indian men who were exiled to the Company port as their punishment, who carried out numerous tasks in early colonial Singapore, particularly the construction of roads and buildings that laid the foundation for the town. "Dog killing" was among the lowliest of duties these men could be assigned. There was only superficial monitoring of such activities, as long as the convicts performed the required labor, with members of the detachment often portrayed as efficient in a responsibility that was "cruel, merciless and brutal." As J.F.A. McNair explained, "only occasionally, an officer of the police came and called roll in order to report to the Government that all were present." The presence of such a taskforce was just part of the colonial landscape, which can be seen in a report from March 1850, when it was reported in a straightforward

---

[55] Anonymous, "Odds and Ends," *ST*, 1 Feb. 1846, p. 1; Anonymous, "Untitled," *SFP*, 8 Apr. 1847, p. 2; Anonymous, "Untitled," *ST*, 26 July 1848, p. 2; Anonymous, "Untitled," *ST*, 19 Jul. 1853, p. 5; Anonymous, "Disbursements," *SFP*, 8 Mar. 1849, p. 1.

manner that "a fine dog was killed by 3 Convicts in the open Verandah of a Gentleman's house in Teluk Ayer Street," for which they received a portion of the reward "for every dead dog, which serve to manure a plantation."[56]

Eventually, the policy of active destruction of dogs soon led to questions about responsibility, and reflected the shifting relationship between humans and animals at the time. Much of this change was rooted in how animals were perceived. There was a distinction between domesticated and wild in English common law, which was linked to property rights. A "wild" animal "should not by habit or training live with or in association with or in the service of man." In this context, a domestic animal could be owned; it was property. The stray dogs of early colonial Singapore, with no perceivable owner, would have been classified as wild, and thus liable to destruction, and the appellation of "nuisance."[57] As dogs were beginning to become domesticated in urban Singapore, their destruction took on new meanings. They were now property.

One case, in 1844, reflected the shifting line between wild and tame in colonial Singapore. It began when a dog owner complained that he found his pet canine—"Revenge"—"lying amongst a heap of slain in a corner of the Road leading to Government Hill." As there had been no announcement of the coming cull printed in the paper, the dog owner was aggrieved. The authorities countered that, although they regretted the death of "some dogs of 'gentle degree'," written circulars were passed to all European inhabitants of Singapore (some 150 people at the time). The dog owner was not angry at the loss of the animal's life, however. He was upset at a loss of property, and this led to larger questions and complaints from the public. For example,

---

[56] Due to the low fertility of the soil in Singapore, many dead animals were used for fertilization purposes throughout the 19th century. Thomas Oxley, "Some Account of the Nutmeg and Its Cultivation," *Journal of the Indian Archipelago and Eastern Asia* 2, 10 (1848): 648–50; Anonymous, "Local," *SFP*, 29 Mar. 1850, p. 3; Pieris, *Hidden Hands and Divided Landscapes*, p. 243; McNair, *Prisoners Their Own Warders*, pp. 39, 38–42; Rajesh Rai, *Indians in Singapore, 1819–1945: Diaspora in the Colonial Port City* (New Delhi: Oxford University Press, 2014), pp. 13–18.

[57] Lye Lin Heng, "Wildlife Protection Laws in Singapore," *Singapore Journal of Legal Studies* (1991): 290.

would the owner be able to request compensation for the loss of a valuable watchdog? It also led to questions related to the brutal nature of the practice, reflecting the changing nature of how the animal was understood in colonial society. As one observer argued, "To kill a stray dog, merely because it be astray, is illegal; to mutilate or half kill, and to have the mutilated or half-destroyed animal exposed to the public gaze is as brutal in its character."[58]

Despite the presence of an active program of culling as an activity "essential to the comfort of the public," mongrels still plagued the streets two decades after the beginning of the program. As one article in *The Straits Times* in 1856 declared, "public thoroughfares are infested and the lives of foot passengers greatly imperiled. There is scarcely a street within the precincts of the town along which passengers can pass with safety even during the day, whilst at night the danger is augmented ten-fold." The problem was particularly bad in Kampong Glam, Teluk Ayer and Bencoolen districts, where "pariah curs keep up almost a continued bark throughout the night."[59]

The practice of culling feral animals continued to create unease in the society throughout the 1850s, although it soon became cloaked in the question of dependence on convicts for the violence during a period of rising fears related to the aftermath of the Indian Mutiny of 1857. Basically, European residents of Singapore began expressing a discomfort with the practice of South Asians roaming the streets, armed with weapons, and beating animals to death. This led to petitions against the public presence of unsupervised convicts in a variety of

---

[58] What Next?, "Correspondence," *SFP*, 10 Oct. 1844, p. 5; Anonymous, "Singapore, Thursday, 10th October 1844," *SFP*, 10 Oct. 1844, p. 5; H.W., "Correspondence"; Anonymous, "Untitled," *ST*, 11 Nov. 1851, p. 4.

[59] In 1856 officials in Calcutta proposed and passed a new Police Bill, which would be applicable in Calcutta, Madras, Bombay as well as Penang, Melaka and Singapore. Towards the end of the numerous regulations and laws was a provision for stray dogs. In Section 116, Act XII, it called for dogs "to be killed at certain appointed periods." Any other stray animal was to be impounded, until the owner was found. This new set of provisions formalized the action to be taken toward dogs in EIC ports throughout Asia, and came into effect in late 1856. Anonymous, "The New Police Bill," *ST*, 17 Oct. 1855, p. 1; Anonymous, "Legislative Council," *SFP*, 8 Nov. 1855, p. 3. Also see William Theobald "Acts of the Legislative Council of India"; Anonymous, "Untitled," *ST*, 9 Sep. 1856, p. 4.

professions, including dog culling. The petitioners described the use of convicts "without any immediate control over them" as a "great evil," as it was "opposed to all ideas of Municipal order and propriety." Although this would result in a rise in expenditures, the uproar was so great that Governor Blundell agreed to remove Indians with clubs tasked with controlling wild animals from the streets by mid-1858.[60]

To entice new dog cullers, the government offered a reward "three times the former amount per head." There was little interest. This led the Commissioner of Police to request that convicts be allowed to continue with the task under the supervision of officers; this request was denied "repeatedly." The solution to the "serious evil arising from the unchecked increase of dogs in Singapore" evolved into new rules in which "European members of the Police Force" would shoot all stray dogs found over the designated three-day periods each month. Under this new policy, 200 dogs were culled in May 1859, with the officers assigned to Rochor Street Station being responsible for 103 of them.[61]

Police officers initially took to dog killing with particular vigor, and their activities received positive coverage in the newspapers. For example, on the morning of a mid-August day in 1859, near a Chinese *wayang* show, the police arrived "armed to the teeth with gun and baton." A dog emerged from a nearby house "unconscious of the fate awaiting him a few yards off." The Police Inspector and his peons waited anxiously as the dog approached. "The Inspector fired, and the dog was astounded—not hurt. The Orderlies rushed in, and by dint of hard blows, the owner of the dog lost $50, through letting him take an airing."[62] After several months, however, police officers

---

[60] SSR: Governor's Miscellaneous Letters, V23 (1858), pp. 160–1; V24 (1858), pp. 78–80; India Office Records, British Library [hereafter, IOR]\L\PJ\3\1069: Straits Collection No. 22: "Discontinuance of Convicts Being Employed as Street Scavengers"; Rajesh Rai, "The 1857 Panic and the Fabrication of an Indian 'Menace' in Singapore," *Modern Asian Studies* 47, 2 (2013): 365–405.

[61] In addition, a "dog tax" was proposed. Once again, this was unsuccessful. Anonymous, "Untitled," *ST*, 16 Apr. 1858: 9; Anonymous, "Municipal Commissioners," *SFP*, 5 May 1859, p. 4; Anonymous, "Thursday Morning, 26th May, 1859," *SFP*, 26 May 1859, p. 2; Anonymous, "Correspondences," *ST*, 28 May 1859, p. 3.

[62] In addition, the police paid $106.09 to freelance dog killers during the financial year of 1858/59. Anonymous, "Singapore: Saturday 4th June," *ST*, 4 June 1859, p. 2; Argus, "To the Editor of The Straits Times," *ST*, 27 Aug. 1859, p. 4.

began to hesitate at the task of publicly killing canines. A proposed alternative was to bring curs to police stations, where they would then be destroyed. This resolution lost its appeal quickly. Ultimately, it became clear that the police and "free persons will not willingly engage in such a task."[63]

In the context of growing official reluctance to participate publicly in dog culling, which was also a further sign of the changing relationship between humans and canines, the municipal commissioners reinstated the use of convicts in late 1859. This renewed system was once again another shift in strategy, reflecting reluctance among the public with carrying out such activities. The new approach called for a "requisite number of Police Peons" to accompany the convicts when they were carrying out the culls as a "precaution necessary to prevent prisoners from becoming embroiled with any individual whose dog they may be instructed to kill." To prevent further disturbance to the public, dog killing would only be carried out between the hours of 10 a.m. and 3 p.m. during the designated days.[64] This program to limit canines in Singapore continued for decades.

In the midst of the debates and passage of regulations related to the role of the police and convicts in dog culling, the continued hope of taming the colonial urban space continued. At this time Governor Blundell proposed that a tax of $2 per annum be imposed on all dogs in "the Town and suburbs, extending in all directions to the 2nd mile stone." This was to allow for dogs in the plantation areas, where they were considered necessary for "protection against thieves," to be maintained. In the city, however, "there are no dogs of a useful description kept by the dog-fanciers," particularly along Waterloo, Queen, Prinsep and Bencoolen streets. The urban dogs were a "tribe of 'yelping curs', and the sooner they are destroyed … the better." Blundell hoped that the imposition of the dog tax would "increase the number of persons unwilling to own dogs and consequently the number of dogs to be destroyed." Each owner that paid the tax would be issued "a numbered collar" or "a brass number to attach to a collar." If a dog did not have a collar it would be subject to culling. This proposal, "like many other good measures," failed to pass due to the inattention of officials in

[63] Anonymous, "Municipal Commissioners," *SFP*, 6 Oct. 1859, p. 3.
[64] Anonymous, "Municipal Commissioners. Local," *ST*, 8 Oct. 1859, p. 3.

Singapore as well as the reluctance of administrators in Calcutta to approve any new taxes.[65]

The debate and consternation over the role of dogs in Singapore continued throughout the 1860s. *The Straits Times* reported that, "There is scarcely a street which you can enter in the suburbs, either by day or night, where you are not in danger of being pounced upon suddenly by dozens of these animals." Stray dogs even attacked horses at the race-track, making training "next to impossible." The result was that "some of the best horses have been rendered skittish and uncertain owing to the sudden attacks" of pariah curs, lamented one newspaper report.[66]

The continuation of the dog nuisance during this period led a resident to submit a rather poorly written poem about the issue. The art piece contains numerous complaints about the nightly howling of mongrels and ends with the following lines:

> Banish all the noisy crew—
> Justice raise your iron hand!
> Spare of worthy dogs a few—
> Crush—oh crush the brawling band.[67]

The feral dogs of Singapore had moved beyond being an irritation. They were now described as "dangerous animals" in the press. If they were not eliminated, warned "Dog Nuisance," the moniker of a letter writer to *The Straits Times*, "Singapore will soon be as much infested with them as Lisbon or Constantinople, where no person, without the most extreme danger, can walk about almost at any hour unaccompanied by a guide."[68]

---

[65] The aversion to taxes was a particular annoyance to Governor Cavenagh, who assumed the post from Blundell in mid-1859, amidst these debates. As Cavenagh bemoaned, in Singapore "the professional and commercial classes benefit by our rule, and how little, comparatively speaking, they contribute to towards meeting the requirements of the state." Cavenagh, *Reminiscences of an Indian Official*, p. 286; Buckley, *An Anecdotal History of Singapore*, p. 383; Anonymous, "Thursday Morning, 26th May, 1859"; Anonymous, "A Dog Tax," *ST*, 17 Sep. 1859, p. 2; Tray, "The Dog Tax," *ST*, 20 Dec. 1862, p. 2; Anonymous, "Correspondences."

[66] Anonymous, "The Dog Nuisance," *ST*, 25 Mar. 1865, p. 1.

[67] Chusan, "Lap Dogs and Curs. A Chorus, by an Invalid," *SFP*, 23 May 1861, p. 3.

[68] Anonymous, "The Dog Nuisance," *ST*, 20 Aug. 1859, p. 2.

Who was at fault for the large number of stray dogs? According to the editors of *The Straits Times*, "we are happy to say that few of the English inhabitants of Singapore are in the habit of keeping kennels, so that in their change of residence to this part of the world, they have, in this respect, brought their good manners with them." Instead, fault was directed toward "the other classes of inhabitants." Although the newspaper editors did not identify one of the worst violators in a diatribe in the late 1850s, they claimed that, "With the exception of the Sepoy Lines, the great majority of the dogs in other parts of town are both owned and fed by one man, a sago manufacturer ... possessing no less than thirty six." The tensions between those who were owners of pets, and those who tolerated commensal animals were widening.[69]

The growing concern over how dog killing activities effected animals living with the elite population of Singapore, which were bred as pets, reached a peak in early 1862 when a police officer shot an English terrier in the middle of the night. The report of the firearm woke Sydney Charles Pass, the owner of the terrier. When he went outside to investigate, the dog ran toward him—"with his face and breast literally battered in by a gunshot"—collapsed and died. Pass found 20 Police Peons standing in the street, and an officer holding a carbine "in his hand still smoking from the discharge." When Pass approached the officer, he realized that the shooter was the Deputy Commissioner of Police, Kenneth B.S. Robertson, who told Pass that he was simply fulfilling his duty. Robertson, Pass declared with exasperation, "was wandering thus at midnight for the purpose of slaying all the dogs that he came across."[70]

This led to a series of discussions that played out in the press concerning dog killing in Singapore, particularly after Pass decided to sue Robertson in court, because the terrier was wearing a collar. Many European residents of Singapore were scandalized, as Robertson was not willing to admit "an ignorance of the error committed." He had, after all, destroyed the property of a European. The Magistrate agreed that an error had occurred, and fined Robertson $50. The violation

---

[69] As Jonathan Saha has argued in his consideration on the role of senses, animals and representation in colonial Burma, "animals are better analysed as having been materially and figuratively entangled in the production of colonial discourses of difference." Saha, "Among the Beasts of Burma," p. 926; Anonymous, "A Dog Tax"; Anonymous, "Thursday Morning, 26th May, 1859."

[70] S.C. Pass, "Untitled," *ST*, 18 Jan. 1862, p. 2.

Image 2.2: Illustration of a European visiting the Singapore Botanic Gardens with domesticated dogs. Illustration by John Edmund Taylor. Courtesy of the Wellcome Collection.

he had committed, however, was the absence of a written notice that dog killing activities were going to take place—under the Police Act of 1857, this was to be done six days in advance—as well as a disregard for noise ordinances.[71]

The entire hubbub over the death of the terrier reflected a change in tone with regard to animals in Singapore, particularly dogs. Many canines were beginning to be viewed as pets. Those with collars were "not the ordinary pariah of the roads." They were "the favorite or play thing of a friend." While the stray dog problem, and the inherent violence related to it, remained an issue, it now took on an air of class and race. The task of dog killing was now to be done with "reluctance," as a culture clash in a multicultural European-controlled colonial port

---

[71] If Robertson had used a cutlass or a club, he would not have violated any noise regulations. Anonymous, "Untitled," *ST*, 1 Feb. 1862, p. 2; Anonymous, "Tuesday, 18th February, 1862," *ST*, 1 Mar. 1862, p. 2; Anonymous, "Untitled," *ST*, 5 Apr. 1862, p. 1.

was developing as the issue shifted from the necessity of carrying out the activity to the methods employed to limit, control, define and differentiate the owners of these dogs.[72]

The problem, according to *The Straits Times*, was rooted in the various communities and how they viewed dogs. European residents, of course, were portrayed as innocent, while Asians were "notorious" for breeding pariah dogs. "An English gentleman," in contrast, maintains a dog that "becomes a pleasure" and provides "protection to his master, but not a nuisance and a danger to others." The key issue was that, although the stray dogs on the streets had no master, the "Natives around us" had "introduced" dogs to the island and then proceeded to ignore them, with the result being their transformations into curs. In light of this debate, the editors of the paper called for "restrictions upon the keeping of dogs by the Natives in the town and suburbs," although this would create two separate laws for residents of the island.[73]

The class and racial implications of the continuing practice of dog culling were coming to the fore by end of the Company period in Singaporean history. The animals—in this case, the dogs—that were the subject of the violence, however, were changing. They were becoming pets, and their status in certain households made the violence less tenable. This violence, however, had served its purpose as it began the process of establishing human dominance over the urban space.

The March of Progress

Even after the Colonial Office in London established direct control over the Straits Settlements in 1867, the dog nuisance continued as did efforts to control it. The police would supervise the killing of curs over three days every month. As one observer noted, however, "although

---

[72] Anonymous, "Untitled," *ST*, 1 Feb. 1862, p. 2.

[73] One of the key issues was the number of dogs each resident kept, or at least protected. In Singapore a pattern had developed in which "any cow-feeder or cooly" could own "a dozen curs of all degrees, provided only he can manage to restrain them within the limited area of his dwelling during the three or four dog shooting days." This resulted in a situation in which, a resident could "own without keeping any number of dogs,—that is, he may successfully assert and maintain a right of property in them, and yet leave them to prowl about the town in search of food." Anonymous, "Friday, 12th May, 1865," *ST*, 13 May 1865, p. 2; Anonymous, "The Dog Nuisance," *ST*, 15 Mar. 1865, p. 1.

a considerable number have met their death, no diminution of their numbers is perceptible." Feral dogs, "under the somewhat nondescript denomination of pariah," continued to plague Singapore and its residents. "They feed in the streets, and sleep in the verandahs or open hovels, whence they rush out at night to attack defenceless pedestrians and to bark and snarl under the heels of the horses."[74]

Taming the wild was an ongoing process of shaping the ecological landscape to fit imperial goals and desires and, in this case, ridding it of pests. Tigers were being eradicated from the forest while dogs that did not follow limitations placed upon them were commonly beaten to death in the streets of the town. This also occurred against a backdrop of converting the island into a cultivated and productive landscape. Raffles' vision of a civilized island had been achieved within decades, and it was accomplished through violence and destruction. One long-term resident of Singapore, John Dill Ross, best summarized the changes that occurred as the island was brought within the orbit of British imperial rule when he wistfully wrote, "The march of progress calls for many a sacrifice and it is useless to bemoan the inevitable, though a seemly sigh for the departed beauty may be permitted."[75]

The relationship between animals and the colonial government as it spread to control the small island of Singapore was a complex mixture of control and limitation, ensuring that the animals that were present had a utilitarian presence, or at least had a commensal relationship with humans. An example of such responses was wildlife legislation that followed in the wake of the deforestation that stripped the island in the first few decades of colonial rule. Long-time residents reported that there had been shifts in the climate, with less rainfall being reported. In addition, without catchment areas and the filtering of water they provided, the streams and rivers of Singapore were drying up and the quality of the fresh water had declined. Providing the basic needs of a society was becoming increasingly difficult. With the imposition of a colonial government that was directly linked to London in 1867, and more attuned to local concerns than the earlier Company overlords from India, institutions began to focus on solutions to address these issues. One of the first steps the new colonial official took was to

---

[74] Anonymous, "Untitled," *ST*, 25 Dec. 1869, p. 2.
[75] John Dill Ross, *The Capital of a Little Empire: A Descriptive Study of a British Crown Colony in the Far East* (Singapore: Kelly and Walsh, 1898), p. 5.

turn to the Singapore Botanic Gardens to help with the reforestation of the island, while water reservoirs were developed in the center of the island.[76]

With this new form of rule came shifting British understandings of wildlife, hunting and sport, as well as a growing understanding of how policies of deforestation had affected the landscape, flora and fauna of its overseas possession. This rapid decline in biodiversity was also addressed through the establishment of new rules and regulations protecting animals. Many of these new policies were directed at limiting the hunting of some of the rich avian wildlife of the region. A new law was passed—The Wild Birds Protection Ordinance, 1884—with no recorded debate in the Legislative Council. The decree made it illegal to "kill, wound or take in any manner whatever any wild bird." The fine for violation of the law was $2 and up to 14 days in jail. There were, however, 31 species excluded from protection as they were considered to be pests or were commonly hunted for sport, such as ducks and pheasants.[77] Twenty years later, the Legislative Council extended protection of fauna with the Wild Animals and Birds Protections Ordinance, 1904, which resulted in a ban on netting and snaring snipe and six additional species of birds (mainly pheasants but also jungle fowl as well as the ground pigeon and wood pigeon) between February and May, their breeding season. Finally, in 1923, the hunting of sambar deer (*Rusa unicolor*) and barking deer (*Muntiacus muntjak*), more commonly known as the *kijang*, was made illegal in Singapore.[78]

The effect of these ordinances was limited, as the native fauna of the island had already been devastated. This led public officials, such as Supreme Court Justice John Bucknill and Raffles Museum Director F.N. Chasen to lament the state of biodiversity in Singapore in 1927. In a book promoting an appreciation of birds found on the island, they urged the public to avoid "haphazard collecting methods" and to stick

---

[76] Barnard, *Nature's Colony*; Lye, "Wildlife Protection Laws in Singapore."

[77] CO276/15: "Government Notification, No. 274," (1884), pp. 695–6; Anonymous, "Shorthand Report of the Legislative Council," *The Straits Times Weekly*, 25 Jun. 1884, p. 8; Lye, "Wildlife Protection Laws in Singapore," pp. 292–3.

[78] Only after World War Two, in 1947, was protection extended to the banded leaf-monkey, slow loris, pangolins and two species of mouse deer. Ordinance No. XVI of 1904; CO276/94: No. 955. Ordinance No. 88 (Wild Animals and Birds), p. 1007; Lye, "Wildlife Protection Laws in Singapore," p. 293; Corlett, "Ecological Transformation of Singapore," p. 414.

to "observation" to enjoy the wildlife around them, as the previous century had left the avian population "destroyed." As they described the situation, "Although it is easy to believe that some of these birds occurred on the island before the settlement was so large," they were now "uncommon," due to "the absence of any extent of old jungle." Bucknill and Chasen went on to add:

> The gradual extension of the city must perforce drive the birds away. It is stated that a few years ago green pigeons were to be seen in the Raffles Museum compound and kingfishers flew up and down the canal in Stamford Road. Such events are now remarkable. So far as birds are concerned, Singapore is not the home of luxuriant, thriving life one is led to expect after the literature dealing with natural history in the tropics.[79]

While some of this biodiversity would re-establish itself in the replanted forests of the interior of the island in the postcolonial era, this would take decades to overcome, and never truly reach the levels of richness and variety that had been lost following the development of man-made landscapes on the island, the creation of an imperial outpost. The first five decades of imperial rule in Singapore ultimately resulted in deforestation and the elimination of native species, as well as control being exercised over beasts in the developing urban landscape. The precolonial landscape was gone. It was replaced with flora and fauna that were more conducive to the expectations of the new immigrants on the island.

Regulations and lamentations given to address this issue, nevertheless, were an important step in the introduction of new concepts related to how animals were understood in the public sphere. This colonial landscape, a tamed island, was part of larger networks of civilization, administration and control. As the British Empire expanded, Singapore was also coming under the influence of shifting understandings of how humans relate to animals, and the manner in which they were present in the lives of all residents of the island.

---

[79] John A.S. Bucknill and F.N. Chasen, *The Birds of Singapore Island* (Singapore: Government Printing Office 1927), pp. 1, 5.

CHAPTER THREE

Fauna in a Colonial Landscape

In the early 1840s the Singaporean elite found entertainment through a "Tiger Club," in which they would rush into the interior of the island after word went out that a beast had fallen into one of the pits that plantation owners had dug around their properties. Privileged residents considered these events to be one of the unique appeals of living in a distant outpost of empire, as it had parallels with hunting rituals in the West that allowed for a symbolic control over nature. Once they gathered around the large hole, these men—and they were always young Europeans—would taunt the captive animal with sticks while they awaited the arrival of their colleagues. After a designated period of time had passed, usually one hour, they then took turns shooting at the trapped creature. The brave sportsman who dispensed the fatal shot was celebrated as the victor, receiving the skin for display as well as the right to brag to his cohorts about the endeavor. In the meantime, the plantation owner presented the head to the government for a reward while the flesh of the tiger was sold in the market to interested consumers.[1]

The joy that the hunters found in the Tiger Club, however, quickly waned, as the opportunity to shoot at a large carnivore in a pit did not occur frequently enough to entertain Europeans hungry

---

[1] Barnard and Emmanuel, "Tigers of Colonial Singapore," pp. 72–3; McNair, *Prisoners Their Own Warders*, pp. 50–1.

for distractions. As W.H.M. Read explained in his memoir, the playing of card games seemed to be the only form of enjoyment that regularly took place in early colonial Singapore. There was "no cricket, football, nor golf; no theatre, no library, no race-course," he lamented. Although he participated in the Tiger Club, Read and his friends began planning for new, more British approaches to passing time in a distant center of empire. This culminated on 4 October 1842 when Read, along with Charles Spottiswoode and William Napier, gathered their peers together and founded the Singapore Sporting Club. One of the main goals of this new association was the development of another symbolic form of control over beasts. They wanted to re-establish horse racing on the island.[2]

Horse racing had taken place in Singapore as early as 1823 in an empty space near the flat, grassy, central plain known as the Padang, where, Munshi Abdullah remembered, "in the evening the white men used to go for walks." Eventually, in 1835, this ground was designated for the construction of St. Andrew's Cathedral, and "the white men" had to pursue new forms of leisure, which included the Tiger Club. After several years, many longed for a revival of the beloved British amusement of watching swift equines run around large ovals. Immediately after discussing the matter with Read and his friends in October 1842, Governor Samuel George Bonham granted the Singapore Sporting Club the right to transform an area of swampy land near the Indian settlement into a racecourse. Construction began, and an announcement of upcoming races appeared in December of that same year. The first meet was scheduled for 19 February, to celebrate "the anniversary of the foundation of this Settlement." Five races were scheduled, with the most prestigious—The Singapore Cup—to be the inaugural contest. It would only be run if there were at least four entries.[3]

---

[2] An Old Resident, *Play and Politics: Reminiscences of Malaya* (London: Wells Gardner, Darton and Company, 1901), pp. 5, 158–60; Sumiko Tan, *The Winning Connection: 150 Years of Racing in Singapore* (Singapore: Bukit Turf Club, 1992), p. 16.

[3] Templeton, "Singapore Races," *SFP*, 8 Dec. 1842, p. 3; Abdullah, *Hikayat Abdullah*, p. 246; Anonymous, "A Century of Sport," in *One Hundred Years of Singapore, Being an Account of the Capital of the Straits Settlements from its Foundation by Sir Stamford Raffles on the 6th February 1819 to the 6th February 1919*, vol. II, ed. Walter Makepeace, Gilbert E. Brooke, and Roland St. J. Braddell (London: John Murray, 1921), p. 348.

On 23 February 1843, a Thursday morning and four days later than scheduled, the elite of Singapore gathered to witness the first official horse race over the new course. The delay in holding the contest may have been due to the racecourse being unfinished, as the crowd that attended the festivities faced difficulties watching the horses from start to finish since the infield of the oval had yet to be "cleared of jungle," thus blocking their views. Despite such an obstacle, the Singapore Cup kicked off events, and six horses had been entered. Colonel was the favorite, although Lady Mary also received strong support from the crowd. Several heats would determine the winner. Following a fair start in the first heat, the favorite won by six lengths. For the second heat Lady Mary took an early lead, but faded in the last quarter of the race, which allowed Colonel to pass and win by three lengths. The jockeys made the difference. One witness praised "the excellent Jockeyism of the Young Amateur who rode the Colonel," which "excited General admiration—indeed we have seldom seen better management." In contrast, "we wish we could say the same for the rider of Lady Mary. Had our friend, the little square built amateur, been mounted on this occasion,—and nothing but his modesty preventing, the result of the race might have been different." The race received little coverage in the local press beyond those brief comments. Even Read, the winning jockey, described it very simply in his own memoir as, "I won the first race run over it, on an Arab named 'Colonel'."[4]

The Singapore Sporting Club existed from 1842 until 1924, when the association changed its name to the Singapore Turf Club. In the first few decades of existence, its popularity was limited mainly to the European community and Malay royalty. Horse racing, nevertheless, was not simply an amusement for the ruling elite of the port. It had a deeper meaning. These contests allowed British administrators and merchants to indulge in their "national pastime" in an outpost of empire. As James C. Whyte argued in his history of the sport published in 1840, most Britons felt horse racing was a manifestation of their identity and authority as it provided a metaphor for their ascendancy

[4] Anonymous, "Singapore Races," *SFP*, 2 Mar. 1843, p. 3; Tan, *The Winning Connection*, pp. 16–20; An Old Resident, *Play and Politics*, p. 5; Arnold Wright and H.A. Cartwright, *Twentieth Century Impressions of British Malaya: Its History, People, Commerce, Industries, and Resources* (London: Lloyd's Greater Britain Publishing Company, 1908), p. 562.

Image 3.1: Two race-going celebrities talk as a race horse is ridden past them, 1881. The figures depicted are Abu Bakar, the Maharaja of Johor, and Chinese Merchant Cheang Hong Lim. The jockey is H. Abrams, who worked closely with the Maharaja in pursuit of this pastime. Illustration by John Edmund Taylor. Courtesy of the Wellcome Collection.

during the century, as the breeding and skills required to raise, train, and ride a successful horse "may be ascribed much our superiority over other nations." A pastime so intimately linked to British character during the age of empire was nurtured, cherished and celebrated in an imperial outpost.[5]

The twice-yearly meets became an important part of the social calendar in Singapore, as they allowed for public displays of status, wealth and power. The Singapore Sporting Club was a place where the privileged went to see others and be seen, and its rituals were part of

---

[5] James Christie Whyte, *History of the British Turf, from the Earliest Period to the Present Day*, Vol. 1 (London: Henry Colburn, 1840), p. vii; Anonymous, *Horse-Racing: Its History and Early Records of the Principal and Other Race Meetings. With Anecdotes, Etc* (London: Saunders, Otley and Co., 1863), p. 442; Anonymous, "A Century of Sport," p. 349; Tan, *The Winning Connection*.

the ebb and flow of life for the elite. When the race season neared, the syces, or native grooms, would begin exercising their mounts in the cool of the early morning, often before the cannon shot at sunrise—at 6 a.m.—from Fort Canning Hill that marked the beginning of the day in the colonial port. Many Europeans would stop by to watch these training sessions with the added provision that "the stewards provide tea on the course, so that it is altogether a very favourite resort for about six weeks before the spring and autumn meetings." During this period, many of the owners of the horses rode them during the races, a practice that continued until the 1870s when professional jockeys began "replacing gentlemen." As membership in the Club was a mark of status, wealthy Chinese Singaporeans eventually began to join for the opportunity to be seen among the powerful of the society since one had to be a member to attend the meets.[6]

The metaphorical control of animals in colonial Singapore was not solely the reserve of the economic, social and political elite of the port. It occurred across all strata of society and was a hallmark of life on the island. The diversity of animal species that lived under the command, or at the will, of humans was remarkable. Horses trotted along the streets alongside plodding bullocks. Pedestrians went for strolls with their domesticated dogs, while the smell of freshly slaughtered meat wafted from nearby markets. In quieter areas of the town, residents could hear the chirping of crickets or the songs of birds, both caged, while a chained gibbon or a macaque furtively glanced at passers-by from a house compound. Singaporeans also could attend a circus, visit a zoo, or marvel at a dead carcass on display at a museum. Animals were everywhere.

The presence of these animals, of course, was not unique. After all, animals exist, and existed, in all communities across the globe. In this case, however, they were understood and reflected larger imperial mores and understandings in the society. Singapore was a port filled with animals, and their presence had implications for how the society perceived its place during the era of imperialism on a small island in Southeast Asia. Animals under human control—whether for utilitarian purposes, emotional companionship, or erudition—reflected a shift in

---

[6] Cameron, *Our Tropical Possessions in Malayan India*, p. 292; Anonymous, "A Century of Sport," p. 349; Anonymous, *Singapore Racecourse, 1842–2000* (Singapore: Singapore Turf Club, 2000), pp. 6–8.

Image 3.2: A Singaporean family participating in a popular colonial pastime, visiting the monkeys in the Singapore Botanic Gardens. Image from Lee Brothers Studio, courtesy of National Archives of Singapore.

the human-animal relationship on the island. The landscape had been tamed, and biodiversity reduced, within decades of the imposition of imperial rule, but animals remained an important part of the Singapore landscape. They became imperial creatures.

The imperial influence in the human-animal relationship in colonial Singapore began with the fact that most of the creatures encountered were not native to the island. Native fauna had been reduced drastically following the arrival of the East India Company, as plantation owners and Chinese agriculturalists began a process of deforestation and cultivation, which left the interior of the island devastated biologically. Writing in the 1930s Roland Braddell exclaimed, "don't imagine that Singapore itself is full of wild animals and snakes, for it is not. You can live on this island for a quarter of a century and see none besides the monkeys in the Botanic Gardens, the animal shops, and the Singapore Zoo."[7] This sentiment was true as early as the 1880s, when American naturalist William T. Hornaday visited Singapore while on a collecting

---

[7] Roland Braddell, *Lights of Singapore* (London: Methuen and Co, 1934), p. 123.

trip for zoos and natural history museums, during which he commented that "with the exception of shells, star-fishes and corals, I found nothing on the island that I cared to either collect or buy."[8]

The absence of native fauna was an important element in the transformation of the society, as all animals on the island were ostensibly under the control of humans. Any fauna external to this control was in danger, much like the occasional tiger that roamed the depleted forests. The last one was killed in 1930, the victim of a hunting party in Choa Chu Kang.[9] The animals that humans cultivated, raised, cherished and employed were everywhere, flourishing due to their ability to fit within the expanding imperial system. The vast majority could be roughly classified as creatures that provided transportation, labor and food. They ranged from bullocks to fish, animals that were present in almost every community worldwide. Tropical fauna, often coming from the Malay Peninsula or wider archipelago, such as birds of paradise or orangutans, supplemented these animals, with their presence a result of the location of Singapore in Southeast Asia and its role in the larger British Empire. The origin of these imperial creatures was of little importance. They were incorporated into a colonial society and they were all clearly under the control of humans, and in the process became metaphors for imperial authority as well as perceptions of Singapore and its place in the tropics and within a landscape that had already been tamed. And, almost all of these animals arrived via the port.

Importing and Trading the Exotic

Singapore owed much of its success during the colonial era not to the growing bureaucracy that oversaw daily interaction, including that involvng humans and animals, but due to its well-functioning port at the center of trade networks. This was the reason the small island was important to the empire. As one observer in the late 19th century noted, "This is Singapore, the great central ganglion of the Malay Archipelago and Southeastern Asia, the hub of the Far East. The spokes of steamship

---

[8] William T. Hornaday, *Two Years in the Jungle: The Experiences of a Hunter and Naturalist in India, Ceylon, the Malay Peninsula and Borneo* (New York, NY: C. Scribner's Sons, 1885), p. 298.
[9] Powell, "People in Peril, Environments at Risk," p. 479.

lines running in almost every direction, to Bangkok, Saigon, China and Japan, Manilla, Sarawak, Pontianak, Batavia, Sumatra, Ceylon, Calcutta, Rangoon, and Malacca."[10] The port connected Singapore to the larger world, the surrounding archipelago, and the island itself. It was the lifeblood of the colony, and the harbor was always filled with ships.

Singapore was an appealing destination due its geographic location as well as the absence of excise duties on all goods, except for opium, alcohol, tobacco and eventually petroleum. Throughout the colonial period the number of ships, and their tonnage, rose continuously. Between 1822 and 1824, 2,889 vessels called at the port—including 333 "square-rigged vessels," meaning larger Western trade ships loaded with cargo from Europe, India, China and many other distant locales— carrying 161,000 tons of cargo. These numbers increased. Twenty years later 870 square-rigged vessels brought in 286,000 tons of cargo out of a total of 340,000 tons in one year. "Prows," Southeast Asian sailing vessels that brought food, supplies and rare products from the forests and plantations of the archipelago as they entered global trade networks, made up the remainder.[11]

The number of ships, and the volume they carried to Singapore, received a significant boost following the opening of the Suez Canal in 1869 as well as improvements to and an expansion of port facilities between 1852 and 1905. The result by the end of the 19th century was "nearly two miles [3.2 kilometers] of steamers, in an unbroken row," along Tanjong Pagar and Borneo Wharves, often with "ships 'double banked' or even three deep on occasion." This allowed for the "aggregrate tonnage of the merchant shipping" to double from 1896 to 1906 to a total of 6,661,549 tons by the later year. In addition, millions of people from throughout the world passed through Singapore

---

[10] Hornaday, *Two Years in the Jungle*, p. 291; Peter Reeves and Noelene Reeves, "Port-City Development and Singapore's Inshore and Culture Fisheries," in *Muddied Waters: Historical and Contemporary Perspectives on Management of Forests and Fisheries in Island Southeast Asia*, ed. Peter Boomgaard, David Henley and Manon Osseweijer (Leiden: KITLV, 2005), pp. 121–3.

[11] A. Stuart, "Exports, Imports, and Shipping. Straits Settlements," in *Twentieth Century Impressions of British Malaya: Its History, People, Commerce, Industries, and Resources*, ed. Arnold Wright and H.A. Cartwright (London: Lloyd's Greater Britain Publishing Company, 1908), p. 162; Wong Lin Ken, *The Trade of Singapore, 1819–69* (Kuala Lumpur: JMBRAS, 2003); Anonymous, *A Short History of the Port of Singapore, with Particular Reference to the Undertakings of the Singapore Harbour Board* (Singapore: Fraser and Neave, 1922), p. 3.

during the colonial era, including massive numbers of migrants from India, China and Southeast Asia, which transformed the social and economic makeup of the region. The statistics related to this trade and the movement of peoples reflect the emergence of the British colonial port as a key node in global trade, and correspond to larger trade statistics. Fundamentally, a small island at the southern reaches of the Melaka Straits developed into a major hub vital to international commerce during the era of high imperialism.[12]

Most animals entered Singapore via the port. It is difficult to account for the actual fauna onboard these ships, however, as it was often done off the books or more commonly conflated into larger categories such as "living animals," with no distinction between a horse and an orangutan, particularly in British trade records. Some differentiation eventually does appear in the early 20th century, with Dutch efforts to account for variations within some of their own broad categories, which provides insight into the role that Singapore played in the trade in live, wild animals. In these records, Singapore is the destination for almost all tropical fauna exported from the Netherlands East Indies. As a matter of fact, it is the only destination. In 1918, for example, 99.9 percent of live animal exports from the Netherlands East Indies officially went through Singapore, while a majority of products such as processed skins and birds-nests also came through the port before entering larger networks of commerce.[13]

Beyond tropical wildlife, the vast majority of live animals that entered Singapore were cattle, horses and fish, as they provided labor and sustenance for the expanding human population of the island. Markets and other facilities quickly developed to handle the transfer and sale of these utilitarian animals. The horses that the Singapore

---

[12] Stuart, "Exports, Imports, and Shipping. Straits Settlements," p. 162; Ross, *Capital of a Little Empire*, p. 6; Goh Chor Boon, *Technology and Entrepôt Colonialism in Singapore, 1819–1940* (Singapore: ISEAS-Yusof Ishak Institute, 2013), pp. 64–92.

[13] In that year 69,211 live animals, out of 69,280, were sent to Singapore. For deerskins and birds-nests, the other markets were Japan, China and the United States. Karel Willem Dammerman, *Preservation of Wild Life and Nature Reserves in the Netherlands Indies* (Weltevreden: Emmink, 1929), pp. 88–91; Fiona L.P. Tan, "The Beastly Business of Regulating the Wildlife Trade in Colonial Singapore," *Nature Contained: Environmental Histories of Singapore*, ed. Timothy P. Barnard (Singapore: NUS Press, 2014), p. 156.

elite enjoyed watching race at the Singapore Sporting Club serve as an illustration. Throughout the 19th century, horses used for labor in Singapore were imported from Southeast Asia, with those from Sumatra being highly prized. Most horses that ran at the track during the colonial era, in contrast, were from Australia. This began following an auction in August 1843, the same year as the first official race. There were 11 horses up for sale at the mart, and the Commercial Square "became rather crowded with Europeans, Jews, Parsees, Arabs and the various tribes of settlers, which presented an animated scene." When the auction was over, the most expensive went for $350 and the cheapest for $100. As one account describe it, "The importation of these Horses &c., was in some degree experimental, and from the satisfactory results of the sales we may expect to see it repeated."[14]

The sale of horses in August 1843 must have been successful, as it became a weekly event for the rest of the century, usually lasting a few hours. These auctions took place in the center of commerce in the port, the Commercial Square, where "all the shipping offices, warehouses, and shops of the European merchants" were located and provided "a great convenience to all, as it was a good opportunity, after tiffin time, to see what was offered." As an observer of the period described in an account of walking through the square (modern day Raffles Place), "An Australian ship has just brought a full consignment of horses. There they are, tethered beneath trees, some of them likely-looking beasts, but somewhat stale after the voyage. One by one they are trotted out by Malays, or Kling grooms, and sold for, from twenty to two hundred dollars a piece."[15]

H.T. Powell, a businessman associated with the Singapore Exchange, developed a virtual monopoly on horse sales in Raffles Place after his establishment of the firm Powell and Co. in 1863. The enterprise oversaw auctions that usually took place on Fridays and were so chaotic that, by 1885, the municipal commissioners refused to provide the necessary licenses for these sales, as it was a "source of danger to passengers as well as an obstruction to traffic." Although Powell tried

---

[14] Anonymous, "Singapore, Thursday, 22nd August, 1844," *SFP*, 22 Aug. 1844, p. 3; Hornaday, *Two Years in the Jungle*, p. 294.

[15] J. Thomson, *The Straits of Malacca, Indo-China, and China; or Ten Years' Travels, Adventures, and Residence Abroad* (New York: Harper and Brothers, 1875), p. 58; Buckley, *An Anecdotal History of Singapore*, p. 628.

to organize the merchants in the area to claim that they welcomed the increased traffic, the commissioners refused to budge, proposing the construction of an alternative horse and cattle market on North Canal Street while owners of various stables offered to host the auctions. The next year, 1886, the situation deteriorated to the point that it became "increasingly difficult to either dispose of or purchase horses and carriage by auction, and the discontinuance has virtually placed the public at the mercy of one or two dealers," as one municipal commissioner described the disruption it caused to the flow of goods and people in the area. Horse auctions shifted to Canal Street that year, officially due to "traffic" issues.[16]

Utilitarian animals, particularly horses, cattle and fish, made up the majority of animals moving through the port, and they were handled through official representatives, companies and fleets of ships before they moved on to the markets, racetracks or butcheries. While this was intimately linked into the economy and providing basic services to the population, the port also functioned as a conduit for tropical fauna from throughout the archipelago, which often caught the eye of commentators as it provided a greater spectacle. As one contributor to a local newspaper wrote in the 1870s, "It is to Singapore that natives [from throughout Asia] ... bring the rare and often most valuable animals of their countries to sell them here for a relatively cheap price."[17]

The trade in tropical animals began soon after the arrival of the East India Company. This led James Low to comment, by the early 1840s, on the vast array of wildlife available, particularly "numbers of the parrot tribe," which arrived in Singapore aboard Bugis trading

---

[16] Debates over the issue dragged into 1887 with a proposal to convert the "southern enclosure in Raffles into a horse and cattle mart" with a levy of 25 cents for each horse, pony, or bullock, and 10 cents on any sheep or goat, sold there. National Archives of Singapore [hereafter NAS] 425: Minutes of the Proceedings of the Municipal Commissioners [hereafter MPMC], 23 Dec. 1885, p. 1094; NAS 425: MPMC, 12 Jan 1887, p. 1289; 20 Jan. 1886, p. 1105; 17 Feb. 1886, p. 1127; 12 Jan 1887, pp. 1263–4; Anonymous, "Municipal Commissioners," *The Straits Times Weekly Issue*, 3 June 1891, p. 5; Walter Makepeace, "The Machinery of Commerce," in *One Hundred Years of Singapore, Being an Account of the Capital of the Straits Settlements from its Foundation by Sir Stamford Raffles on the 6th February 1819 to the 6th February 1919*, vol. II, ed. Walter Makepeace, Gilbert E. Brooke, and Roland St. J. Braddell (London: John Murray, 1921), p. 214.

[17] W., "A Local Zoological Garden," *ST*, 16 May 1874, p. 4.

vessels from the eastern archipelago. For a month after the monsoons pushed their ships toward the port, "the streets resound with the discordant screams of beautiful birds." This remained true for decades. British travel writer Anna Brassey visited Singapore in 1877 and described an active market for all birds, ranging from "curious pheasants and jungle-fowl from Perak, doves, pigeons, quails, besides cockatoos, parrots, parakeets, and lories." The vendors, "all with parrots in their hands and on their shoulders," surrounded her, which she found "a very amusing sight." American journalist Thomas Knox also had a similar experience. Bird sellers swarmed him at the dock, where the "parrots, and members of their family, were generally secured by strings to little perches, and they kept up an incessant chattering in the Malay and other Oriental tongues." He was offered parakeets for 25 cents each, while a talking cockatoo would have cost him $6. Knox decided not to buy the cockatoo, however, as its English "vocabulary consisted of a half-dozen words of profanity."[18]

Accounts describing the array of exotic animals (from a Western perspective) available in the port were so common that they became a standard section in most memoirs describing a visit to the island in the 19th century. Although he had complained about the absence of native fauna on the island, Hornaday saw this traffic as something that made Singapore special. It was a place where—seemingly—any Southeast Asian animal could be purchased. As he proclaimed, "had I been a showman or collector of live animals, I could have gathered quite a harvest of wild beasts in Singapore, at a very small cost."[19] The industrialist Andrew Carnegie met Hornaday in Singapore on this trip, and was amused at the wonder the American zoologist exuded over this matter. According to Carnegie, with a bit of the humor, salesmanship and exaggeration for which he was known, Hornaday gushed that in the informal mart in the harbor:

---

[18] Anna Brassey, *A Voyage in the 'Sunbeam': Our Home on the Ocean for Eleven Months* (New York: John Wurtele Lovell, 1881), p. 411; Thomas W. Knox, *The Boy Travellers in the Far East: Part Second, Adventures of Two Youths in a Journey to Siam and Java, with Descriptions of Cochin-China, Cambodia, Sumatra and the Malay Archipelago* (New York, NY: Harper and Brothers, 1880), p. 303; Low, "Extracts from an Unpublished Journal of a Residence at Singapore during Part of 1840 & 41," *SFP*, 16 Dec. 1841, p. 3.

[19] Hornaday, *Two Years in the Jungle*, p. 298.

Image 3.3: Malay bird seller.
Illustrated London News
Collection, courtesy of
National Archives of
Singapore.

> Tigers are still reported "lively;" orang-outangs "looking up;"
> pythons show little animation at this season of the year; proboscis
> monkeys, on the other hand, continue scarce; there is quite a run
> on lions, and kangaroos are jumped at with avidity; elephants
> heavy; birds of paradise drooping; crocodiles are snapped up as
> offered, while dugongs bring large prices.[20]

Such was the variety and availability of wildlife in the port of Singapore,
making it an important commercial hub for the trade, that Carnegie
and his traveling companion even delivered two live orangutans to
Madras as a favor to Hornaday.[21]

Although animals were onboard almost all vessels in the harbor,
the trade in tropical creatures was associated with Malays who, during
the colonial era, were thought to have "skill in taming birds and

---

[20] Andrew Carnegie, *Round the World* (New York, NY: Charles Scribner's and
Sons, 1884), p. 161.
[21] Carnegie, *Round the World*, pp. 158–65.

animals."[22] Most of these Malay entrepreneurs, who bought the birds and apes "on speculation" from "the many islands south of Singapore that form the Malay Archipelago," were actually Bugis seamen, as Low had mentioned in the 1840s. Upon arrival in Singapore these sailors would sell the animals to other crewmen, who would often buy the animals collectively to reduce risk from bad deals or animals dying on the voyages, and from there they would enter international markets. The ultimate goal was to resell the animal in European or American ports. This created an atmosphere in the harbor in which disembarking travelers were met with animal sellers before they moved into the city. This experience mirrored that of Thomas Knox, who not only was offered birds upon arrival but also primates as well as other animals. Knox refused all of the initial offers made to him, and then proceeded to move along the dock. He finally stopped, hoping that he had moved beyond the cacophony that accompanied most arrivals into Singapore. He then bent over to examine the contents of a nearby basket. Inside, "it proved to be a large snake," which he declined, offering up the excuse "we are not buying snakes just now."[23]

The presence of such a plethora of tropical fauna in the port "helped to put Singapore on the world's 'animal' map." The wild animal trade was so profitable, and the port was such a nexus for these activities, that beginning in the late 19th century "not a month" passed, "without some representative of a foreign zoological society calling at Singapore in search of animals, reptiles and birds." These representatives would meet with collectors, both Asian and European, who gathered wild animals from Malaya and the Netherlands East Indies in compounds throughout the island, before shipment was arranged to circuses and zoos throughout the world. When they were not coordinating the sale of these animals, these entrepreneurs would travel throughout the region trapping, collecting or purchasing creatures, or just simply venturing down to the harbor when word went out that a particularly rare animal was available from a newly arrived ship. The most famous of these businessmen was Frank Buck, who developed a reputation as

---

[22] In British parlance, Malay meant anyone from island Southeast Asia. Bird, *The Golden Chersonese*, p. 381.

[23] Low, "Extracts from an Unpublished Journal," *SFP*, 16 Dec. 1841, p. 3; Knox, *The Boy Travellers in the Far East*, pp. 303–5; Charles Mayer, *Trapping Wild Animals in Malay Jungles* (Garden City, NY: Garden City Publishing, 1921), p. 26.

a reliable supplier of exotic beasts to the West in the 1910s and 1920s, which he parlayed into a career in Hollywood and book publishing.[24]

An earlier counterpart to Buck in the wild animal trade centered in Singapore was Charles Mayer, who first came to Asia as part of the Fryer Circus, which toured much of the region in the mid-1880s and attracted large audiences with acrobats and "various clear and amusing tricks by ponies, dogs, and goats."[25] In his memoir Mayer recounts that the first time he visited Singapore he met Mahommed Ariff, a "Malay dealer who held a monopoly on the animal trade." Ariff invited Mayer to his compound. When he entered, Ariff "was squatted in the center of his courtyard, surrounded by cages containing the animals brought in form the jungle by his native agents." The American left with "a tiger, several monkeys and a pair of leopards." A few years later, in 1887, Mayer decided to stay in the region. He eventually bought and developed a compound on Orchard Road, and his enterprise became one of the main conduits for wild animals that were exported to the West for several decades.[26]

To help ensure his place in these trade networks Mayer immediately began studying the Malay language, as it was the lingua franca of Singapore as well as the wider archipelago. After a dispute with Ariff —who, according to the memoir, was famous for cheating customers and collectors—Mayer set up business with "a Malay hadji" from Palembang.[27] This was most likely Haji Marip, who became a mainstay of the animal trade in Singapore over the next 30 years. He and Mayer

---

[24] Frank Buck and Edward Anthony, *Bring 'em Back Alive* (New York: Simon and Schuster, 1930); Timothy P. Barnard, "'Sufficient Dramatic or Adventure Interest': Authenticity, Reality and Violence in Pre-War Animal Documentaries from South-East Asia", in *The Colonial Documentary Film in South and South-East Asia*, ed. Ian Aitken and Camille Deprez (Edinburgh: Edinburgh University Press, 2017), pp. 223–35; Braddell, *Lights of Singapore*, p. 123; Tan, "The Beastly Business," p. 149; Anonymous, "Officialdom and the Zoo," *The Morning Tribune*, 24 Feb. 1936, p. 11; Matthew Minarchek, "Plantations, Peddlers, and Nature Protection: The Transnational Origins of Indonesia's Orangutan Crisis," *TRaNS: Trans— Regional and—National Studies of Southeast Asia* 6, 1 (2018): 101–29.

[25] Mayer, *Trapping Wild Animals in Malay Jungles*, p. 12; Anonymous, "Fryer's Circus," *ST*, 30 Aug. 1886, p. 2.

[26] Once, after a successful trip in which he captured dozens of elephants, Mayer transferred them back to Singapore, leading them through the streets to the compound. Mayer, *Trapping Wild Animals in Malay Jungles*, pp. 13, 20–7.

[27] Mayer, *Trapping Wild Animals in Malay Jungles*, pp. 26–7.

created a common business interest that funneled animals, mainly from Sumatra and the Malay Peninsula, through Singapore. Mayer became so interlinked with this commerce that he eventually received right of first refusal for any of the animals the Sultan of Johor decided not to keep from the many that were presented to him. From these various relationships, and with profitable contracts from an array of global entities ranging from the Melbourne Zoological Society to Barnum and Bailey Circus, Mayer sent Southeast Asian fauna into the wider world over several decades.[28]

By the early 20th century the wild animal trade had become an acceptable, albeit hidden, part of the local economy. The informal market in tropical fauna slowly became organized under a variety of sellers, many of whom had shops or compounds in the town, particularly along Rochor Road and Trengganu Street, where interested visitors could purchase an animal, or even put in an order for one. In 1932 an article in *The Malaya Tribune* gave pointers on how the public could use their services, using the purchase of a "waw-waw" (gibbon, g. *Hylobates*) as its exemplar. The anonymous author recommended interested buyers contact "a reliable dealer," such as Herbert De Souza, who would have "bought the animal young and broken it in to eat suitable food." After ensuring the gibbon had fur that "is consistently soft and glossy, that its limbs are fairly hard and that its stomach is not enlarged," nor exhibits any skin disorders on its fingers and toes, the buyer was supposed to check its stool. "If the stool is very loose refuse to take the animal, because stomach disorders are a prolific cause of deaths among animals in captivity." Once the gibbon was taken home, it was recommended that it be kept on a diet based around sweet potatoes with bread, guava, and bananas included for variety, and kept restrained with a collar or chain if it was not in a cage.[29]

This trade in tropical animals was one of the key factors in creating an exotic aura for the port. Singapore was a gateway that allowed access to the riches of Southeast Asia, and through which they were distributed globally. Not all animals were transferred to other ships, however, as the gibbon purchased from De Souza in 1932 illustrates.

---

[28] Mayer, *Trapping Wild Animals in Malay Jungles*, pp. 50–1, 82–3, 97–8; Braddell, *Lights of Singapore*, p. 123; Anonymous, "Elephant Catching in Tringganu," *SFP*, 7 Sep. 1897, p. 6.

[29] Anonymous, "The Care of Pets in Malaya," *The Malayan Tribune* [hereafter, *MT*], 24 Sep. 1932, p. IV.

Singapore. The wellknown dancing Monkey.

Image 3.4: "The well-known dancing monkey, Singapore." Postcard from the early 20th century. Courtesy of National Archives, Singapore.

Many stayed in Singapore, where they became part of the created imperial landscape. Some of these animals had a utilitarian function, such as horses and bullocks that carried goods and people throughout the island. Food animals also made up an important component of the fauna of the port, as they provided protein for an expanding society. Other animals were put on display, paraded before the public, occasionally for education but mainly for amusement and a reflection of the power that humans held over the wild. They were in Singapore to provide companionship and entertainment for humans on the island through their mere presence, and to reflect the status of the master.

Domestic Pets

Animals have been important human companions, for both utilitarian purposes and amusement, for millennia in all societies throughout the world. Their roles and functions, nevertheless, have transformed constantly alongside dynamic changes within these societies. An example of this is the development of "pets," a complex concept with obscure origins. As Katherine Grier and Keith Thomas have described, in Western societies the term originally referred to a spoiled child and eventually any small animal that could be fondled or indulged, which, in its earliest phases, was associated with lambs. After the 15th century, a variety of animals slowly transformed into pets, a concept that can be identified by three main characteristics. The animal was allowed in the house; it was given an individual name; and, it was never eaten.[30]

Dogs serve as an example of the complexity and subtlety of the transformation of a utilitarian, work animal into a pet. In both Asian and Western societies, canines have a long history of living alongside humans and developed a relationship in which they served in various capacities such as acting as guards, controlling livestock and hunting. Dogs were even attached to carts to provide transport for goods and people. Their role as emotional companions, or pets, was one that developed slowly over time and in all societies was initially limited to the elite, who could afford to expend resources for their upkeep. In China this began with the cultivation of Pekingese dogs, which were used as tributary items in the 7th-century Tang court, and eventually became a fashionable accessory in elite households by the 18th and 19th centuries. Similar developments occurred in Europe during the same period, with dogs transitioning from helpers in hunting parties to sitting in salons alongside elite Victorian ladies.[31]

Dogs were one of the most common animals seen in Singapore, and their presence represented the complex and changing nature of the relationship between humans and other animals. The stray dogs that roamed the town were tolerated at best. Since they did not provide a utilitarian function or companionship, they were to be eliminated as humans began to gain control over the landscape. At the same time, other canines were being imported and incorporated into households, leading to concerns with regard to their treatment, particularly if they were mistaken for a cur. This transition was one fraught with numerous

---

[30] Katherine C. Grier, *Pets in America: A History* (Chapel Hill, NC: The University of North Carolina Press, 2006), pp. 6–7; Thomas, *Man and the Natural World*, pp. 112–5.

[31] Shuk-Wah Poon, "Dogs and British Colonialism: The Contested Ban on Eating Dogs in Colonial Hong Kong," *The Journal of Imperial and Commonwealth History* 42, 2 (2014): 311; John D. Blaisdell, "The Rise of Man's Best Friend: The Popularity of Dogs as Companion Animals in Late Eighteenth-Century London as Reflected by the Dog Tax of 1796," *Anthrozoös: A Multidisciplinary Journal of the Interactions of People and Animals* 12 (1999): 76–87; Harriet Ritvo, "Pride and Pedigree: The Evolution of the Victorian Dog Fancy," *Victorian Studies*, 29 2 (1986): 227–53.

Image 3.5: Portrait of a modern Chinese woman, with her favorite pet, c.1920. Image from Lee Brothers Studio, courtesy of National Archives of Singapore.

threads of the imperial experience. Dogs that roamed the town were seen as savage, and required destruction. Bred dogs that provided emotional companionship—pets—were to be cherished, with much of this occurring initially in the homes of the elite. These bred dogs began arriving in Singapore in the mid-19th century, which mirrored the culture of domesticated dog ownership developing in Victorian England.[32]

Dogs quickly became the most popular domestic pet in colonial Singapore, and one newspaper report in the 1930s described a system in which ownership had fractured and become so complex that preferred breeds of canine could be linked to the different ethnic communities in the port. The anonymous author claimed, "Chinese fanciers pick dog pets in extremes," maintaining either "massive dogs like great Danes or collies, or, at the other extreme petite Pomeranians and Pekinese," while Europeans preferred "pets such as wire-haired terriers or Airedales." Along with these animals came the various cultural practices and

---

[32] Skabelund, *Empire of Dogs*; Ritvo, "Pride and Pedigree."

accouterment of elite pet ownership, including specialty shops catering to dog owners by the late colonial period. Grooming aids, medicines and other items, for example, could be found at The Federal Dispensary, a store that had branches in Singapore and larger towns in Malaya, while puppies—including fox terriers and dachshunds, "all from prize winning stock"—could be purchased from kennels throughout the island, such as the Singapore Boarding Kennels on Bukit Timah Road. To treat these new domestic companions, owners could even buy specialist dog biscuits at Cold Storage, a grocery store that catered to the elite of society.[33]

In addition to dogs, residents of colonial Singapore had "many good and faithful domestic pets," which were "a great source of pleasure, amusement, and instruction to their owners." While dogs were the most common domestic companion, monkeys and birds were in "a tie for second place" in the tropical, colonial society, while cats did "not rank as popular pets in Singapore." Among these runners-up, the most popular simian was the "Java monkey" (crab-eating macaque, *Macaca fascicularis*), while "love birds" (budgerigar, *Melopsittacus undalatus*) and canaries dominated the bird market, which also had ethnic differentiation. Malay bird keepers were partial to exotic fauna from deep in the jungle, such as cockatoos or parrots from the archipelago, usually tied to a perch on a string, while Chinese aficionados maintained cages in which they placed birds that were known for their voice, such as the oriental magpie robin (*Copsychus saularis*) and zebra dove (*Geopelia striata*), both of which are native to Southeast Asia, to supplement the Australian love bird.[34]

---

[33] Anonymous, *Catalogue of the Singapore Dog Show* (Kuala Lumpur: Charles Ward-Jackson for the Malayan Kennel Association, 1936), pp. 2–3 and 29; Anonymous, "Singapore's Favourite Pets are Dogs, Monkeys, Birds," *ST*, 14 Aug. 1938, p. 3.

[34] Beyond ethnic considerations related to pet ownership, class was also one of the main factors, as costs influenced who was able to purchase the animal and maintain it. A well-bred canine cost $100 to $500 in 1938; a gibbon ranged from $15 to $50, and a Siamese cat was $20–25 depending on the dealer. In contrast, a Java monkey could be had for $2, while love birds and canaries were $3 and 35–50 cents respectively. The price for the gibbon is from 1932. Anonymous, "The Care of Pets in Malaya"; Anonymous, "Singapore's Favourite Pets are Dogs, Monkeys, Birds"; Koo Tiang Hye, "Domestic Pets," *MT*, 21 Jan. 1932, p. 2; Brassey, *A Voyage in the 'Sunbeam,'* p. 393; Lesley Layton, *Songbirds of Singapore: Growth of a Pastime* (Singapore: Oxford University Press, 1991), p. 21.

The popularity of many of these domestic animals was often transitory, as can be seen in a "new Singapore craze for keeping goldfish" that arrived aboard Chinese vessels in the mid-1930s. Crew members from these ships would buy thousands in Hong Kong, along with canaries, and take them to ports throughout the world. As long as there were interested consumers, the trade remained vibrant. Once any of these fads waned, the consequences could influence the biodiversity of Singapore, as the Javan myna (*Acridotheres javanicus*) demonstrates. This rare songbird was introduced to Singapore, most likely in the 1920s, as a highly desired companion for bird aficionados due to its ability to mimic sounds, including human speech. When the fad passed, Javan mynas were released into the wild, proliferating throughout the island over the subsequent decades. While they remain a vulnerable, rare species in Java, they are considered a pest in modern Singapore.[35]

Another aspect of domestic pets in colonial Singapore was the range of animals taken into the home. John Thomson, for example, mentioned that he saw an "ape" and "tamed otter" aboard a boat he took around Singapore, while visitors to the botanic gardens often came across a tapir named Eva that lived with the first director, H.N. Ridley. Eva even accompanied Ridley to work, and had a special bed in the corner of his office.[36] The exotic diversity of pets in Singapore is best exemplified in a tale that Anna Brassey told following her visit in the late 1870s. During this period, the Maharaja of Johor, Abu Bakar, entertained her party over several days. When she was to depart, he presented her with a new pet, a "live little beast, not an alligator, and not an armadillo or a lizard; in fact I do not know what it is; it clings round my arm just like a bracelet."[37] It was a pangolin (*Manis javanica*).

---

[35] This also happens through religious and social practices, such as the release of birds and other animals from Buddhist temples on Vesak Day as a symbol of liberation. W.B. Paterson, A Scotsman Looks at Malaya," *The Sunday Tribune (Singapore)*, 1 Dec. 1935, p. 12; Lim Kim Seng, *Birds: An Illustrated Field Guide to the Birds of Singapore* (Singapore: Sun Tree Publishing, 1997), p. 104; Navjot S. Sodhi and Ilsa Sharp, *Winged Invaders: Pest Birds of the Asia Pacific with Information on Bird Flu and Other Diseases* (Singapore: SNP Reference, 2006), p. 55; Layton, *Songbirds of Singapore.*

[36] Ridley also maintained a python in his residence to help limit the number of rats. Thomson, *Glimpses into Life in the Far East*, p. 213; Barnard, *Nature's Colony*, pp. 109–10.

[37] Brassey, *A Voyage in the 'Sunbeam,'* p. 417.

The pet Manis.

Image 3.6: Anna Brassey with a pangolin. Source: Brassey, *A Voyage in the "Sunbeam"*, p. 393.

The presentation of the pangolin to Brassey and the keeping of pets in an imperial society represented the domestication of animals that had been imported to Singapore to provide emotional companionship. Whether originally from the forests of Southeast Asia or the breeding kennels of England, such animals made up the faunal society of the island. They were part of a colonial landscape in which animals were controlled and viewed for the support they could provide, often reflecting the status or ethnicity of the owner. Beyond this role of companionship, these animals could also entertain.

Entertaining Spectacles

While particularly rare animals occasionally found their way into the possession of individuals, many others were placed on display in zoos and menageries. These institutions in colonial Singapore also reflected a transition that was occurring globally. Menageries were usually private collections that the elite maintained as a reflection of their power and ability to gather rare fauna that they then would put on display. Elites had participated in these exhibitions for millennia, which often took on the tone of the society producing them, from the spectacles that Roman emperors staged to the private collections of Chinese emperors or French monarchs. Scholars have pointed out the power politics of these endeavors, which were transforming in the 19th century when such animals became more accessible to the public. In this process, zoos transitioned from privately owned and displayed endeavors to government-sponsored presentations of a social power over the natural world.[38] This also took place in the imperial society of Singapore, where animals were exhibited in private menageries, government-sponsored zoos and profit-centered circuses that produced a theater of control over savagery.

The most famous private, elite menagerie in mid-19th-century Singapore was at the home of Ho Ah Kay, better known as Whampoa, "an enterprising entrepreneur" and leader among the Chinese community. He was particularly well known for his spacious estate in which he had "one of the finest gardens in the world" with a vast array of plants as well as a "collection of tropical animals," including an orangutan and macaques. Even the topiary was trimmed to resemble animals, making the grounds of the compound "the only site worth seeing in Singapore" for many years. Whampoa had an "open house" policy for Western visitors who wished to see his gardens, while Asian visitors were allowed entry on special occasions, such as Chinese New Year. When visitors entered the compound, they were met with "quite a collection of live animals, including tortoises of three species, argus pheasants, golden and silver pheasants, a gazelle, porcupine, kangaroo, and some mandarin ducks." William Hornaday enjoyed seeing all of these beasts, but was most fascinated with an orangutan, which he found to be "as savage as a tiger." The primate was a large specimen,

---

[38] Nigel Rothfels, *Savages and Beasts: The Birth of the Modern Zoo* (Baltimore: The Johns Hopkins University Press, 2002), pp. 31–7; Lewis Pyenson and Susan Sheets-Pyenson, *Servants of Nature: A History of Scientific Institutions, Enterprises and Sensibilities* (New York: W.W. Norton and Company, 1999), pp. 169–72.

"a perfect monster in size," that Whampoa kept in a wooden cage. It survived for about a year on "leaves, plantains, and pineapples."[39]

In addition to this private menagerie, residents of Singapore could visit "another garden," which opened after the transition of power in Singapore from the East India Company to the British imperial government. This zoo operated from 1875 until 1905 and was "the property of the city; it contains more animals than the private one, and fewer trees," and was located within the confines of the Singapore Botanic Gardens. It featured fauna ranging from leopards and orangutans to parrots and pythons that were mainly gifts from Asian rulers, such as the King of Siam, to colonial governors. It was a popular attraction, although the lack of interest among botanists as well as the cost in maintaining it, was a continual subject of concern. This zoological collection, which was free to visit, was featured in travel guides, and one of the most popular attractions among all levels of society in Singapore, with particularly large crowds gathering around the enclosures on the weekends. As Knox observed, the collection at the Gardens contained "what the tropics can produce in the way of animals and birds."[40]

These menageries were metaphors for the imperial process, and the transition that was occurring in the display of animals, mirroring the efforts humans had made to gain control over an island in the midst of a diverse, tropical region. These exhibitions were an act of power, the submission of a wild animal to the gaze of humans. The transition between these two venues—one, a private residence with limited access, and the other, a free, government-sponsored public garden—also reflected the transition and imposition of the colonial administration upon the fauna of the island, as it moved from unknowable and unseen, or at least a symbol of the financial and social power of an individual, to

---

[39] After its death, the orangutan was given to the Raffles Museum where it was put on display. Hornaday, *Two Years in the Jungle*, pp. 299–300; Wellcome Collection: MS5958: "Sunday, 15th Jan 1854," *Journal of a Voyage from London to the Far East, and Voyages between Bombay, Singapore and Hong Kong*, p. 20; Anonymous, "The Late Hon'ble Hoh Ah Kay Whampoa, C.M.G. and M.L.C," *The Straits Times Overland Journal*, 31 Mar. 1880, p. 2; Knox, *The Boy Travellers in the Far East*, pp. 295–8.

[40] Knox, *The Boy Travellers in the Far East*, p. 297–8; B.E. D'Aranjo, *A Stranger's Guide to Singapore* (Singapore: Sirangoon Press, 1890), p. 6; Walter Fox, *Guide to the Botanical Gardens* (Singapore: Government Printing Office, 1889), p. 14; Barnard, *Nature's Colony*, pp. 84–113.

publicly accessible venue representing the glory of imperial rule controlling the flora and fauna of a region.[41]

Metaphors of control over animals in Singapore extended beyond menageries. It also included exhibitions of the human ability to tame the savage beast, which became one of the most popular pastimes in the port. These were traveling circuses that featured displays of bravery, acrobats, clowns, and, most importantly, performing animals. Although circuses have a variety of foundations and influences, the modern version originated in 18th-century Britain amid theatrical presentations and changing relationships between humans and animals. Fundamentally, to summarize an argument historian Helen Stoddart has made, circuses were the site of "hierarchical ordering of both the forces of chaos and … those of order."[42] Humans maintained order, tamed the savage beast, at these spectacles and to attend a performance was to witness humanity's triumph over the natural world. This made circuses the venue for popular global entertainments beginning in the 18th century, as humans were also industrializing and extending their mastery over the landscape, just as observing animals kept in a menagerie was also reflecting the power of control and display over the wild.

There were numerous traveling circuses in Southeast Asia, known in the Malay world as "*komedi kuda*" (horse show), which toured a circuit of the major ports in the region. One of the earliest circuses in Singapore was the Olympic Circus, which performed in February 1851 in front of the London Hotel, which was located on High Street near the Esplanade and among the first formal hotels in the port as it contained a restaurant and a theater. Jugglers, an acrobat, two clowns

---

[41] With the closure of the zoo in the Singapore Botanic Gardens, Singaporeans could still view animals in a very imperial setting during special occasions, such as when they were gathered prior to shipment to the Malaya-Borneo Exhibition in Singapore in 1922, which then traveled to England and acted as a present from the Prince of Wales to the London Zoo, all in an effort to display the riches of empire, including its living fauna. Anonymous, *Guide to the Malaya-Borneo Exhibition 1922 and Souvenir of Malaya* (Singapore: Malaya-Borneo Exhibition, 1922), p. 65; Anonymous, "The Prince's Zoo: Arrival of Animals from Malaya," *ST*, 24 June 1922, p. 9; Wong Lee Min, "Negotiating Colonial Identities: Malaya in the British Empire Exhibition, 1924–1925," unpublished Master's Thesis, Department of History, National University of Singapore, 2013.

[42] Helen Stoddart, *Rings of Desire: Circus History and Representation* (Manchester: Manchester University Press, 2000), p. 5.

and the "nymph of the floating vale," as well as prancing horses drew a large audience over several weeks.[43]

Circuses were a frequent highlight of the colonial entertainment calendar by the end of the 19th century.[44] In this atmosphere the presence of such an extravaganza became an event, with breathless newspaper coverage, which attracted even larger crowds. An example is "Wilson's Great World Circus," which performed in Singapore in 1883. Before an "appreciative audience," acrobats and plate spinners entertained the crowd while "trained horses did wonders" before the grand finale involving "the entrance of the immense cage of five large lions, some of which appeared rather savage." At the urging of their "intrepid African tamer," two of the beasts jumped "through a fiery hoop, over hurdles, and the like." This climax was "the great sensation of the evening," according to one witness. Another example was "Messrs. Kaler and Olmans' Circus," which was a popular attraction along Tank Road in late 1890. While the program highlighted "equestrian performances," a reviewer of the show gave particular praise to the dogs and monkeys that entertained the many patrons. They were "remarkably well trained animals."[45]

William Batty Harmston was the proprietor of perhaps the most famous circus in colonial Southeast Asia. He had founded his

---

[43] This early circus may have had difficulties, despite the "throngs" of people who attended. Two months later, all items related to the Olympic Circus were auctioned off, including 5 horses. Anonymous, "Notice," *ST*, 22 Apr. 1851, p. 3; Anonymous, "Olympic Circus," *ST*, 4 Feb. 1851, p. 4; Anonymous, "Tuesday, Feb. 25th 1851," *ST*, 25 Feb. 1851, p. 11; Matthew Isaac Cohen, *The Komedie Stamboel: Popular Theater in Colonial Indonesia, 1891–1903* (Athens, OH: Ohio University Center for International Studies, 2006), p. 12.

[44] Historian Nadi Tofighian has identified at least 28 different circus companies that were present in the region at the end of the 19th century. Nadi Tofighian, "Mapping 'the Whirligig of Amusements' in Colonial Southeast Asia." *Journal of Southeast Asian Studies* 49, 2 (2018): 288.

[45] Many of these circuses, however, appeared to be fly-by-night affairs, often outrunning creditors as the transportation and maintenance of animals and humans was quite costly. Charles Mayer often sponsored the smaller ones when they visited, putting in a good word for their ability to meet their debts. Mayer, *Trapping Wild Animals in Malay Jungles*, pp. 15–8; Anonymous, "Wilson's Great World Circus," *The Straits Times Weekly Issue*, 7 June 1883, p. 4; Anonymous, "Untitled," *ST*, 20 Oct. 1890, p. 2; Anonymous, "Harmston's Circus," *SFP* 15 Dec. 1891, p. 3; Anonymous, "Cooke's Circus," *SFP*, 21 Feb. 1895, p. 3; Tofighian, "Mapping 'the Whirligig of Amusements'," p. 292.

extravaganza in England in 1880. After succumbing to bankruptcy in 1886, Harmston reconstituted his business and brought it to Asia, where it became a popular draw in commercial ports from the 1890s until the 1930s, following a circuit that took it from Calcutta to Shanghai. Unfortunately, William Harmston died in Singapore in 1893; he was buried in the Bukit Timah Cemetery. His wife, Jane, and her new husband—Robert Love—went on with the show, maintaining the name along with one of the great entertainment spectacles of colonial Southeast Asia. When Jane retired, her son—Willie Harmston—continued to entertain Asian audiences until his own death in Saigon in 1936. Animals were the main draw at many of these circuses. At one point, the Harmston Circus featured "30 European Artists and 50 Performing Animals and Menagerie including 3 Lions, 4 Tigers, 4 Elephants, 2 Panthers, 3 Bears, 15 Monkeys, 10 Geese, 2 Kangaroos, 1 Llama, 35 Cocacatoos, 14 Horses and 9 Ponies."[46]

Residents of Singapore would flock to the temporary circus compounds to watch a wild animal perform at the whim of a human, as well as the possibility that they could cross the line separating tame and wild. This occurred in March 1895, when Harmston's Circus, was set up along River Valley Road to entertain Singaporeans with a mixture of acrobats and animals. A leopard named "Beauty," escaped after "some one maliciously let it out of the cage," and over the next two days Singaporeans closely followed the developments. On the first night, Beauty returned to the circus grounds and attacked an elephant, most likely due to hunger. The elephant fought back and Beauty fled again. Leo Hernandez, the big cat tamer, leapt into action and created an entertaining sideshow. Riding an elephant, followed by 11 other men on horseback, Hernandez led 60 "Kling and Malay trackers, with 14 dogs from Johore" on an expedition through Singapore to track the escaped leopard. When the party found it, Beauty "promptly killed one dog and vanished." The next morning the trackers once again found the leopard, this time "near the water tank on Fort Canning Hill." Hernandez approached the feline and skillfully threw a net over it.

---

[46] Anonymous, "Deaths," *SFP*, 13 Nov. 1893, p. 2; Anonymous, "The Municipality," *ST*, 22 Dec. 1893, p. 3; Anonymous, "Harmston's Circus," *ST*, 24 Sep. 1895, p. 2; Anonymous, "Death of Mr. W. Harmston," *MT*, 1 Feb. 1936, p. 15; "Harmston on the Net." (https://sites.google.com/site/harmstanonthenet/The-Harmston-Circus, accessed on 18 Aug. 2017; Tofighian, "Mapping 'the Whirligig of Amusements'," p. 284.

"The leopard looked in the tamer's eye and became again a menagerie beast." Following an investigation, the authorities determined that Beauty killed a goat, two dogs and two bullocks during its escapade, forcing Love and his wife to pay compensation of $111 to the owners of the animals. Visitors to the circus on the night of its capture saw Beauty on exhibit, and within days it was, once again, performing before a paying crowd.[47]

Such violence combined with spectacle was the cornerstone of many of the interactions between humans and animals in colonial Singapore. It was part of the process of domestication, as animals transitioned from savage beasts to entertaining companions or loyal servants that provided labor. Beyond the cage and whip, residents participated in this process through their fascination with animal-animal contests, which were among the most popular pastimes in the region. These clashes ranged from competitions of speed, such as the horse races at the Singapore Sporting Club, to fights to the death between various animals. All of the different ethnic communities in Singapore enjoyed these amusements, with the main difference being the types of animals involved, which also often reflected the class status of the audience, much like the maintenance of domestic pets. This resulted in reports that "the Chinese are in the habit of amusing themselves with fights between insects of the species called the 'Praying Mantis,' which they keep for the purpose," while Malays enjoyed cockfighting. For the elite, the animals in blood sport involved ceremony and splendor, and were usually mammals. An instance of such a performance occurred when Prince Albert and Prince George visited the region in 1882. Maharaja Abu Bakar of Johor hosted the two English royals with a ram fight in his garden, a contest that was portrayed as being common in Southeast Asia. Most importantly, in this instance, it was a confrontation staged for the elite.[48]

---

[47] Anonymous, "A Leopard Hunt in Singapore," *ST*, 15 Mar. 1895, p. 3; Anonymous, "Wild Animals," *The Mid-Day Herald*, 18 Mar. 1895, p. 2; Anonymous, "Tuesday, March 19, 1895," *SFP*, 26 Mar. 1895, p. 3; Anonymous, "A Leopard at Loose," *SFP*, 19 Mar. 1895, p. 7; Cohen, *The Komedie Stamboel*, p. 18.

[48] Brooke, "A Century of Sport," pp. 320–67; Winstedt, *A History of Johore* (JMBRAS version), p. 118; CO273/180/32044: "Ordinance 14, 1902, Prevention of Cruelty to Animals," p. 64; Thomson, *Glimpses into Life in the Far East*, p. 203; Anthony Reid, *Southeast Asia in the Age of Commerce, 1450–1680. Volume One: The Land Below the Winds* (New Haven: Yale University Press, 1988), p. 183.

Image 3.7: "A Menagerie Race at Singapore." By John Charles Dollman. *The Graphic*, August 1881. Courtesy of National Archives of Singapore.

Another form of animal entertainment that was not quite as violent, and was a regular feature of sports days in the late 19th century among the European community of Singapore, was menagerie racing. In these contests, each human participant would choose an animal and follow it on a string or leash along a set track. The contestants were often distinguished officials, usually military officers, and their frustration at dealing with the animals usually led to "uproarious mirth" among the crowd of spectators. The animals were allowed to go wherever they chose and, as one guide reminded, "there need be no cruelty of any kind." One account of a menagerie race in Singapore from 1881 described it as "an odd affair." The participants were a dog, a turkey, a goat, a pig, a monkey, a cat, a chicken, a goose, a duck, a pelican, a frog, and a crab.[49] "The animals, driven by means of a string tied to the legs, were handicapped according to their respective abilities." Following a false start by the pelican, which slipped its string and flew to a nearby tree, the other animals began to play with each other or refused to move; the one exception was the goose. "Held steadily by its owner," Sage, as it was known, "ran straight for the winning post, and won the race by a good yard over the frog, which, being constantly poked up, was hopping along for the goal." This particular race was of such interest that *The Graphic* illustrated magazine from London republished an account of it from the Singaporean press later that same year.[50]

While such amusements were imported from the home societies of residents of the port, it was the animals themselves that were being subjugated and controlled to represent metaphorically the characteristics of their human owners. Whether a horse raced around a track, a leopard jumped through hoops in a circus, or a spider participated in a fight to the death, animals were seen as agents of larger contests in society. Their obedience and victories were allegories on their place in

---

[49] Each animal had a name. The pig was named "Pride of China," while the monkey was "Darwin" and the frog "Jean Crapeau." Anonymous, "The Regimental Athletic Sports," *The Straits Times Overland Journal*, 9 June 1881, p. 6; Mary Grant Bruce, *A Little Bush Maid* (Melbourne: Ward, Lock and Co., 1910), pp. 26–34; Anonymous, "Police Sports," *ST*, 12 Apr 1900, p. 3; "A Menagerie Race in a Garden," http://messybeast.com/history/menagerie.htm, accessed 03 Oct. 2018.

[50] John Charles Dollman, "A Menagerie Race at Singapore," *The Graphic*, 20 Aug. 1881, p. 189; Anonymous, "The Regimental Athletic Sports."

society as the ability of humans to exhibit mastery over animals meant dominance over the environment. While this was limited to a few animals in most instances, ranging from a horse to an insect, it also expanded out to institutions that soon came to display their expanding power and control over the island and its place in the region, bringing the natural world under the imperial gaze. These institutions were developed to support the science of gathering, collecting and identifying animals—zoology—in Singapore, ultimately becoming an important component in networks of understanding fauna and British control over the island and region.

Documenting the Wild

In 1909, Frank Matthew, an eight-year-old living with his two sisters in Chelsfield, England, sent a dead squirrel to Oldfield Thomas, who oversaw the mammal collection at the British Museum (Natural History) in London. In the attached note, the young man explained that the animal had been sent to him from Singapore "nearly 2 years ago," lived on "fruits and nuts," and had died the previous winter. The animal was *Sciurus prevostii* (more commonly known as an Asian tri-colored squirrel) and it had already been "stuffed."[51]

This squirrel is one of thousands of animals from Singapore and Southeast Asia listed in the Ascension Books of the Natural History Museum, a meticulous record of all animals the institution received, with columns to record the species, the date of their arrival, and who sent them. Two weeks before Matthew mailed his dead squirrel to Thomas, for example, the logs note that H.C. Robinson and C. Boden Kloss sent hundreds of specimens collected from the Malay Peninsula and the Riau Archipelago to London, which supplemented another shipment from the year before. During this same period the museum also received specimens from J.D. Gimlette, the Secretary for Chinese Affairs in the Chinese Protectorate office as well as from W.L. Abbott, an American who lived in Singapore and collected animals from the Malay World for the Smithsonian Institution. These specimens were among the hundreds, and often thousands, that made their way from Singapore and Southeast Asia to the British Museum as well as other

---

[51] Natural History Museum (London) [hereafter, NHM]: DF ZOO/232/1/15: Frank Matthew to Oldfield Thomas, Received 10 Mar. 1909, Letter 121.

institutions throughout the world via various scientific networks every year, helping to support and expand imperial knowledge of biodiversity throughout the globe.[52]

The tendrils of Western science also extended into the center of plant research in the region, the Singapore Botanic Gardens. While the scientists at the Gardens worked as part of a vast system of imperial botany, and served the empire through the introduction of acclimatized plants such as rubber, they also occasionally found unusual animals within the grounds. One example was *Tylonycteris pachypus*, a species more commonly known as the lesser bamboo bat, and one of the 25 species of the animal that are found in Singapore. These particular bats are quite unique due to their size. They are tiny, weighing as little as 2.5 grams although they can grow to an equally unimpressive 9 grams. Their limited mass allows them to roost in small, vertical slits in bamboo during the day, gaining access to the internodal compartments within the plant by squeezing their skull through openings as narrow as 5 millimeters. Based on specimens collected in western Java, C.J. Temminck first identified these bats in 1840, while W. Peters coined their modern scientific name in 1872, based on another sample collected in southern Luzon.[53]

In May 1908, workers brought this unique species to the attention of Henry Nicholas Ridley, the Director of the Singapore Botanic Gardens, after they saw several fly out of a clump of bamboo. The coolies tied up a length of the plant and presented it to Ridley, who then took it for examination to Richard Hanitsch, the Director of the Raffles Museum. Inside, the 2 scientists found 23 bats, 4 adults and 19 "young ones." As each septum, or segment, of the bamboo was unbroken, they realized that "the only possible entrance was made by

---

[52] NHM: DF 218/3/3: Zoological Ascensions, Mammalia, 1904–1910, pp. 202v–203; 204v–205; 205v–209, 210v; NHM: DF ZOO/232/1/15: C. Boden Kloss to Oldfield Thomas, Written 27 July 1908, 19 Sep. 1908, 2 Oct. 1908, Letters 101–3.

[53] Nick Baker, "Bats in the Bamboo," *Gardenwise* 43, (2014): 12–3; Barnard, *Nature's Colony*; C.J. Temminck, *Monographies de Mammalogie, ou Description de Quelques Genres de Ammiferes, don't les Especes ont ete Obersvees dan les Differens Musees de l'Europe* (Leiden: C.C. Vander Hoek, 1840), p. 217; W. Peters, "Uber den Vespertilio calcaratus Prinz zu Wied und eine neue Gattung der Flederthiere, Tyloncteris," *Königlich Preussicschen Akademie Wissenschaften zu Berlin* (1872): 699–706.

a crack on one side." Ridley went on to add "through this very small space all these bats must have crept." The botanist returned to the bamboo grove and inspected other felled plants nearby. In one stem with similar cracks he found approximately 30 dead bats that filled the joint. In the meantime, Hanitsch sent "two adult and five young bats" to Oldfield Thomas at the British Museum, asking if he could identify them. Hanitsch went on the describe the animal as one that "Mr. Ridley had discovered within the joint of a living Bamboo. The Bamboo had a double split in one side," and the gap was only "¼!!" of an inch. Thomas identified the gift as *Tylonycteris pachypus*.[54]

It is through this process that various species of animal have been discovered, identified, and classified, as part of larger efforts to achieve a greater understanding of their habits and range in Southeast Asia. When Europeans sent descriptions, illustrations or even physical specimens of animals to Europe for classifying and control, the natural landscapes, and its creatures, were also falling under another form of metaphorical power beyond the development of a domestic pet or the antics of a circus animal. A small island and its inhabitants were being mapped into global networks of knowledge of the natural world that ranged from a small bamboo grove in Singapore to a house in Chelsfield, England.

This transformation in understanding and documenting animals was revolutionary, and interlinked with philosophies and governance that had arisen in the 18th and 19th centuries as a result of the Enlightenment. Much of this was rooted in institutions, often government sponsored, which reflected and supported the research that made this possible. Within networks of imperialism, and knowledge, Singapore became a gathering station for information on the fauna, and flora, of the region as well as a producer of this knowledge. Once this information was gathered, it would then re-enter the society in the form of new policies and approaches to controlling the animals in Singapore, and how they interacted with humans. This can be seen in the institutions created, as well as policies such as wildlife preservation, which mimicked the ability of the state to control nature itself.

---

[54] The specimens arrived "in spirit" on 18 May 1908. NHM: DF 218/3/3: Zoological Ascensions, Mammalia, 1904–1910, p. 157v; NHM: DF ZOO/232/1/14: R. Hanitsch to Oldfield Thomas, Written 12 May 1908, Letter 65; H.N. Ridley, "Bats in the Bamboo," *Journal of the Straits Branch of the Royal Asiatic Society*, 50 (1908): 103–4.

The collection of fauna from Singapore for global networks of science and imperialism began soon after the arrival of East India Company officials in 1819. William Farquhar and Thomas Stamford Raffles were active collectors of specimens, competing with each other to document their surroundings. Others soon followed, including Thomas Hardwicke. A soldier with a keen interest in nature, he collected depictions of Indian fauna from throughout the subcontinent in the first two decades of the 19th century. Along with J.E. Gray, Hardwicke published *Illustrations of Indian Zoology*, in the 1830s. While the collection contained hundreds of illustrations depicting the fauna of South Asia, it also featured sketches of animals from Singapore, reflecting how British scholars of the time visualized the continent and their position within it, with the Southeast Asian port being an appendage of imperial and economic efforts in governing India for the first 40 years of its colonial existence.[55]

These illustrations of Singaporean fauna were from commissioned artists, who sent their work to Bengal. Hardwicke would collate, classify and organize each of these images into a record of the natural world that the Company was expanding to control. The drawings of these species were one avenue from which exotic specimens were publicly presented to the British scholarly community in the 19th century, usually accompanied by a dead specimen that was either stuffed or stored in jars of formaldehyde, both of which allowed for collectors to appreciate a variety of features, such as the coloration and size of the animal. Such works of art and science were also a visual device in which an image of an animal that had come under the gaze of imperial rule was captured metaphorically. In this manner, illustrations of animals, and often specimens, became an important part of the archives of scientific institutions, where they awaited classification and placement within structures of understandings, as well as control. This was part of the development of knowledge of the natural world. In this case,

---

[55] Noltie, *Raffles' Ark Redrawn*; Anonymous, *Natural History Drawings*; Warren R. Dawson, "On the History of Gray and Hardwicke's Illustrations of Indian Zoology, and Some Biographical Notes on General Hardwicke," *Journal of the Society for the Bibliography of Natural History* 2, 3 (1946): 55–69; Thomas Hardwicke and J.E. Gray, *Illustrations of Indian Zoology, Chiefly Selected from the Collection of Major-General Hardwicke*, 2 vols. (London: Treutell, Wurtz, Treutell Jun. and Richter, 1830–4).

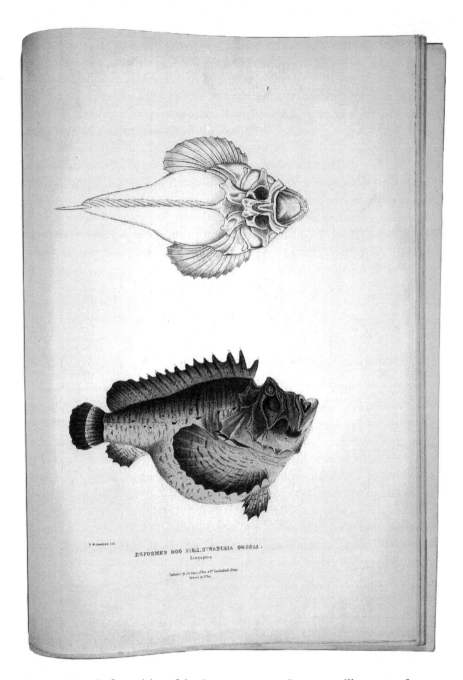

Image 3.8: Deformed hog fish, *Synanceia grossa*. Singapore. Illustration from Hardwicke and Gray, *Illustrations of Indian Zoology*. Courtesy of the New York Public Library.

the illustrations also emphasized their Singaporean origin, specifically citing that they were collected in the British controlled port.[56]

The animals Hardwicke and Gray highlighted from Singapore were unusual, with a deformed hog fish (*Synanceia grossa*, now known as *Synanceia horrida*) and an ornamented trygon (*Trygon ornatus*, now known as *Teniura lymma*) serving as primary examples. Both of these species were curiosities, even in the region, and scholars desired information about them as they crossed various categories, thus challenging classification schemes. As Harriet Ritvo has argued, they were "idiosyncratic anomalies," which "undermined previous taxonomic assumptions and structures," thus creating "a vacuum of zoological authority, if not of power." To document and identify them reversed the "traditional relationship between humans and the natural world," as these oddities represented the limits of knowledge. To understand their existence gave humans power over the environment. The result was an obsessive need to document the fauna of the region. In this sense, Singapore was and is not unique. It was part of a global network that sent examples of fauna—and the more anomalous the better—to a central collection station, in this case Calcutta and then London, where understandings of the natural world were constructed, making them an important component of the conquest and control of a vast empire.[57]

The reputation of Singapore among naturalists in the 19th century was based not only in the early work of Raffles, Farquhar and other collectors who brought back magnificent illustrations, but also in its position as an international port that attracted goods (and animals) from throughout Southeast Asia. Among the explorers who ventured into Singapore was Alfred Russel Wallace, who used the British outpost as the base for his wider exploration of the Indonesian Archipelago in the 1850s and 1860s. He spent a total of seven months on the island during this period, leaving his more famous work for Borneo and the

---

[56] Anonymous, *List of the Specimens of Birds in the Collection of the British Museum, Part III: Gallinae, Grallae, and Anseres* (London: George Woodfall and Son, 1844).
[57] Harriet Ritvo, *The Platypus and the Mermaid, and Other Figments of the Classifying Imagination* (Cambridge, MA: Harvard University Press, 1997), pp. 6–18; Bernard Cohn, *Colonialism and Its Form of Knowledge: The British in India* (Princeton: Princeton University Press, 1996); Phillip B. Wagoner, "Precolonial Intellectuals and the Production of Colonial Knowledge", *Comparative Studies in Society and History* 45, 4 (2003): 783–814; David Arnold, *The Tropics and the Traveling Gaze: India, Landscape and Science, 1800–1856* (Seattle: University of Washington Press, 2006).

Maluku region. While in Singapore, however, Wallace collected insect specimens on Bukit Timah Hill and Pulau Ubin, and used the port as the site where his collection—which he assembled mainly for profit—was gathered prior to export to Britain. This exemplified the role that Singapore played within larger administrative and economic structures of the East India Company, as well as the early legacy of British imperial understandings of nature. It was a hub from which knowledge of the flora and fauna of the region was gathered, traded and then returned for dissection and study.[58]

Beyond illustrations and specimens, local administrators also actively conducted surveys of nature, publishing their accounts in scholarly journals and books. While these often trickled back to publications in London, some of these interested scientists turned to publishing their research in Southeast Asia, where it could play a role in developing a greater understanding of cultures, societies and nature in the region. Among the most preeminent in this regard was J.R. Logan, a lawyer in Penang who founded the *Journal of the Indian Archipelago and Eastern Asia* in 1847.

"Logan's Journal" was one of the first scientific publications in English from Southeast Asia, and was founded to republish, and occasionally refute, much of the interesting research Dutch scientists were carrying out in the East Indies. Each issue contained a vast array of information on the region, ranging from reports on ethnic groups on nearby islands to meteorological data, providing details of peoples and landscapes that were to fall under imperial control, including a survey of Singapore zoology, which appeared in 1849. While the journal only lasted 16 years, fading away following the death of its founder, it reflected the growing importance of studying the natural world of Southeast Asia, and its link to larger imperial enterprises.[59]

---

[58] Alfred Russel Wallace, *The Malay Archipelago: The Land of the Orang-Utan, and the Bird of Paradise. A Narrative of Travel, with Studies of Man and Nature*, vol. 1 (London: Macmillan and Co., 1869); John van Wyhe, "Wallace in Singapore," in *Nature Contained: Environmental Histories of Singapore*, ed. Timothy P. Barnard (Singapore: NUS Press, 2014), pp. 85–109; Jeyamalar Kathirithamby-Wells, "Peninsular Malaysia in the Context of Natural History and Colonial Science," *New Zealand Journal of Asian Studies* 11, 1 (2009): 361.

[59] Guan Jingwen, "*The Journal of the Indian Archipelago and Eastern Asia*, 1847–1863: A Study in Colonial Knowledge and Context," (unpublished B.A. (Honours) Thesis. Department of History, National University of Singapore, 2011); Oxley, "The Zoology of Singapore."

Prior to 1867, information about the fauna of the island and the surrounding region may have traveled via Singapore, but the ultimate goal was to gather it in Calcutta—the East India Company headquarters —before sending it back to Britain. It was the beginning of a complex web of publications, displays and classification that documented the natural world of Southeast Asia. Through knowledge of its flora and fauna, imperial efforts to control and manipulate the landscape could take place. With the reconfiguration of British imperial control, following the Indian Mutiny of 1857, the East India Company was replaced with more formal, and direct, governmental control from Britain. The administration of direct colonial rule meant that the Colonial Office in London, in contrast to the Company, oversaw the administration of the Straits Settlements by 1867. They then began instituting more formal methods to document the animals in a colonial landscape that was centered in Singapore, and assist people ranging from young Frank Matthew to high colonial officials in the collection and display of this fauna from a perspective more closely linked to the region.

Organizing Knowledge

Singapore entered a new era of imperial control, British influence, and international science when it fell under direct rule from the Colonial Office in London. Much of this was aided by the development of new modes of understanding and organizing the surrounding world that resulted in an expanded control over the landscape and the implementation of new approaches to flora and fauna. Animals quickly came under the scrutiny of a variety of institutions, where they could be organized and studied, and the work of early explorers in the region would now expand and fall under direct oversight of the government. While there was rarely a direct, profitable application for such efforts, such as limiting the spread of disease and the development of hygienic markets, the continued collection of knowledge about the natural world allowed for an enhanced metaphorical control over the colonial landscape. To understand the flora and fauna, the nature, of a region implied control over all its creatures. The expansion of imperial rule, therefore, resulted in the introduction of new institutions that went beyond having a pet or companion in your home. They were focused on the massive biodiversity and potential of the region, and Singapore, and bringing it into the orbit of a foreign and imposed government, society and gaze.

Beginning in 1873 the Legislative Council of the Straits Settlements proposed the establishment of direct governmental control over two institutions dedicated to the study of the natural world. The first was the Singapore Botanic Gardens, which had operated as a private park for the elite since 1859, but had also suffered from mismanagement during its first 15 years of existence. The second institution was a library and its attached museum.[60] The initial proposal arose out of a desire to support the collection of materials for a colonial exhibition in London that was to focus on "objects of interest of whatever kind, illustrating the ethnology, antiquities, natural history and physical character of the country." Out of these efforts there was a scheme to establish a more substantial museum in Singapore for "the collection of objects of Natural History." As H.L. Randell, the Colonial Secretary, argued, the specimens would be "easily procured," due to Singapore's position in the region, and "be of immense value and interest to the scientific world." The proposals to create formal government institutions related to science wound their way through the bureaucracy over the next few years, and were finally approved in 1874. They quickly became an integral component of the British imperial presence in the region and, in 1878, the government officially placed the Singapore Botanic Gardens and the Raffles Library and Museum "under more immediate government control."[61]

---

[60] Along with his publishing efforts Logan promoted the development of an early library in Singapore, and he sustained a limited one that existed for much of the East India Company period of colonial rule. As European residents became more interested in living in the region, and governing it, this small collection expanded to meet the needs of administrators and merchants to understand its landscape and peoples. A small museum that focused on the archaeology and "objects of General History" was soon attached to the library. Much of this fell into financial difficulties in the 1860s, however, due to changes in governance in port of Singapore and larger Straits Settlements. R. Hanitsch, "Raffles Library and Museum, Singapore," in *One Hundred Years of Singapore, Being Some Account of the Capital of the Straits Settlements from Its Foundation by Sir Stamford Raffles on the 6th February 1819 to the 6th February 1919*, Vol. I, ed. Walter Makepeace, Gilbert E. Brooke and Roland St. J. Braddell (London: John Murray, 1921), pp. 532–42; Guan Jingwen, "*The Journal of the Indian Archipelago and Eastern Asia*," pp. 30–6.

[61] CO273/98/3680: "The Agri-Horticultural Gardens and the Raffles Library and Museum," pp. 335v–7; CO276/06: "A Bill to Provide for the Permanent Establishment of a Public Library and Museum, and Horticultural and Zoological Gardens, in Singapore"; Barnard, *Nature's Colony*; Kevin Tan, *Of Whales and Dinosaurs*; Hanitsch, "Raffles Library and Museum, Singapore," pp. 542–3.

In its initial stages, the Raffles Library and Museum was a depository for ethnographic items and, of course, reading material. The occasional animal specimens that trickled in between the 1870s and early 1890s were usually gifts from local collectors or had died in the zoo at the Singapore Botanic Gardens. Among the first of these donations was a rhinoceros, which the museum received in August 1877 after it spent two years entertaining visitors in the Gardens. Other dead animals soon joined the rhinoceros, including a collection of stuffed fish the 1880s that T.I. Rowell, who was the Colonial Secretary at the time, worked on, which reflected the convergence of administrators and scientists during the period. Rowell prepared an estimated "200 or 300 specimens," and made sure to record "their Malay names and scientific names." Unfortunately, these fish were seen as a failure at developing the institution, as "they were little attractive, as no attempt was made to paint them."[62]

The Raffles Museum came under more sustainable leadership in the late 1880s, when the government hired William Davidson to curate the collection. Davidson was an ornithologist, who not only oversaw the development of a more substantial natural history collection that was based in the fauna of Southeast Asia but also the move to its new premises, the site of the current National Museum of Singapore, in 1887.[63] In the next decade the institution came under the leadership of Richard Hanitsch, a German entomologist who specialized in cockroaches, who served as the curator and then director from 1895 until his retirement in 1919. Supported by a staff including taxidermists Valentine Knight and P.M. de Fontaine, Hanitsch developed a systematic collection of animals and "succeeded in that important part of a Curator's work, keeping the Institution in touch with other museums, and scientific men." Hanitsch also oversaw a renovation of the building, which was completed in 1906, so that it could fulfill its remit of

---

[62] Colonial administrators taking on extra responsibilities related to natural history was common during this period. One of the early curators of the library and museum was Nicholas Belfield Dennys, whose main job was "Assistant Protector of Chinese." For this supplemental work, Dennys received an additional $100 per month. CO273/152/6507: "Annual Report on the Raffles Library and Museum, for the Year Ending 31st December, 1887"; Hanitsch, "Raffles Library and Museum, Singapore," pp. 552–3, 560–1; Barnard, *Nature's Colony*, pp. 97–8; Tan, *Of Whales and Dinosaurs*, pp. 20–2.

[63] Hanitsch, "Raffles Library and Museum, Singapore," p. 554; Tan, *Of Whales and Dinosaurs*, pp. 40–50.

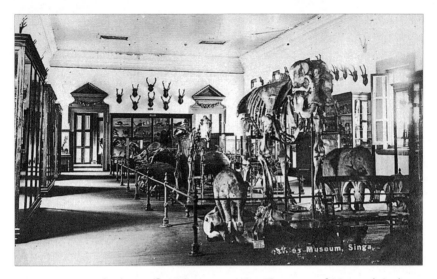

Image 3.9: Inside the Raffles Museum, 1920s. Courtesy of National Archives of Singapore.

presenting the fauna of a region that was "one of the most interesting in the world."[64]

The animals collected in the museum continued to come from donations, particularly in the 19th century, as big game hunters and explorers ventured into the interior of peninsular Malaya. Among the most consistent donors was the Sultan of Johor who sent a range of specimens, including a tiger and black panther that were displayed prominently in the museum. Other benefactors included Ridley, who provided a sambar deer (*Cervus unicolor equinus*) he had shot near Changi in 1891, while wild animal trader Charles Mayer contributed any animal that died under his care, including "a group of eight orangoutangs, from babies to full grown, and a baby elephant." Perhaps the most famous acquisition in the Raffles Museum was a 13-meter skeleton of a blue whale that had washed up on a beach near Melaka in 1892.[65]

---

[64] R. Hanitsch, *Raffles Museum and Library Annual Reports, 1901* (Singapore: Government Printing Office, 1902), p. 5; Hanitsch, "Raffles Library and Museum, Singapore," p. 567; Tan, *Of Whales and Dinosaurs*, pp. 56–62.

[65] Megan S. Osborne, "Early Collectors and Their Impact on the Raffles Museum and Library," *The Heritage Journal*, 3 (2008): 1–15; Hanitsch, "Raffles Library and Museum, Singapore," pp. 561–2; Mayer, *Trapping Wild Animals in Malay Jungles*, p. 97.

Museum officials also often played a part in this collecting process, as occurred after the Johor sultan killed an elephant near Senai in his polity in 1909. The sultan contacted Hanitsch, who caught a train, ferry and automobile to the site along with Knight and De Fontaine. The three Europeans then engaged 25 Malay, Chinese and Tamil coolies to help guide them and their equipment "through lalang, bracken and finally swampy jungle," before they came upon the "magnificent specimen and looked a veritable mountain of flesh, lying partly on its side, with the trunk doubled up under its head." They skinned, removed "large lumps of flesh on the back and sides of the body," and gutted the animal. This final act before tiffin resulted in "a fearsome noise like that of a huge steam whistle, repeating itself several times." The "frightful odor" that escaped from the carcass left the coolies scrambling for whiffs from discarded durian shells to cover up the stench. Hanitsch then had a lunch of "Malay curry in true Malay fashion, without forks or spoons, washed down with bottled beer." After a few more attempts were made at dressing the elephant, Hanitsch returned to Singapore. He eventually sent more men with instruments and preservatives, and the entire process took four days. When the German curator returned to the site, the bones of the elephant were being boiled in large iron pans borrowed from a nearby gambier plantation. The skeleton was then taken back to Singapore, where it was assembled for display.[66]

At other times, museum officials went on collecting expeditions, which became more common in the 20th century. These outings were mainly focused on the Malay Peninsula, Borneo, Sumatra and Christmas Island. Scientists who eventually succeeded Hanitsch, such as C. Boden Kloss and F.N. Chasen, used these trips to expand the museum collection with their own expertise on birds and mammals. Kloss was particular active in making these journeys. A "cruise" he took in 1900 in the South China Sea with W.L. Abbott serves as an example. The two naturalists spent 11 weeks on a schooner with the intent, according to Kloss, "to make collections of mammals and birds

---

[66] "The boiling and bubbling Elephant soup drew many visitors, and Chinese and Malays came with huge ladles and a good supply of bottles to scoop off the thick layer of fluid fat and store it in their bottles. Rheumatism and similar ailments will in Senai and neighborhood be cured for some time to come by application of Elephant fat!" R. Hanitsch, "My First (and Last?) Elephant," *SFP*, 22 Nov. 1909, p. 1; Tan, *Of Whales and Dinosaurs*, p. 65.

and of any other objects zoological that might fall in our way." They gathered fruit bats on Lingga (by discharging a shotgun upward into a tree and picking them up off the ground), shot a blue-and-white kingfisher and reef heron on a small islet nearby, and discovered a new subspecies of macaque on Benoa in the Tambelan Archipelago. That was only the beginning of the riches of the natural world they collected, as they eventually documented more than 50 new unique species solely on that journey.[67]

The process of presenting these discoveries was the focus of periodic meetings of local officials and members of the scientific community. The first one occurred at the Raffles Library in 1877. At that particular gathering, scholars and administrators founded a society with the goal of "collecting and recording scientific information in the Malay Peninsula and Archipelago." Two years later they launched a journal, *The Journal of the Straits Branch of the Royal Asiatic Society*, to bring recognition to their efforts.[68] This publication was a continuation of "Logan's Journal," in that it provided a forum for the research being conducted on their expanding regional influence, as British imperialism began to spread from the Straits Settlements into Malaya. The articles that appeared, particularly during the first few decades of its existence, were decidedly focused on natural history with topics ranging from birds and fish to minerals. The editor during this period was usually a scientist, beginning with Ridley and ending with Kloss, all of whom were associated with the Raffles Museum or the Singapore Botanic Gardens. Other journals, such as the *Raffles Bulletin of Zoology*, and guides, such as *The Birds of Singapore Island*, supplemented these initiatives.[69]

---

[67] C. Boden Kloss, "Notes on a Cruise in the Southern China Sea," *Journal of the Straits Branch of the Royal Asiatic Society*, 41 (1904): 53–80; Barnard, "The Raffles Museum and the Fate of Natural History in Singapore," pp. 188–90; Tan, *Of Whales and Dinosaurs*, pp. 87–90.

[68] The name of the society and the journal shifted over time to reflect changing political configurations in the region. In 1923 it became the Malayan Branch, and in 1963 the Malaysian Branch.

[69] Choy Chee Meh née Lum, "History of the Malaysian Branch of the Royal Asiatic Society," *Journal of the Malaysian Branch of the Royal Asiatic Society* 68, 2 (1995): 85–93; Tiew Wai Sin, "History of *Journal of the Malaysian Branch of the Royal Asiatic Society* (*JMBRAS*) 1878–1997: An Overview," *Malaysian Journal of Library and Information Science* 3, 1 (1998): 43–61; Kathirithamby-Wells, "Peninsular Malaysia in the Context of Natural History and Colonial Science," p. 367; Bucknill and Chasen, *The Birds of Singapore Island*.

The Raffles Museum was a scientific institution in which documenting the fauna of Singapore and the region was among its primary responsibilities. Beyond the gathering of unique specimens and scientific research, the public understood it as place to view animals. The display of these animals was not only "an introduction to the study of the fauna of the Malay region," as Hanitsch described it in a guide from 1908, but also a metaphorical mastery of the natural world.[70] Visitors could observe the diversity of species—the museum was a particularly popular place during Chinese New Year during the colonial era—at their own pace. The centerpiece of this experience was the range and majesty of the animals they saw with immense whale and elephant skeletons dominating rooms lined with display cases filled with stuffed birds, crabs and a plethora of other fauna. They were all animals that had come under the imperial gaze entering networks of colonial knowledge that reflected continual efforts at exerting control over the natural world.

Government, Animals and Institutions in Late Colonial Singapore

Throughout the colonial era Singapore was part of a larger web of collection, commerce, display and domestication of animals that linked scientific institutions, administrators, the port, businessmen and residents on the island with the region, empire and world, making it a primary location for imperial creatures. The participation of individuals such as Charles Mayer, Haji Marip, H.N. Ridley and F.N. Chasen established networks to display many of these animals for scientific study and entertainment, or even their incorporation into the household as domestic pets. As these individuals retired or passed away, new participants began to maintain these formal and informal institutions, often providing new ways of presenting and understanding animals. Some came from unexpected places, or only influenced how these networks developed after their deaths, such as Karl Van Kleef, who died in Haarlem, the Netherlands in June 1930.

The passing of a businessman who had lived in Singapore in the late 19th and early 20th centuries normally would not merit much

---

[70] R. Hanitsch, *Guide to the Zoological Collections of the Raffles Museum, Singapore* (Singapore: Straits Times Press, 1908).

attention. In his will, however, Van Kleef bequeathed the net proceeds from the sale of his estates to the Municipality of Singapore with the wish that the money be used "for the embellishment of the town" with the provision that "churches and other institutions connected to worship in general" not benefit. Faced with a sudden gift of some $100,000, the municipal commissioners were unsure how to proceed. After J.A. Elias elicited proposals for the use of the funds, his colleagues and newspaper contributors threw out various suggestions including statues, fountains and even an ornamental flower garden at the abandoned site of the Turf Club, which had recently shifted to Bukit Timah Road. Elias countered with a proposal to establish a zoo.[71]

In February 1931, "E.L.S." wrote to *The Malaya Tribune* and suggested that the Van Kleef funds be used in the construction of an aquarium, an idea that the Natural History Society of Singapore had proposed as early as 1922. An aquarium was a necessity for this British imperial outpost to be considered a modern city, he argued, as "it is well known that long ago public aquaria were established in Europe, America, Japan, Java, Manila, etc., and that their value and importance has been fully recognized." In addition, "in no other place in the world is the sea so well stocked with fish suitable" for such an institution. Such an establishment, E.L.S. also reasoned, would provide an educational site for young Singaporeans to learn the "vital principals of living organisms." Otherwise, these young ne'er-do-wells might otherwise "roam the streets at night" or be "visiting movies." To consider all of suggestions being offered for the use of the funds, the Municipal Commission appointed a Van Kleef Committee. Two years later, they concurred with E.L.S., recommending the establishment of an aquarium at the site of the former racecourse. It was a decision that, according to the Director of Fisheries, W. Birtwistle, was "admirable."[72]

The members of the Municipal Commission soon thereafter changed their mind, deciding that the green space at the former Turf

---

[71] Anonymous, "Former Resident's Bequest," *MT*, 15 Sep. 1930, p. 8; Y.C. Bee, "Van Kleef Bequest," *ST*, 10 Feb. 1931, p. 18; Kevin Khoo, "Remembering Karl Van Kleef and the Van Kleef Aquarium" (http://www.nas.gov.sg/archivesonline/article/remembering-karl-van-kleef. Accessed 26 Apr 2018).

[72] E.L.S., "An Aquarium for Singapore?," *MT*, 25 Feb 1931, p. 10; Anonymous, "Five Year-Plan for Municipality," *ST*, 31 Jan. 1933, p. 12; Anonymous, "An Aquarium for Singapore," *SFP*, 17 Feb. 1933, p. 7.

Club was better used "for football and other games and also tennis courts." They then proceeded to debate the benefits of several different locations for another two years before it was announced that the aquarium would be located at the base of Fort Canning Hill as it would have easy access to water storage tanks located nearby. The construction of the aquarium was delayed for several more years as architectural plans and additional funding were debated. Ultimately, all work on the project was suspended in 1939, as the municipal commissioners grew concerned over the outbreak of World War Two in Europe and the influence it might have on budgets. The Van Kleef Aquarium only opened in 1955.[73]

The inability to complete an aquarium prior to the Japanese Occupation represents a number of different themes related to animals in late colonial Singapore. The first of these is that the imperial government played an outsized role in how these issues were understood and presented. As they wielded power, the voice of British residents in both the government and among the merchant community had tremendous influence, allowing them to dictate the parameters for suggestions and debates. From the wish to construct an aquarium, as a symbol of a modern city, to the continual delays in its construction, the government helped set much of the tone for how the society operated, and the rules that were established. This would be a theme for all activities related to animals, ranging from definitions of cruelty and regulations related to domestic pets, to how meat was processed in the markets. Imperial understandings and considerations imposed from afar, as well as locally, permeated the decision-making process. While this often took time and was somewhat messy in its implementation, as with the construction of the aquarium, it established and rationalized human-animal relations in the society, and the relationship between ruler and ruled, master and subject.

---

[73] By the late 1930s, some of the delay was based on considerations related to the origins of the water. Birtwistle argued that it was necessary for the aquarium to use circulated, and stored, seawater as the available water near the harbor was "too heavily polluted and cannot be used." CO275/150: "Annual Report of the Fisheries Department, Straits Settlements and Federated Malay States for the Year 1938," p. 475; Anonymous, "Deleted Item Replaced in Municipal Budget," *SFP*, 1 Apr. 1933, p. 7; Anonymous, "An Aquarium for Singapore," *SFP*, 17 Feb. 1933, p. 7; Khoo, "Remembering Karl Van Kleef and the Van Kleef Aquarium."

The government and British residents, however, were not the only active participants in how these societal standards were set. In a society that was composed entirely of immigrants from the throughout Asia, with only a minimal number of Europeans present, there were numerous other influences on the human-animal relationship. Among these other participants, as Roland Braddell mentions in his memoir, were Indian, Eurasian and "several Chinese dealers" who were active in the animal trade and operated establishments, many located along Rochor Road. Among these individuals was W.L.S. Basapa.[74]

When the Van Kleef Aquarium was first mooted, another proposal had been the establishment of a public zoo in Singapore. While the Singapore Botanic Gardens contained a zoo from 1875 until 1905, the absence of one had meant that the city did not contain an important public symbol of modernity. A zoo, however, did exist. It was a private encampment that Basapa operated on the far eastern shore of Singapore, in Punggol. Basapa was an Indian entrepreneur who was the trustee of the estate of his father, Hunmah Somapah, who had parlayed his civil service job as a bill collector for the municipality into extensive land and property holdings throughout Singapore. When Somapah died in 1919, Basapa inherited control over these properties, using this real estate empire to support his interest in the business of supplying wild animals to interested parties throughout the world.[75] The maintenance of these networks began at home, as he routinely donated animals that had died before shipment to the Raffles Museum. As a 1926 report mentioned, "Donations from Mr. W.L. Basapa have as usual been numerous and include several gibbons one of which, *Hylobates lar albimanus*, from Sumatra, is new to the Museum." Meanwhile, in July of that same year, he shipped "nine tigers and several other wild animals" to England. Perhaps his greatest impact on the display of wild animals globally came in the late colonial era, when Basapa provided "the majority of the animals from Malaya" in the epic Mann Expedition,

---

[74] Braddell, *The Lights of Singapore*, p. 123.

[75] Basapa was the son-in-law of Somapah's best friend and associate, Appasamy Kandasamy. Basapa also inherited the extensive Kandasamy trusteeship following his death in 1919, giving him control over vast swaths of Singaporean real estate. Lakshmi Naidu, National Archives [Singapore] Oral History Centre, 000110/11, Reel 1.

which supplied the National Zoo in Washington DC with many of its pre-war tropical Asian fauna.[76]

Despite the role he played in the animal trade, Basapa is best known in Singapore as the owner of the small zoo, of some 8 hectares, in Punggol that existed from the 1920s until the Japanese invasion in 1942. The menagerie consisted of various animals that Basapa gathered for trade, although he displayed some from his private collection. "It was a novelty," one visitor remembered, and the menagerie came to be one of the highlights of a visit to Singapore in the 1930s, when admission was 40 cents.[77] According to *Willis's Singapore Guide* of 1936:

> The Malayan animals collected here are still in their primitive state, and not so tame as the ones we are used to seeing in the zoos at home. There are two Chimpanzees here, that are always ready to make friends with one, and especially so if you have anything to give them to eat. They will pose for photographs, enabling you to get very useful souvenirs for your album.

Jean Cocteau visited this attraction that same year. According to the French writer and artist, Basapa mainly displayed "recent captures" that were uncomfortable in their new environment. While Cocteau felt these animals represented the "vast reserves of energy [with which] the Orient can challenge an exhausted Europe," he was sadly resigned to the imperial certainty that they "would learn obedience." The main attraction at the zoo was a tiger named Apay, one of the few animals that was a constant at the site. It famously was led around on a chain and had learned the obedience that colonial rule demanded. Braddell claimed that the large feline would "roll on his back and purr like a cat," if visitors spoke quietly to it, while Cocteau simply described it as "docile, almost blind, with moonstone eyes."[78]

---

[76] In popular culture, the expedition was described as a "modern Noah's Ark." Anonymous, "Cross-Section of Malayan Fauna for Washington," *ST*, 8 Aug. 1937, p. 4; Anonymous, "Raffles Museum," *ST*, 24 May 1926, p. 11; Anonymous, "Untitled," *ST*, 29 July 1926, p. 8.

[77] Mohinder Singh, National Archives [Singapore] Oral History Centre, 000546/65, Reel 58; Lakshmi Naidu, National Archives [Singapore] Oral History Centre, 000110/11, Reel 1.

[78] Jean Cocteau, *Round the World Again in 80 Days (Mon Premier Voyage)*, tr. Stuart Gilbert (London, Tauris Parke, 2000), pp. 123–5; A.C. Willis, *Willis's Singapore Guide* (Singapore: Advertising and Policy Bureau, 1936), p. 119; Braddell, *The Lights of Singapore*, p. 24.

Image 3.10: William Basapa with Apay. Image from Roland Braddell, *The Lights of Singapore*.

The Punggol Zoo was a late colonial attraction in Singapore and closely interlinked with the animal trade, domestication of exotic species and their display before an interested public. It also intersected with government attempts to monitor and regulate fauna in Singapore, which shaped the imperial experience. In this case, it is related to attempts to address the threat that such trade on the biodiversity of the region, out of fears of hunters and collectors ravaging the forests of Malaya in search of unique animals for circuses, zoos and collectors globally. This resulted, in 1934, in the colonial government banning "the capture and sale of live animals and birds in the Malay States," which was a blow to the commerce that Basapa had inherited from Frank Buck and Charles Mayer.[79] Such restrictions, which were part of larger global efforts on behalf of imperial governments to monitor the wildlife trade, meant that Basapa had to find new solutions. He

---

[79] Basapa then began to focus on Sumatra and Siam to supply the animals he needed. Anonymous, "Officialdom and the Zoo," *The Morning Tribune*, 24 Feb. 1936, p. 11.

found one in a loophole that allowed for trade to occur if it was done on a system of animal exchange. Under this scheme, he "shipped 12 elephants, 12 tigers, 20 black panthers and over 20 pythons" to Europe, America, Australia and India in 1935, and received other animals in return, such as three sea lions, a pair of mountain lions and a pair of elks that arrived from California the next year. He would then feature these new acquisitions in his zoo for brief periods before shipping them on to new destinations.[80]

Due to his ability to participate in such exchanges, which allowed him to display animals to the public, Basapa soon faced a range of accusations and regulations related to shifting understandings of cruelty throughout the 1930s. This was part of new understandings of the relationship between humans and animals that had resulted in harsh criticism of the animal shops along Rochor Road, and even Basapa's zoological collection. Although the authorities usually approved his facilities, in contrast to his downtown counterparts, the criticism was constant throughout the decade. In 1937, for example, Basapa faced accusations that he kept panthers and tigers "in cages where the animal can hardly move." He countered that this was only true for "animals awaiting shipment to other Zoos," and employed statements from the Director of the Raffles Museum and several large European zoos as proof that he enjoyed their support in this matter.[81]

Each of the various pressures that the Van Kleef Aquarium and the Punggol Zoo faced were reflective of how animals fit into colonial

---

[80] The collection, for example, featured a lion, from an Australian zoo in Perth. Basapa claimed that the zoo and the animal trade, which were based in his "love for animals and birds," was a drain on his resources, as he estimated in 1936 that it had cost him almost $100,000 over the 15 years he had been active in these endeavors. Anonymous, "Animals Shipped to Singapore," *MT*, 9 Nov. 1936, p. 12; Anonymous, "Officialdom and the Zoo."

[81] Despite the active trade that took place, the monitoring of the authorities, and the exotic thrill of seeing the animals for many Singaporeans, the zoo did not survive the imminent arrival of the Japanese. The British military took over the land, which faced the Johor Straits, on the eve of the invasion and ordered Basapa to evacuate the animals within 24 hours. When he was unable to do so, soldiers freed the birds and shot all of the mammals and reptiles. The zoo was closed. When the Japanese arrived, they confiscated the cages and a generator. Anonymous, "W.L.S. Basapa: The 'Animal Man'." http://www.singaporebasapa.com, accessed 24 Apr. 2018; W.L.S. Basapa, "The Ponggol Zoo," *MT*, 22 Oct. 1937, p. 14; Anonymous, "Officialdom and the Zoo"; Tan, "The Beastly Business of Regulating the Wild Animal Trade in Colonial Singapore."

Singapore, and mirrored developments that had occurred since the late 19th century regarding the relationship between humans and animals in an imperial port. The imposition of British perspectives on the relationship, attempts to monitor and control animals, and how such rationalizations reflected understandings of the relationship between government, science and larger society. In Singapore, every animal lived under a colonial government that influenced how the interaction between the various species took place, a relationship that was fraught with metaphors of power, control and spectacle. As the British Empire expanded, Singapore was also coming under the influence of shifting understandings of how humans relate to animals, and how they should be treated. It was at this time, in the second half of the 19th century, that Britons introduced new notions of what constituted cruelty, transforming how animals were perceived in the colonized landscape of Singapore.

CHAPTER FOUR

Defining Cruelty

In 1872 Alexei Alexandrovich, better known as Grand Duke Alexis, the fifth child of Czar Alexander II of Russia, visited Singapore along with a squadron of naval vessels. His sojourn in the capital of the Straits Settlements was part of a longer diplomatic journey that involved an extended tour of the United States as well as stops in Rio de Janeiro, Cape Town and Batavia, and eventually Hong Kong, Canton and Shanghai. Grand Duke Alexis was headed to Japan, where he was to meet with members of the Meiji government and participate in discussions on Russo-Japanese diplomatic relations. While in Singapore he met with Governor Harry Ord and attended dinners and balls in his honor, amidst surging crowds and all of the trimmings of pomp and circumstance. The presence of foreign royalty brought some life to the colonial port. As one observer opined, it was "an agreeable interlude in the sleepy monotony and sameness which characterizes life in this so-called Paradise of the East." The visit was originally scheduled for three days, but went so well the Grand Duke extended his stay for over a week, and even made a visit to Melaka.[1]

One of the highlights of this brief sojourn in the Straits Settlements occurred on 31 August. That morning, accompanied by the Governor and much of the elite of Singapore, Grand Duke Alexis boarded the government steamer *Pluto* and sailed around the island

---

[1] CO273/59/10138: Arrival and Departure of Corvette "Sveltana" with Grand Duke Alexis Aboard; Anonymous, "The Grand Duke Alexis at Johore," *ST*, 7 Sep. 1872, p. 1; Anonymous, "The Grand Duke Alexis," *ST*, 31 Aug. 1871, p. 1; Anonymous, "Untitled," *Straits Times Overland Journal*, 7 Sep. 1872, p. 11.

to the newly founded town of Johor Baru. The visitors alighted at the bungalow of the Maharaja of Johor, Abu Bakar, who was an influential supporter of the British presence in the region. The Johor royal family, Chinese entrepreneurs and the European elite of the port had been closely interlinked since 1819. The grandfather of the Maharaja was the Temenggong of Singapore who had signed the original treaties with Thomas Stamford Raffles and John Crawfurd in 1819 and 1824 respectively, which transferred sovereignty of the island to the British East India Company. Abu Bakar and his father continued to support the colonial government and its policies in the following decades as they expanded their influence and agricultural policies into the southern portions of the Malay Peninsula. The Maharaja eventually became so intertwined with the imperial elite, and their culture, his British friends referred to him as "Albert Baker," and the visit of the Grand Duke to Johor was part of the larger theater-state of colonial society in Singapore.[2]

The Maharaja greeted his guests upon their arrival and accompanied them to a large tent in the courtyard of the bungalow, where a sumptuous breakfast was laid out. After the meal and several speeches, everyone retired to an area behind the building, where they saw a large cage consisting of "long poles driven into the ground and tied together with thongs, and made firm by strong cross-pieces at the top." The Maharaja of Johor was about to entertain his guests with a contest between a "royal tiger and a buffalo bull."[3]

Such spectacles were commonly staged in royal houses throughout Southeast Asia in the premodern era. As Anthony Reid states in a survey of such entertainment, "No great feast passed at the courts of Java, Aceh, Siam and Burma without some spectacular fight between elephants, tigers, buffaloes, or lesser animals." J.F.A. McNair, a Briton who served as Head Engineer for the Straits Settlements and attended the breakfast that morning in Johor, described such events as "the grand national sport" of Malay polities. It was not the first time McNair had

---

[2] R.O. Winstedt, *A History of Johore (1365–1941)* (Kuala Lumpur: Malaysian Branch of the Royal Asiatic Society, 1992), p. 137; Carl A. Trocki, *Prince of Pirates: The Temenggongs and the Development of Johor and Singapore, 1784–1885* (Singapore: NUS Press, 2007), pp. 128–60; Anonymous, "She Cannot Sue the Sultan," *The Chicago Sunday Tribune*, 5 Nov. 1893, p. 1; Anonymous, "The Grand Duke Alexis at Johore."

[3] Anonymous, "The Grand Duke Alexis at Johore."

attended such a contest in Johor. Only three years earlier, he was present when the Duke of Edinburgh witnessed a similar confrontation—which would have the same outcome—during his visit to the Straits Settlements.[4]

A curtain divided the cage in half and, after Grand Duke Alexis and the other guests were readied, the two animals were admitted into opposite sides of the pen. As described in a newspaper report:

> The curtain was raised, but the tiger, a female, proved an arrant coward, and utterly indisposed to fight, seeing which the buffalo was inclined to let her alone, but after a while made a rush at her and jammed her against the poles of the cage. This was repeated several times, during which the buffalo received little or no injury, and the tiger then lay down and could not be urged on more. Fire-crackers were burned in the cage in the vain hope of getting her into a rage, but the tiger only moved away from them and again lay down. Seeing this, the Prince and party left the platform, after which the Malays let down a rope from the top of the cage, and a noose having been slipped round one of the tiger's hind legs, she was suspended in the air, when the buffalo was goaded on and butted and gored the poor tiger till life was extinct.[5]

The outcome of the battle had been preordained. In these contests, it was important for the tiger to lose, as it was the symbol of danger, lawlessness and disorder. The representative of civilization—the buffalo —was required to defeat the wild, savage beast.[6]

Beyond the symbolism of such a contest in a Southeast Asian polity, this staged spectacle, held for the elite of the Straits Settlements in 1872, was also a metaphor for a shift in animals and their importance in Singapore. The tiger was no longer much of a concern for residents of the growing port. The jungle had been tamed, its predators destroyed, and in this case even converted into a form of symbolic entertainment. In contrast, the buffalo—or, more specifically its close relative, the bullock—was about to become the most important animal

---

[4] J.F.A. McNair, *Perak and the Malays* (Kuala Lumpur: Oxford University Press, 1972), pp. 266–8; Boomgaard, *Frontiers of Fear*, p. 14; Reid, *Southeast Asia in the Age of Commerce, 1450–1680. Volume One*, p. 183.

[5] Anonymous, "The Grand Duke Alexis at Johore."

[6] Anonymous, "The Grand Duke Alexis at Johore"; Reid, *Southeast Asia in the Age of Commerce, Volume One*, pp. 183–91; Boomgaard, *Frontiers of Fear*, pp. 146–66.

on the island, where it would play a role in transporting peoples and goods while reflecting attitudes towards animals that would reveal many of the permutations of British imperial rule in Southeast Asia as well as the development of colonial Singapore. The bullock thus would play a role in transforming the island during a period when animals provided much of the labor in transporting goods and people throughout the region, and power structures within the colonial government were becoming clearer. This also would be reflected in how humans perceived other animals, and treated them, particularly those that provided labor.

Horses, Cattle, and Transport in Late 19th-Century Singapore

In the mid-19th century the residents of Singapore moved about the island by walking or being conveyed by either an animal or a human. The use of an animal for these purposes was a relatively new phenomenon in the port. In the first few decades of colonial rule, almost every resident had been "chiefly pedestrian."[7] The town was compact, and residents could move easily within and between districts. Singapore, however, was developing. The population was increasing—for example, the number of residents almost doubled from 97,000 to 178,000 in the 20 years between 1870 and 1890—while dwellings and other buildings pushed beyond the immediate environs of the port. As the population grew and the town expanded, over the remainder of the century, alternative methods of transportation were needed to convey people and goods.

The heyday of the bullock and the horse in Singapore was between the 1870s and 1900, when they were the primary method of moving humans and goods away from the port into the expanding urban landscape.[8] In 1877 there were almost 6,000 "horned cattle" and

---

[7] An Old Resident, *Play and Politics*, p. 6; Cameron, *Our Tropical Possessions in Malayan India*, pp. 290–2.

[8] Rickshaws existed, but they only became the main form of transport for humans after 1893, when their numbers skyrocketed from approximately 4,000 in 1892 to over 20,000 by the beginning of the 20th century. Warren, *Rickshaw Coolie*, p. 61; Peter J. Rimmer, "Hackney Carriage Syces and Rikisha Pullers in Singapore: A Colonial Registrar's Perspective on Public Transport, 1892–1923," in *The Underside of Malaysian History: Pullers, Prostitutes, Plantation Workers*, ed. Peter J. Rimmer and Lisa M. Allen (Singapore: Singapore University Press, 1991), pp. 130–1.

1,600 horses present on the island.[9] The number of work animals had increased throughout the first decade of direct colonial rule, reflecting their importance in the development of colonial infrastructure. The key year was 1871, when the number of bullocks in Singapore doubled to 5,988, a figure that was relatively stable for the remainder of the century. There were 543 horse drawn carriages plying the streets in 1872, a number that increased to 896 by 1879. By 1900 the bullock population declined to 4,000 while the number of carriages also decreased to 500, mirroring a lessening of their influence, as the society turned to more mechanized forms of transport, such as railroads and trams, as well as human-powered rickshaws.[10] It was during this 20-year period that notions related to the treatment of animals in an imperial port were established, and it focused around the horse and bullock. These conceptions were developed in a busy and chaotic atmosphere.

The streets of Singapore in the late 19th century were a mélange of various forms of transport, mixing the raw muscle power of humans and animals. As one contemporary guidebook described the scene, the streets were "crowded and busy at all hours of the day.... Carriages, hack-gharries, bullock-carts, and jinrickishas pass and repass in a continual stream." This is further supported in an account of an American visiting the port in the 1880s. "As the steamer drew near," he wrote, "we saw many natives, with bright-colored garments, which gave a dash of color to the scene; queer looking bullock-carts, for merchandise; gharries, drawn by ponies, waiting for the passengers." Another visitor reported that, when preparing for departure, he sent "the heavy baggage ahead on a bullock-cart in charge of one of the hotel runners, we bade Raffles Hotel and its smiling manager good-bye and drove to the docks in a 'ticca-gharry,' one of the box like cabs of India and the Straits." Meanwhile, in a similar passage, American Thomas Knox praised the

---

[9] As bullocks were imported under the catch-all rubric of "cattle," it is difficult to determine how many were used for labor or slaughtered for food. Anonymous, *Straits Settlements Blue Book for the Year 1867* (Singapore: Government Printing Office, 1868), p. 513. There were 1,269 sheep and 960 goats in Singapore that same year. CO277: *Straits Settlements Blue Book for the Year 1877* (Singapore: Government Printing Office, 1878), X4.

[10] CO277 (1871), p. X5; CO277 (1874), p. 248; CO277 (1877), p. X6; CO277 (1900), p. X4; Warren, *Rickshaw Coolie*; Rimmer, "Hackney Carriage Syces and Rikisha Pullers in Singapore," p. 132.

Image 4.1: Horse Gharry in late 19th-century Singapore. Courtesy of the Rijksmuseum, Amsterdam.

use of bullock carts to transport luggage, while horse-drawn carriages were more "expeditious."[11]

As Knox implies in his description, the role of horses and bullocks in transporting people and goods in Singapore was not only related to the speed of the vehicle but also class differences. Horses were for the well-to-do in society. They pulled hackney carriages—often called "gharry," and of which there were 1,075 registered in 1883. These carriages were almost exclusively available to the elite. Further emphasizing

---

[11] Reflecting the changing, and exploitative nature of transportation in colonial Singapore, James Low described how, in 1840, "Ponies with small carts have lately been introduced; and the Chinese, in order to evade the tax on carts drawn by cattle or horses, have started a three-man cart or truck, which is propelled by them, one man guiding it with a pole, and one pushing at each hind quarter of the cart." James Low, "Extracts from an Unpublished Journal," *SFP*, 2 Dec. 1841, p. 2; Knox, *The Boy Travellers in the Far East*, p. 315; G.M. Reith, *Handbook to Singapore, with Map* (1907), p. 35; J.E.L., *Ten Days in the Jungle* (Boston: Cupples, Upham and Company, 1885), p. 8; Arthur S. Walcott, *Java and her Neighbors; A Traveller's Notes in Java, Celebes, the Moluccas, and Sumatra* (New York: G.P. Putnam's Sons, 1914), p. 34.

the financial differences between their users, a horse could be purchased for £50, while a bullock went for £7 10s at that time.[12] Ownership of a horse became di rigueur for anyone hoping to impress, with one observer commenting that "The Anglo-Saxon instinct for respectability (or for some more subtle reason) prescribes the use of a ghari, which is practically a four-wheeled cab with venetian blinds substituted for windows," with the accompanying servants. Open carriages and gigs were also common, with one horse pulling each one. These horses were "led, not often driven, by a groom, with an occasional out-rider behind."[13]

Gharries also operated like taxis in 19th-century Singapore. According to one travel guide the cost was 15 cents for one or two passengers for the first half-mile (800 meters), and 20 cents for any subsequent distance. In contrast, a rickshaw cost 3 cents over the the first half-mile, reflecting how gharries were limited to a financial class that could afford it. Visitors staying for longer periods could hire private carriages with two horses at F. Clarke and Co. on Hill Street or The Straits Horse Repository and Livery Stables at the corner of North Bridge Road and Bras Brasah Road for $5 for the day. Costs went down to as little as $2.50 per day for a carriage with one horse if leased for more than a month. Most Europeans residents, however, had their own "rather motley vehicles" and this often led to traffic jams "for half an hour every morning" on the two bridges leading across the river into town. These privately owned carriages were well maintained, as they mirrored the owners standing in society. "On the whole both the private conveyances and horses of Singapore are creditable," John Cameron commented, "though the same cannot be said for the miserable pony hack-gharries that are let out on hire."[14]

---

[12] For a comparison, annual wages for an agricultural laborer in 1874 were a bit more than £12 (£12.15.0), while a domestic servant received a bit more (£15.6.0). CO277 (1871), p. X5; CO277 (1874), p. 248.

[13] Wellcome Collection: MS5963: "Monday, 6th Mar 1857," *Journal of a Voyage from London to the Far East, and Voyages between Bombay, Singapore and Hong Kong*, p. 64; W. Basil Worsfold, *A Visit to Java with an Account of the Founding of Singapore* (London: R. Bentley, 1893), p. 281; Buckley, *An Anecdotal History of Singapore*, p. 362; Knox, *The Boy Travellers in the Far East*, p. 292. Low, "Extracts from an Unpublished Journal," *SFP*, 2 Dec. 1841, p. 2; Warren, *Rickshaw Coolie*, p. 60.

[14] G.M. Reith, *Handbook to Singapore, with Map and a Plan of the Botanical Gardens* (Singapore: The Singapore and Straits Printing Office, 1892), p. 82; Cameron, *Our Tropical Possessions in Malayan India*, pp. 295–6.

Horses, as 19th-century travel writer Ida Pfeiffer noted on her visit, were not bred in Singapore, mainly due to the absence of grazing land. The horses found on the island were mainly imported from a variety of Southeast Asian societies. As James Low described in his report from 1840–1, "With the exception of a few Arabs [horses], the residents content themselves with ponies. They are chiefly obtained from Java. But they are not so smart and powerful as those from Sumatra." John Thomson went on to add that these Sumatran ponies were "the perfection of symmetry; with small well-formed heads, full tender eyes, and neck that arch gracefully beneath a profusion of mane. Their chests are broad, their limbs fine, their hoofs round and compact; and so full of spirit are these fiery little animals that many of them, if given the rein, would keep their pace up until they dropped down." Basically, with regard to horse-drawn transport, one British visitor in 1854 summarized the scene as one in which the "many covered carriages" were "drawn by remarkably small and active poneys", which were from Southeast Asia.[15]

Larger horses of "Arabian" stock were imported from Australia in increasing numbers throughout the 19th century, and any "meadow-grass" that could be grown in Singapore was reserved for their consumption, according to McNair. For these animals, "the climate seems to agree with them; they grow fat and sleek and live long, though they can scarcely go through the same amount of work as in their native country; each horse has its groom and grass-cutter, and probably the additional attention they receive compensates for the exhausting temperature." As appreciation of these animals grew, their use in transport became a symbol of the status of the owners throughout the society, leading the Chinese and Malay elite to maintain beautiful horses and stables, as well as the workers to support their needs. The coachmen were all Malay—the only English coachman in Singapore worked for the Sultan of Johor while a German resident, G. Kuglemann, was

---

[15] Pfeiffer, *A Woman's Journey Round the World*, p. 120; Low, "Extracts from an Unpublished Journal," *SFP*, 2 Dec. 1841, p. 2; Wellcome Collection: MS5958: "Sunday, 15th Jan 1854," *Journal of a Voyage from London to the Far East, and Voyages between Bombay, Singapore and Hong Kong*, p. 20; Thomson, *The Straits of Malacca, Indo-China, and China*, p. 61; William Gervase Clarence-Smith, "Southeast Asia and Southern Africa in the Maritime Horse Trade of the Indian Ocean, c. 1800–1914," in *Breeds of Empire: The 'Invention' of the Horse in Southeast Asia and Southern Africa, 1500–1950*, ed. Greg Bankoff and Sandra Swart (Copenhagen: NIAS Press, 2007), p. 29.

renowned for his ability to break the animals. He boasted that "he had never been thrown in his life," and was often seen lifting a horse by its forelegs and backing it between the shafts of the carriage.[16]

While horses were the main form of transport for the well-to-do in 19th-century Singapore society, and were also used in horse races that entertained this same elite, bovines did most of the work of hauling goods and materials. They were an important component in the development of the island, as without them human energy could not be directed to other activities. They carried the society into a civilized colonial modernity. In the main account of the metaphorical clash between civilization and savagery that Grand Duke Alexis witnessed in Johor in 1872, the animal opposing the tiger is described as both a "bullock" and a "buffalo," reflecting the interchangeability of the term at the time. In such contests in the Malay World it usually was a water buffalo (*Bubalus bubalis*) confronting a tiger.[17]

Within Southeast Asia there were two types of bovine: water buffalo and cattle. For our purposes, cattle are members of the subfamily that were used to produce beef for consumption while, in British territories, bullock referred to a male bovine, specifically meaning a young male that had its testicles removed. In colonial Singapore it referred to a work animal. The interchangeability of the terms for bovines often makes it difficult to trace the various subspecies in the records. Buffaloes, according to McNair, were "a large and heavy kind of ox, domesticated by the Malays. There are two varieties, called the white and black; but the former is more of a pink tint. They are used by their owners both as draught cattle and as beasts of burden." He went on to add, "When attached to one of the long, narrow, roughly-made country carts, they can draw very heavy loads; but in this task they are rarely yoked in pairs, on account of the narrowness of the roads and the width of the buffaloes' horns, the points of which are more than four feet from tip to tip." While the water buffalo remained the most

---

[16] The English coachman for the Sultan of Johor was named "Arthur Holley." Anonymous, "The Inquest of the Body of C. Kruger," *ST*, 8 May 1880, p. 1; Thomson, *The Straits of Malacca, Indo-China, and China*, p. 60; Anonymous, "A Lady on Singapore," *The Straits Times Weekly Issue*, 5 Oct. 1892, p. 7; McNair, *Perak and the Malays*, p. 73; Cameron, *Our Tropical Possessions in Malayan India*, p. 296.

[17] Water buffaloes are members of the subfamily Bovinae, which includes cattle, bison, buffalo, yak and some antelopes. Anonymous, "The Grand Duke Alexis at Johore."

important bovine throughout Southeast Asia, where it was integrated into agricultural cycles and social communities, the bullock was used "for drawing carts and for other agricultural purposes," particularly in a colonial settlement such as Singapore.[18]

The bullocks that arrived often varied in appearance. "Some are dirty white, some of cream color, some almost pink, and a few are of the darker shades," Rounsevelle Wildman described in 1891. In contrast, those imported from Bali could vary from black to brown in color, while "the horns are sharp and diverging." Wildman went on to explain how bullocks commonly seen pulling a cart in Singapore had horns "generally tipped with curiously carved knobs, and often painted in colours."[19] He went on to describe:

> Their necks are always 'bowed to the yoke,' … and seem almost to invite its humiliating clasp … a simple pole with a pin of wood through each end to ride on the outside of the bullocks' necks. The burden comes against the projecting hump when the team pulls. To the centre of this yoke is tied, with strong withes of rattan, the pole of a cart … [with which] all the heavy traffic of the Colonies it down within its rude board sides. It has two wheels with heavy square spokes that are held on to a ponderous wooden axletree, by two wooden pins. A platform bottom rests on the axletree, and two fence-like sides.[20]

A female visitor to the port supported this description. "All carts here are drawn by bullocks. They are not like home cattle, but have a slight hump on the shoulder, and are generally of a dun or a white colour. A rope is passed through the nostrils, and with this the bullock driver guides his team, standing on the shafts between the bullocks—a veritable study for a painter or sculptor."[21]

---

[18] McNair, *Perak and the Malays*, p. 112; Worsfold, *A Visit to Java*, p. 190.

[19] Adapting bullocks to tropical conditions was often difficult, with various diseases often affecting the community. As mentioned in the extremely informative report of James Low from 1841, "Buffaloes and oxen are chiefly used for draft, but are very expensive, as they are subject to frequent murrains [red water fever] and are not reared on the island, but are brought from Malacca, Penang, and other countries." Low, "Extracts from an Unpublished Journal," *SFP*, 2 Dec. 1841, p. 2; Rounsevelle Wildman, "Indian Bullocks," *The Straits Times Weekly Issue*, 27 Oct. 1891, p. 3.

[20] Wildman, "Indian Bullocks."

[21] Anonymous, "A Lady on Singapore," *The Straits Times Weekly Issue*, 5 Oct. 1892, p. 7; Buckley, *An Anecdotal History of Singapore*, pp. 316, 362.

Image 4.2: Draught bullock, 1881. From the John Edmund Taylor Collection. Courtesy of the Wellcome Collection.

The cultivation and maintenance of bullocks in Singapore was centered in the Indian community. This was true throughout Southeast Asia. In Siam, it was even believed that "Klings and Tamils from Southern India" introduced the "bullock cart as a convenient method of carrying heavy goods."[22] They were the drivers, the dairymen and

---

[22] As one account of Malaya defined, "Klings is a name given to the lowest classes of native immigrants, who clear the jungles, do the rough part of road-making, and drive bullock-carts." Arnold Wright, *Twentieth Century Impressions of British Malaya: Its History, People, Commerce, Industries, and Resources* (Singapore: Lloyd's Greater Britain Publishing Company, 1908), p. 218; Ernest Young, *The Kingdom of the Yellow Robe. Being Sketches of the Domestic and Religious Rites and Ceremonies of the Siamese* (Westminster: A. Constable, 1898), p. 14; James Low, *A Dissertation on the Soil and Agriculture of Penang or Prince of Wales Island, in the Straits of Malacca: Including Province Wellesley on the Malayan Peninsula. With Brief References to the Settlements of Singapore and Malacca, and Accompanied by Incidental Observations on Various Subjects of Local Interest in these Straits* (Singapore: Singapore Free Press, 1836), p. 182.

the owners of these cattle. In the Straits Settlements these tasks often fell to former Indian convicts—approximately 1,100 were brought in under the East India Company in the 1830s and 1840s—who were mainly "employed in making roads and digging canals." After achieving emancipation, some took up employment as "a keeper of cattle, or a letter-out of bullock carts, carriages and horses." As this practice developed, an area where the cattle herders gathered and lived soon came to be known as Kadang Kerbau (Cattle Pen, in Malay), sometimes referred to as Buffalo Village in old records.[23]

The drivers of these cattle were seen as both noble drovers and cruel taskmasters. Wildman painted a picture of a human that "belabours his bullocks in turn, calling down upon their ungainly humps the curses of his religion. The scene has grown so familiar that it hardly seems worth recording." He went on to add that it was common to see "a long line of these bullock carts, laden with the products of the tropics; pineapples, bananas, gambier, coffee, urged on by a straight and graceful driver, winding slowly along a palm and banyan tree-shaded-road." Another account mentioned, "The drivers are usually Klings or natives of India, and are fine handsome fellows with bronze-coloured skins. Their usual costume is a cloth round their loins and a scarlet turban on their heads." Finally, Eliza Scidmore, the first female board member of the American National Geographic Society, described them as one of the more picturesque aspects of the colonial port. "The array of turbans and sarongs give color to every thoroughfare; but the striking and most unique pictures in Singapore streets are the Tamil bullock-drivers, who, sooty and statuesque, stand in splendid contrast between their humped white oxen and the mounds of white flour-bags they draw in primitive carts."[24]

---

[23] As Low described, "The Malays are not a pastoral race. Few of them keep any sort of cattle except buffaloes. The settlers from India are the chief graziers. They rear cattle for dairy." Most of these cattle came from Kelantan and Siam. Buckley, *An Anecdotal History of Singapore*, p. 364; A. H. Keane, *A Geography of the Malay Peninsula, Indo-China, the Eastern Archipelago, The Philippines and New Guinea* (London: E. Stanford, 1892), p. 20; Jacob T. Child, *The Pearl of Asia: Reminiscences of the Court of a Supreme Monarch or Five Years in Siam* (Chicago: Donohue, Henneberr and Co, 1892), p. 11; Rajesh Rai, *Indians in Singapore*.

[24] Eliza Ruhamah Scidmore, *Java: The Garden of the East* (New York, The Century Co., 1899), p. 4; Anonymous, "A Lady on Singapore," *The Straits Times Weekly Issue*, 5 Oct. 1892, p. 7; Wildman, "Indian Bullocks."

The role of bullock carts for basic transportation tasks made them a common sight in colonial Singapore, although they rarely merited mention in the records, unless it was related to their contribution to a chaotic traffic system. As one call for increased regulations in 1892 noted, it was common to encounter "a number of bullock carts wandering about in an aimless way." Another mentioned that, "it is common thing in our streets to see a bullock cart overloaded.... One of these carts was heavily loaded with rattans, and while crossing the Singapore River over Elgin Bridge, the shaft broke," and the bullocks were immediately covered with tumbling vines.[25]

The state of these draft animals—the bullock and the horse—was a key motivator of reform in Singapore related to the roads, sanitation and transportation. It also allowed for the infusion of a very imperial perspective into a society far from Great Britain. This was achieved through a promotion of a concern for the well-being of such animals, which could be a conduit for greater reforms, as well as a commentary on the distance between the colonizers and colonized. The focus on how animals were treated in Singapore began to gather steam in the mid-1870s, just as the colonial government was beginning to exercise greater control over the society, which occurred following the transfer of power from the East India Company to direct British government control of the Straits Settlements of Singapore, Melaka and Penang in 1867. Part of this control was an advocacy for creatures, such as the bullock, which were important in the functioning of the society and would come through the Society for the Prevention of Cruelty to Animals. And, once again, it could be linked back to the contest that Grand Duke Alexis witnessed.

---

[25] Their role in this regard, and the people who oversaw them, is highlighted in a letter to the editor of *The Straits Times* in November 1874 protesting the closing of a bridge on Serangoon Road. The author claimed that horse owners "no doubt can and will stand up for themselves." In contrast, he wrote as an advocate, "on behalf of the poor, the grass and wood cutters and owners of Bullock Carts, whose livelihood depends on their ability to bring grass and wood in quantities daily and expeditiously into town. I ask what are they to do during the time that this bridge is closed?" One of the Public?, "The Municipal Commissioners," *ST*, 28 Nov. 1874, p. 4; Anonymous, "The Regulation of Street Traffic," *The Straits Times Weekly Issue*, 15 Mar. 1892, p. 8; Anonymous, "Local and General," *The Daily Advertiser*, 21 June 1892, p. 3.

"A Defective Civilization"

The staged tiger-buffalo confrontation that Grand Duke Alexis of Russia and Straits Settlements officials witnessed in Johor in 1872 merited attention in Singapore. Although it took place in a neighboring Malay polity, outside the purview of the colonial government, it occurred in front of the imperial elite during a period when they were attempting to establish British law and culture in a newly recognized colony, as well as create an image of civilizational superiority. This led to criticism of the effort to entertain the Grand Duke. According to a letter to the editor of *The Straits Times*, such a staged fight was evidence of "a low tone of morals, and a defective civilization," much like cockfighting in Britain and bullfighting in Spain. The anonymous critic, going by the moniker "Censor," continued with this line of thought, condemning officials, who "cannot escape the responsibility of having sanctioned a spectacle which, first and last, was worthy only of some uncivilized tribe." "Such exhibitions arose out of, and produce, a recklessness of bloodshed and cruelty alike wicked and disastrous," and was unsuitable behavior for any Briton, including those in the colonies, as "the higher demands of the Christian law, which enacts that tenderness and compassion and mercifulness shall be prominent in our characters."[26] As the event may have been contrary to British cultural practices, the presence of Britons made it particularly inexcusable. After all, in the understandings of the times, the formation of the Straits Settlements in 1867 "was but the natural outflow of the spirit of our age and race, or in other and plainer words, the fulfillment of England's destiny to civilize by colonizing the uttermost parts of the earth."[27]

Newspapers in Singapore often highlighted cases of animal cruelty, usually framing it within such civilizational discourse. In this regard, the account of the tiger-buffalo contest in September 1872 was not even the first complaint of this nature in the local press that month. The editors of *The Straits Times* also highlighted criticisms the Registrar of Hackney Carriages received about the use of unbroken ponies, which would often stop in the street and refuse to proceed. This would cause

---

[26] Censor, "The Tiger and Buffalo Fight," *ST*, 7 Sep. 1872, p. 3.

[27] Anonymous, "Thursday, 4th February, 1875," *The Straits Observer*, 4 Feb. 1875, p. 2. Similar efforts occurred in all colonies. For an example of such issues in Africa, see Brett L. Shadle, "Cruelty and Empathy, Animals and Race, in Colonial Kenya," *Journal of Social History* 45, 4 (2012): 1097–116.

an inconvenience if the passengers were "far from a stand and no other gharry obtainable at the time," which often resulted in abuse directed at the intransigent horse. "The poor pony is beaten and belaboured, sometimes with a heavy stick." Such behavior, however, was not illegal at the time, although the complainant argued that such behavior bordered on the criminal, particularly if Singapore had "a branch of the Society for preventing cruelty to animals."[28]

The pressure was kept up. The next month a letter complaining about cockfighting in the Straits Settlements appeared, placing it in the context of the recently viewed tiger-buffalo contest in Johor. The presence of British officials, the writer argued, reflected the tacit approval of the imperial authorities in attendance. "It says but little for the power for good of a British government, that, 50 years after its establishment at each end of the Straits, such inhuman and cowardly slaughter should prevail without an effort being made to put a stop to it. If our authorities have not the courage to perform an evident duty, should not the public voice call upon them, in the name of humanity and civilization, to interfere to prevent barbarities which cause a shudder even when committed by savages and cannibals."[29]

Accounts such as these appeared throughout the colonial era in Singapore, and were directed toward different animals and varying forms of cruelty at different times. For example, in early May 1874, a dog was found in a state of "*assommé*" along North Bridge Road as the authorities had not properly killed it. The canine suffered further when a gharry ran over it; the dog still did not die. It remained paralyzed on the road. Witnesses were horrified, claiming that such cruelty stigmatized Singapore as a "heathen land," and was unacceptable "in a country which has the name of being a Christian one."[30] While concern over the suffering of a dog in Singapore was relatively rare in the 19th century, it was rooted in changing British understandings of what constituted proper behavior.

The concept of cruelty directed toward animals and its prevention was not a common feature of civilizational discourse prior to the era of high imperialism. In the early 19th century the English were famous for their acceptance of animal abuse, ranging from widespread

---

[28] Anonymous, "Legislative Council", *ST*, 14 Sep. 1872, p. 2.
[29] Aquila, "Barbarity in the Straits," *ST*, 5 Oct. 1872, p. 4.
[30] Philokoun, "Dog Killing," *ST*, 9 May 1874, p. 5.

mistreatment of oxen and workhorses to cruel forms of entertainment. The prevalence of such cruelty prior to the Victorian era is reflected in a proposal before Parliament in 1800 to prohibit bullbaiting—in which a bull was tied to a stake and taunted before being attacked with specially trained dogs. The motion was soundly defeated, with newspapers claiming it to be beneath the dignity of the institution to even question a common practice in the nation. More importantly, the legislation was not proposed to protect animals. It was done out of a concern that bullbaiting demoralized human witnesses, and subsequently made them unfit for work. This outlook, in which the rights of the animal was secondary, would quickly transform, as the nation became increasingly industrialized, resulting in a shift in the economic priorities from rural areas to urban centers while energy and instruments of the economy became increasingly mechanized. The tool for transforming understandings of acceptable human-animal behavior, in the words of historian Brian Harrison, was "a powerful combination of evangelical piety, romantic poetry and rational humanitarianism," which "gradually alerted the public to the plight of animals."[31]

The changing human-animal relationship in Britain became more apparent in proposed legislation by the 1820s, which was part of a larger movement to make animal protection an English virtue, one that differentiated between a pure British core and the foreign. In such a system, it came to be accepted that cruelty to animals became an indicator of moral depravity that foreshadowed greater potential to commit brutality. The benefits from protecting animals, therefore, were twofold. Preventing cruelty not only rescued defenseless victims but also suppressed dangerous elements in human society. One of the key leaders in this moral campaign was Richard Martin, an Irish politician who succeeded in passing the Cruel Treatment of Cattle Act 1822, one of the first pieces of animal welfare legislation in Britain. The Act, which prohibited the abuse or ill treatment of four-legged farm and draft animals, passed easily after receiving public support from London magistrates and the clergy.[32] Two years after the passage of the Cruel Treatment of Cattle Act 1822, Martin met with like-minded individuals

---

[31] Brian Harrison, "Animals and the State in Nineteenth-Century England," *The English Historical Review* 88, 3 (1973): 788; Ritvo, *The Animal Estate*, pp. 125–6.
[32] Ritvo, *The Animal Estate*, pp. 126–34.

in a London tavern and founded the Society for Prevention of Cruelty to Animals with the goal of creating a "revolution of morals."[33]

The subsequent Royal Society of Prevention of Cruelty to Animals (RSPCA) was to become a product of the imperial age. Over the next few decades it acted as a "cause group," reflecting the shifting attitudes of British society while promoting issues and legislation that were vital in the creation of a Victorian worldview. To do so, the Society walked a fine line between professionalism and activism, always ensuring that their activities were seen as being in support of government regulations and not protesting or countering authority. Following the activism that Martin envisioned, the organization influenced the passage of numerous acts that forbade fighting and baiting between animals, creating an atmosphere in which commercial and recreational exploitation of animals was increasingly limited and, more importantly, seen as contrary to the British national image.[34]

There were limitations to the definition of animal cruelty, however, and these were rooted in the class system of Britain. The Society and its supporters were from the upper classes and most of their vitriol and crusading were directed at the treatment of animals in the daily lives of the lower classes. Regulations, for example, were passed to protect draft and farm animals, while little criticism was directed at fox hunting or others pastimes of the elite. By 1839 Vicount Mathon, the Chair of the RSPCA, verbalized these attitudes when he stated that "innocent amusements, such as fishing and shooting," do not fall under the purview of the Society as elite sportsmen "protect from causeless pain those sources of our amusements, and incentives to wholesome exercise."[35]

Within decades Britons began to perceive their nation as one in which a humane approach toward animals was the norm, with it becoming closely associated as a trait of English Protestantism, held in contrast to Catholic societies throughout Europe and even more distant communities, which were portrayed as being cruel toward all life.

---

[33] Edward George Fairholme and Wellesley Pain, *A Century of Work for Animals: The History of the R.S.P.C.A., 1824–1934* (London: J. Murray, 1934); Ritvo, *The Animal Estate*, pp. 126–7.

[34] Harrison, "Animals and the State in Nineteenth-Century England"; Ritvo, *The Animal Estate*.

[35] This quote is taken from the 1839 report of the RSPCA, and is featured in Ritvo, *The Animal Estate*, pp. 133–4.

Kindness towards animals soon became a British characteristic, just as its empire was reaching its height, with continental Europe portrayed as a site of French vivisection practices or Spanish bullfighting, while much of the rest of the world was a location of even more savage practices. It is in this context that much of the elite of Singapore, and Grand Duke Alexis, witnessed the tiger-buffalo fight as guests of the Maharaja of Johor.[36]

In 1872 Singapore was a relatively new Crown Colony, in a larger global context of expanding British imperial power. Five years earlier the Colonial Office in London began to exercise direct oversight of the Straits Settlements of Singapore, Penang, and Melaka, thus taking over the administration of British interests in the region from the quasi-corporate-government entity of the British East India Company. This resulted in the posting of a Governor in Singapore and the creation of administrative departments, along with their administrators, all supported with direct communication to the metropole through telegraph, steamships and the others tools of high imperialism. Singapore was to become the main focus of British imperial activity in Southeast Asia at the height of the Victorian Age. Such imperial rule would transform how Singapore and the Straits Settlements were ruled, as well as British civilizational notions related to animal cruelty in a distant colonial port.

Mounting grievances related to animal cruelty, and particularly the implication that such activities were reflective of an inferior civilization, took place in the context of proposals regarding a new Criminal Jurisdiction Bill, which the Legislative Council approved in October 1872, and were a continuation of the regulations originally promulgated in Calcutta for all British ports in Asia in the mid-1850s.[37] The Bill had originally been passed two years earlier but resulted in a series of riots in 1871 that involved Chinese secret societies rebelling against new

---

[36] Harrison, "Animals and the State in Nineteenth-Century England"; Ritvo, *The Animal Estate.*

[37] This legislation was known as the 1855 New Police Bill. It allowed for the destruction of stray dogs and had provisions that included fines "for misbehavior in driving cattle; [and], for ill treating animals." A key component of these regulations, however, was that it did not focus on the well-being of any of the animals mentioned. Instead, concern was directed toward "mischief or obstruction" they may cause. Anonymous, "The New Police Bill," *ST,* 17 Oct. 1855, p. 1; Anonymous, "Legislative Council," *SFP,* 8 Nov. 1855, p. 3.

restrictions or, as John Thomson described the events, they wanted "to resist the rough interference of the police."[38] Following the outbreak of violence, as the government was attempting to gain control over the society that the East India Company had ignored or just allowed to function on its own, many members of the government elite believed it should become a formal law, and not just an ordinance. Although much of the Bill focused on fines and punishments related to a variety of minor infractions, including the use of music at processions and rallies as well as the failure to follow the instructions of a police officer, there were several sections that exposed the changing human-animal relationship in the Straits Settlements. Among these provisions were prohibitions against the grazing of horses and cattle along public thoroughfares, or allowing pigs to stray from their pens. Horned cattle were also now required to have a bar of wood across their horns, while "any ferocious dog" had to be muzzled. In addition, carriage operators were no longer allowed to use unbroken horses to pull their vehicles, while dogs were prohibited from "barking or running at any persons, carriages, horses, or cattle, passing along any public thoroughfare." This was supplemented with numerous provisions related to how horses and cattle were to be led throughout the Straits Settlements, while driving or leading an elephant or camel through the streets was banned outright (although it is difficult to imagine that this was really an issue). Finally, the Bill banned cockfighting.[39]

The varied references to creatures in the Crime Jurisdiction Bill reflect how animals were present in the daily lives of Singaporeans during the colonial era. They were more than simply pests or beasts that were to be hunted or killed. Animals conveyed goods and people. They were pets. They were consumed as meat. Animals were everywhere. Most of these animals were treated with disdain, much like the pariah dogs that roamed the island. It was common, for example, to see a distressed horse or bullock on the side of the road, in addition to the teams of government supervised "cullers" that beat stray dogs to death to limit their scavenging or trained public health personnel who oversaw the slaughter of animals for meat. Essentially, animals were overworked, overstressed, eaten or even hunted in colonial Singapore.

---

[38] Thomson, *The Straits of Malacca, Indo-China, and China*, p. 46.
[39] Anonymous, "The Summary Jurisdiction Bill," *ST*, 19 Oct. 1872, p. 1.

Much of this was rooted in a society that was largely rural, and dependent on animal labor. As Singapore became increasingly deforested, as the jungle was tamed, and the port expanded, however, a more urban orientation to the society was emphasized. While Singapore continued to have a vast rural area, the main focus of administration, economic activity and society was the urban core.

The focus on increasingly urban lifestyles was translated in the colony through shifting attitudes toward animals, and it also had parallels with the expansion of British imperial control over society. Animals, as promulgated through legislation and debates among the elite, were a vital tool in the expansion and imposition of colonial ideals in the region, and reflect the desire for moral and religious progress that motivated many of society's leaders.[40] Such efforts to regulate the treatment of animals reflect new attempts to gain control over a colonial society in which formal, direct British rule had arrived. Rules needed to be established, and they needed to be in line with the civilizational discourse as it was understood in Britain. This resulted in concern, and regulation, being directed initially toward the treatment of work animals in Singapore, particularly bullocks and, as a part of these efforts, the creation of a Society for the Prevention of Cruelty to Animals. Once proper treatment of these animals could be established, control of the society could subsequently be expanded and monitored so that it fulfilled colonial understandings of how the port should function, and how humans and animals could relate to each other, thus exposing how Singapore was a site of imperial control.

A Society for the Prevention of Cruelty to Animals

A renewed call to protect labor animals, which was also steeped in the rhetoric of civilizational discourse, appeared in *The Straits Times* in March 1876.[41] It came from D.F.A. Hervey, a civil servant who arrived in the Straits soon after the British government assumed administration from the East India Company. Hervey, who would eventually serve

---

[40] Harrison, "Animals and the State in Nineteenth-Century England."

[41] In 1875, there was a rare mention of cockfighting that equated it with cruelty. The complainant, H.J. Rous, argued that it was "a relic of past days when people did such shocking things and apparently thought little of them," and it was "a most barbarous, debasing amusement" that took place at "Teluk Blangah or Pulo Brani, or any other quiet place." H.J. Rous, "Cock-fighting," *ST*, 24 July 1875, p. 1.

on the Legislative Council and at the time was the Second Police Magistrate, called for the establishment of a society for the prevention of cruelty to animals. He argued that, while some may believe the police were "sufficiently empowered by the law to deal with offences of this nature," they rarely availed themselves in their enforcement. A solution—as occurs in the "mother country"—was the creation of an organization that could apply "extraneous influence." This would result, according to Hervey, in not only improving the condition of animals in the region, but also would allow for "the humanizing effect" that would instill "merciful precepts" in the residents of Singapore. Although the "Natives of the East" are open to such influences, "though in a less degree perhaps," the aid of such a society could, "bring about a change in the Native way of looking at these matters." Among the common issues related to the treatment of animals, according to Hervey, was "the maltreating of hack-horses, and ponies, and bullocks, by over-riding and over-loading them, and driving them when lame or with sores under the harness or the yokes, and in the case of bullocks, the beating and goading of them, and wrenching and twisting of their tails, the last a refinement of torture." Hervey went on to bemoan the "manner in which pariah dogs are killed; possibly the mode of slaughtering cattle" as well as "the baiting of animals of any kind to fight."[42]

A week later, another letter made the same argument. The anonymous author, "IOTA," wrote:

> Every one actuated by a spark of humanity must approve of the proposal to oppose, so far as possible, and punish cruelty to animals here, particularly those patient animals which administer to Colonial necessities, either social or commercial.
>
> There is one quarter where the most reprehensible cruelty is practised systematically; and that is where sugar canes being conveyed at the instigation of Chinese planters, by Kling bullock cart drivers. The former heap the carts until the animals can scarcely move; whilst the kling drivers resort to the most cruel means to compel the animals to exert themselves beyond their powers. Selfishness overloads the carts, and actuated by a bribe probably of a few cents, the drivers thrash and twist the animals tails, until a regular break down appears to the only likely issue of the struggle."[43]

---

[42] D.F.A. Hervey, "Cruelty to Animals," *ST*, 4 Mar. 1876, p. 2.
[43] IOTA, "Cruelty to Animals," *ST*, 11 Mar. 1876, p. 6.

IOTA then recommended that fines be instituted, as he believed they would reduce the occurrence of such behavior.

Debates in newspapers, particularly between rival journals, were among the amusements of Europeans in Singapore during the colonial era. "As the parties are generally those best acquainted with the subjects under review, this exchange of opinions is found both amusing and instructive, for the inhabitants are enabled to see both sides of the question, and may therefore judge for themselves." Attempts to define cruelty in the 1870s quickly became a point of public debate between the editors of the *The Straits Times* and *The Straits Observer*, mainly through anonymous letters to the editor. Much of it originated out of a letter criticizing calls for the creation of a Society for Prevention of Cruelty to Animals as "maudlin sentimentalism" in *The Straits Observer* in 1876. This resulted in responses that anyone who opposed such a development, "belongs to that class who are always railing at any scheme intended for the improvement of the morals of mankind in general and the Temperance League in particular."[44]

Fundamentally, the critiques of the potential founding of an organization to prevent animal cruelty bemoaned its use of the journal *Animal World*—the official journal of the RSPCA—and that its members were "too *'goody goody'*," promoting "gushing sentiment" that was "ungenuine and impractical."[45] These critics, supporters of having a society argued, "overlook the difficult nature of the objects which the Society has at heart; viz on the one hand the propagation of a kinder tone, especially among the young, towards all the animal world, and on the other the suppression and prevention of existing cruelties, which can only be done by the relentless prosecutions and punishment." Finally, the supporters went on to argue that, "it is not unreasonable to expect every English Colony to follow in some degree the examples set by England and America, and to cover the dumb creation with adequate legislative protection." The author of the original offending letter—"Beagle"—responded that, "the police have quite sufficient power in their hands to correct abuses," which is better situation as the

---

[44] Otter Hound, "Society for the Prevention of Cruelty to Animals," *The Straits Observer*, 17 Mar. 1876, p. 2; Earl, *The Eastern Seas*, p. 359.

[45] Italics in the original. A Member, "Prevention of Cruelty to Animals," *The Straits Observer*, 17 Mar. 1876, p. 3.

officers of a society would be acting "entirely from personal motives—the principal one being that of bringing themselves before the public in a moral light."[46]

On 27 March 1876, Hervey oversaw a "fairly attended meeting" at which a Society for the Prevention of Cruelty to Animals (SPCA, to differentiate from its British version, RSPCA) was established in Singapore. A committee, consisting of prominent Britons in the colony, including W.H. Read and John Cameron, was formed to oversee the Society with William Adamson acting as its Chair and Hervey as the Honorary Secretary. The attendees wholeheartedly believe the Society was needed. As one account of its founding stated, "Every one who has had the smallest experience of daily life here in Singapore and the treatment to which hack ponies and bullocks etc. are subjected must acknowledge that there were ample cause and scope for the institution and existence of such a Society." The committee was to "inquire into the present law and to suggest such amendments and additions to it as may seem necessary for the carrying out of the objects of the Society." After reviewing the recently passed Police Ordinances, the committee decided there was no need to alter the existing laws.[47]

The main activity the SPCA leadership recommended was to support the police in their enforcement of existing laws. In order to do so, the committee proposed, "The appointment of an officer to report all cases of the kind he may discover." The SPCA officer was to receive "the miserable pittance" of $20 per month, which reflected—according to the editors of *The Straits Observer*—the "impolitely termed 'great cry and little wool,' as might be looked for from shearing a pig." This critic of the Society not only portrayed the salary as a lack of commitment, but also as an insult directed at the ability of the police to carry out their duties. It was argued that if Samuel Dunlop, a member of the SPCA committee as well as the Inspector-General of Police, "only told his myrmidons that he expected them to do their duty, and it would have been done under the Police Act." The issue was "as ridiculous

---

[46] Beagle, "Society for the Prevention of Cruelty to Animals," *The Straits Observer*, 21 Mar. 1876, p. 3; A Member, "Prevention of Cruelty to Animals."

[47] Anonymous, "The S.P.C.A.," *ST*, 13 July 1878, p. 1; Anonymous, "Tuesday, 28th March, 1876," *The Straits Observer*, 28 Mar. 1876: 2; Anonymous, "Untitled," *ST*, 1 Apr. 1876, p. 5.

and comical an affair that has occurred in Singapore for some time."[48] In addition to the inspection officer, the public was to play an important role in protecting animal rights by providing information and making suggestions on how to enforce the laws, which they had often proposed. Such vicarious intervention in governmental programs became increasingly common in Victorian Britain, and was ultimately transferred to the colonial society.[49]

The Straits Observer continued to question the new Society, and its role in the Straits, when it reported three days later on a case of "two or three native boys with five or six live sparrows fastened to a string suspended from the rails, and the boys were amusing themselves with playing 'puff and dart' at them and firing at them with a pea shooter." When a concerned citizen approached a nearby policeman to report the incident, "he only shrugged his shoulders and said he had nothing to do with it."[50] The editors of the newspaper kept up the pressure over the next few months, pointing out cases of animal cruelty that the SPCA officer had failed to report. This mocking coverage reached its apex when it was reported that the crowd at the spring meet at the Singapore Sporting Club began chanting "Hervey" following the appearance of a lame horse named Chin Chin that was entered in a race. The horse was allowed to start, and tragedy ensued. "By some mischance or another Chin Chin broke her shoulder in the course of the race and had to be shot the same evening." Under such circumstances, "it is difficult to see how the newly started Society to put down cruelty to animals can gain any character for consistency when it strains at a gnat and swallows a camel by hauling a gharrywallah before the Bench for 'establishing a raw' on his pony and allowing a horse to be ridden to death on a race course."[51]

---

[48] The use of an officer to represent the group with the police in the enforcement of legislation it promoted was a tactic the RSPCA developed in England. Harrison, "Animals and the State in Nineteenth-Century England," pp. 793–8; Anonymous, "Tuesday, 2nd May, 1876," *The Straits Observer*, 2 May 1876, p. 2.

[49] Harrison, "Animals and the State in Nineteenth-Century England," p. 799.

[50] Anonymous, "Friday, 5th May, 1876," *The Straits Observer*, 5 May 1876, p. 2.

[51] Anonymous, "Tuesday, 16th May, 1876," *The Straits Observer*, 16 May 1876, p. 2; Anonymous, "The Spring Meeting," *ST*, 20 May 1876, p. 1; Anonymous, "The S.C.P.A.".

By the end of May, "a competent European" named Edward Burton, "with very good testimonials from the Gaol and Police authorities," was appointed as the officer of the SPCA. His role was to act as a liaison between the police and British cultural mores being introduced to Singapore. In this regard, Burton would not actively promote legal proceedings against anyone accused of cruelty, but would "warn them to desist and amend their ways under penalty of being taken up and dealt with according to their desserts." In addition, "to prevent any ignorance," the committee issued notices in Chinese, Malay and Tamil "explaining the objects of the Society and the bearing of the law upon acts of cruelty to animals."[52]

To start this process, Burton began placing notices in "prominent positions, warning those who drove animals in a sickly state, that they offend against the law." He then would institute proceedings against "every day cruelty" directed towards "a wounded bullock, or horse." Once a fine was imposed, the Society would publicize it in the hope that news would spread and set an example, thus reducing the likelihood of the offense being repeated. This was important as Burton would be, it was assumed, trying to change the attitudes of Asian residents, who were "long habituated … to the exercise of what *we* consider cruelty to their animals," and "look upon what is, undoubtedly, an offence against the law as a mere matter of every day custom; and probably, any interference with this custom they may characterize as an act of unjustifiable tyranny."[53]

Over several months in mid-1876 numerous fines and citations were given out against humans who inflicted pain on work animals in Singapore. In June there were 21 convictions of cruelty directed at bullocks or horses, while there were 15 convictions the next month. For the remainder of the year, there were approximately 20 cases of cruelty prosecuted in Singaporean courts with the assistance of the Society, with the reduction being trumpeted as a reflection of the effectiveness of its approach (although it may have been due to less vigilant enforcement). In the first six months of its existence, the efforts of the Society

---

[52] Anonymous, "Singapore Chamber of Commerce," *Straits Times Overland Journal*, 27 May 1876, p. 8.

[53] Italics in original. Anonymous, "The Society for the Prevention of Cruelty to Animals," *ST*, 10 June 1876, p. 1; Anonymous, "Friday, 21st July," *ST*, 22 July 1876, p. 5.

for the Prevention of Cruelty to Animals led to the enforcement of fines in 107 cases, of which 94 involved horses or ponies.[54]

A court case related to animal cruelty took place in August 1876 and reflects how animal cruelty laws were enforced with assistance from the Society, and clashed with local cultures. The case was Miang versus Kuglemann, and while the disagreement was over wages and position, the role of animal cruelty played an important role. The dispute was over the monthly wage of $12 that Kuglemann owed Miang as a driver for one his omnibuses. In the course of his daily activities, Miang supposedly "severely whipped one of his horses" to the point that it annoyed Kuglemann, who approached Samuel Dunlop and asked him to cite the employee for animal cruelty. Considering Miang a threat to his horses, Kuglemann then demoted the syce from driver to stable boy. Miang considered the demotion an insult, and quit his position and enticed two of his relatives—who also worked for Kuglemann—to join him. Miang then claimed he was owed back wages. Chief Justice Thomas Sidgreaves decided that this amounted to blackmail and, since Miang had left of his own accord, rather than suffer the indignity of grooming horses instead of driving them, the case was dismissed. "The *syce* was taught a lesson which may be of service to him." In this case, however, the charges of animal cruelty were considered quite minor to their entire affair, and it was the act of defiance (or blackmail) that the court found offensive.[55]

In such an atmosphere, after one year the Society for the Prevention of Cruelty to Animals faced much disgruntlement over limits placed on its position within the colonial society and bureaucracy, despite the appearance of effective enforcement of regulations related to the treatment of work animals. The SPCA was described as "a fifth wheel to a coach" in one account as only the police had the authority to fine and prosecute cases. In addition, several members took part in petty bickering over their position in the organization, which was compounded when Burton was accused of "defalcation," or misappropriation of funds, for which he was sent to prison. This resulted in several members refusing to pay their subscription for membership of

---

[54] Anonymous, "The S.P.C.A."; Anonymous, "Tuesday, 1st August," *ST*, 5 Aug. 1876, p. 2; Pegasus, "Cruelty to Animals," *The Straits Times Overland Journal*, 22 Jul 1876: 1; Anonymous, "Untitled", *ST*, 1 June 1878, p. 3.
[55] Anonymous, "Thursday, 17th August," *ST*, 19 Aug. 1876, p. 4.

$3 per year, or $25 for lifetime membership, leaving the Society in financial difficulties. The result was, "That there should be grumbling against the Society amongst its members after a year's existence is, for Singapore, nothing to be wondered at. We possess the most fickle of publics. Like the Athenians of old, we are always on the look out for something new, and soon tire of it when we get it." To counter these developments, Adamson made a request to the government in March 1877 that all fines related to animal cruelty cases should go toward the Society and its upkeep a year after the institution had been established. The government approved this request in late May. By September 1877, J.L. Green replaced Burton as the official SPCA agent on a salary of $50 per month. Despite such problems swirling around the Society, during 1877 it continued to assist the police in enforcing animal rights laws, with 175 cases, of which 159 involved horses and ponies.[56]

In July 1878 the Society for the Prevention of Cruelty to Animals published its first annual report, which highlighted that overburdening of draft animals still continued in Singapore.

> No matter how small they may be, weak or strong, sick or well, they are employed in conveying loads frequently above their strength, as for instance a cart load of bricks, about 400 to the load, weighing … 1 ton 8 cwt [1.4 metric tons]. They are often beaten throughout the journey, and goaded on with those favourite native methods of torture – twisting the tails or progging with a point in tender places.[57]

The report continued with a plea that greater concern be directed toward the treatment of all animals, citing how pigs were transported stuffed into baskets, and lame animals often were abandoned on the roadside and left to die.

---

[56] Anonymous, "Tuesday, 10th September, *ST*, 14 Sep. 1878, p. 3; Anonymous, "The S.P.C.A."; Nemo, "Variorum," *ST*, 2 June 1877, p. 24; Anonymous, "The S.P.C.A."; Nemo, "Variorum," *ST*, 29 Sep. 1877, p. 1.

[57] While some of this criticism could also be directed at hackney carriage syces, who reportedly mistreated many of their animals, regulations passed in this period—known as the Hackney Carriage Ordinance 1879—reflected the lack of focus on issues related to cruelty in most government legislation as it simply proscribed where hackney stands could be located and the prices the drivers could charge. Anonymous, "The Governor's Address to Council, *ST*, 16 Nov. 1878, p. 1; Anonymous, "The S.P.C.A."

Image 4.3: Malay bullock cart. Courtesy of the New York Public Library.

Despite the existence of the Society for the Prevention of Cruelty to Animals, brutality directed at fauna continued. The type of brutality mentioned, however, quickly expanded beyond draft animals in their daily tasks. As one letter writer described, "Fowls and Ducks are still thrown on the beach and at the landing places with their legs tied, 4 and 6 birds together, and then thrown across a long pole and carried head downwards through the streets of the market. Bullocks and Horses are tossed over the side of cargo boats." Another letter writer decried commonly seen brutalities, such as "cock fighting, the wholesale branding of bullocks" in addition to the employment of sick horses and the overloading of bullock carts and omnibuses. Throughout these complaints, the civilizational discourse that represented a cultural gulf between Westerners and Asians was a constant. For example, one letter commented that anyone who witnesses "the unloading of boats on the Quay every morning must be struck with the cruelty inherent in the Chinese character."[58]

---

[58] Anonymous, "Cruelty to Animals," *SFP*, 20 Apr. 1892, p. 3; Pegasus, "Cruelty to Animals"; Anonymous, "Friday, 21st July"; Anonymous, "Friday, 6th September," *ST*, 7 Sep. 1878, p. 4.

In this context a plea regarding the developing definitions of cruelty and civilization with regard to animals appeared in *The Straits Times* in September 1878. The newspaper published an essay, titled "A Dog's Howl," which implored readers to consider the plight of canines in Singapore. It was one in which an "indiscriminate war" was waged against them, "a war indeed of extermination, as well as oppression and ignominy, for when not in fear of our lives from official brutality, we are subjects to kicks and curses from every one we meet." While the Society for the Prevention of Cruelty to Animals focused on the treatment of bullocks, horses and even fowl, little compassion was directed toward other animals. Due to dog culling practices, all canines in Singapore had to be confined, usually with chains, for several days every few months to ensure that they were not mistaken for a stray. If a dog wandered onto the street, it was likely to see "a Kling man beating out the brains of one of [its] intimate acquaintances." This led to complaints that, "The present mode of beating dogs to death in the street is at any rate clumsy and disgusting, and a bad example to the native children."[59]

In 1879, two cases of "the zealous Klings who are entrusted with the unpleasant duty" of destroying stray dogs highlight these shifting attitudes. These public servants came under criticism due to their ignorance of desired breeds and the manner in which they completed their tasks "on the days appointed for the slaughter." In the first instance, a European girl was taking her "valuable King Charles' dog" on a walk on Dhobie Green, where it "fell a victim to the baton of the iconoclast who presides over the orgies." As the girl was overcome with grief, "a good natured native" took her home. In the second instance, outside of Emmerson's Hotel, a rather "ugly" dog was being beaten when its master intervened, but not before one of its eyes was knocked out of its head. The dog was condemned to wandering about, "a suffering cripple." In light of these cases, local commentators recommended that new approaches be taken, such as capturing stray dogs in nets, and poisoning them after three days if no one has claimed them, instead of beating them in public. After all, the "style of cruelty" in Singapore, "which may pander to the taste of a class of low born Indians" was

---

[59] Ten, "A Dog's Howl," *ST*, 21 Sep. 1878, p. 5; Anonymous, "S.P.C.A."; Anonymous, "The S.P.C.A.," *ST*, 13 July 1878, p. 1.

"distasteful to the more refined feelings of Englishmen."[60] Despite such early calls to expand the scope of the SPCA to include domestic pets, it continued to act as quasi-governmental representative in the enforcement of the Crime Bill, and its efforts were directed toward cruelty that fit British understandings of such behavior. In this manner, the Society continued to focus on work animals and those that were consumed.

When alerted to issues related to cruelty, an SPCA representative would visit the accused and assess the situation. Between July and September 1878, for example, J.L. Green brought 84 cases of animal cruelty before the courts in Singapore. "Of these 3 were for cruelty to omnibus horses, 60 for cruelty to hack ponies, 17 for ill-treatment of oxen while landing them from the 'Tongkangs' &c., and 4 for causing suffering to birds by shooting them with 'sumpitans.'"[61] Only 26 of these cases resulted in fines or warnings. Green, however, participated in follow-up visits to verify that the "wounded animals and those unfit for labor were not made to work until condition was improved." By the mid-1880s the SPCA held regular meetings to promote its activities, while its representatives actively monitored cases involving the mistreatment of animals. Much of this was done under the authority of E.F. Paglar, who was hired in 1884 as the Inspector. In his new position, he reported 225 cases of animal abuse that resulted in convictions in the courts, with nine of those cases leading to incarceration for the offenders, in 1885.[62]

For the remainder of the 19th century the Society for the Prevention of Cruelty to Animals in Singapore promoted a relationship between humans and others animals based in British ideals and mores. Its activities became so well ensconced in the port they rarely merited coverage in newspapers and other reports, subtly infusing notions of proper behavior and disciplining the human-animal relationship. In public forums, British officials described the efforts of the SPCA as noble, and much of it was rooted in discourse on race and civilization in British Empire. Any brutality directed toward animals was, therefore, the result

---

[60] Anonymous, "Dog Killing," *Straits Times Overland Journal*, 19 June 1879, p. 8.
[61] In the parlance of the day, a "tongkang" was a light wooden boat used to carry goods along rivers while a "sumpitan" was a blowgun. Anonymous, "Thursday, 3rd October," *ST*, 5 Oct. 1878, p. 4.
[62] Anonymous, "Thursday, 3rd October"; Anonymous, "Society for the Prevention of Cruelty to Animals," *The Straits Times Weekly Issue*, 8 Sep. 1886, p. 4.

of "Ramsamys and others who think it of no consequence," or "China-men" who "had very little idea of what cruelty was."[63] While new officials from Europe had created a semi-independent organization that worked alongside the police to promote their British understanding of civilization and cruelty, the government had not been directly involved. This was about to change, however, as the municipal government began to expand it powers over the port of Singapore.

A Municipal Effort

The municipal government was the most important bureaucratic presence in the lives of most Singapore residents during the colonial era. The area under its purview was the main focus of British colonial activity on the island, consisting of the port, administrative and business offices as well as the main areas of the settlement. While a few tendrils of influence ran out from this core along Pasir Panjang, Serangoon and Thomson roads, the main focus was on five designated districts: Tanjong Pagar, Tanglin, Rochor, Kallang and Central. Under the Municipality Ordinance of 1887, its employees focused their efforts on providing government health services, as well as the modernization of utilities and sewerage. Essentially, it was a series of bureaucratic depart-ments tasked with overseeing the development of a British imperial city.[64] Under their efforts, the urban core of Singapore was to become a modern space in which issues related to a "defective civilization" could be addressed and corrected to fit a British vision of global power.

A meeting of the Society for the Prevention of Cruelty to Animals in 1890 reflects the role that the Municipal Commission would play with their expanded powers in colonial society in Singapore. Attending the meeting were several important members of the government, including

---

[63] Anonymous, "Local and General," Daily Advertiser, 6 Jan. 1893, p. 3; Anony-mous, "Society for the Prevention of Cruelty to Animals," The Straits Times Weekly Edition, 6 Aug. 1890, p. 2.

[64] CO276/18: Straits Settlements Government Gazette (1887): "Government Notification, No. 475," pp. 1871–5; F.J. Hallifax, "Municipal Government," in One Hundred Years of Singapore, Being an Account of the Capital of the Straits Settlements from its Foundation by Sir Stamford Raffles on the 6th February 1819 to the 6th February 1919, vol. I, ed. Walter Makepeace, Gilbert E. Brooke, and Roland St. J. Braddell (London: John Murray, 1921), p. 315; Brenda S.A. Yeoh, Contesting Space: Power Relations and the Urban Built Environment in Colonial Singapore (Kuala Lumpur: Oxford University Press, 1996).

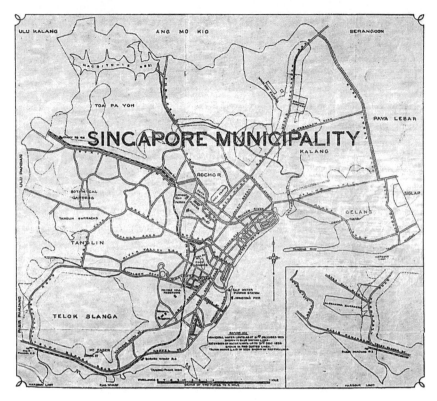

Image 4.4: Map of the municipal boundaries, 1924. Courtesy of National Archives of Singapore.

James MacRitchie and Alexander Gentle, who were prominent officials in the municipal government. Up to that time the SPCA had relied solely on the efforts of its Secretary, A.M. Skinner. While "the Society was undoubtedly doing very good work," it needed to rationalize the reporting of cases of cruelty, one account of the meeting argued. Previously, people would write to the newspapers—thus, centering the efforts in the miniscule English literate public. Instead a new system was proposed in which "people would report cases of cruelty directly to the Society's inspector." This would supposedly "save a good deal of trouble." The attendees quickly formed a committee consisting of such important colonial figures as Lewis Fraser and E.W. Presgrave as well as Gentle, to enact these changes, bringing it within the orbit of governmental programs and monitoring. To help with this new approach, the home address of the Inspector was provided in newspaper advertisements, and the general public was encouraged to contact him when they saw cases of cruelty being committed.[65]

Although this new system of reporting cases of animal cruelty still kept it within the cultural circles of the European elite, there were attempts to reach out to the rest of society. More importantly, in this new system members of the SPCA began to openly debate the definition of cruelty in the port, with the stated goal of promoting education and not punishment, reflecting a shift in the belief that the Asian populace could learn to follow British imperial standards. These discussions, however, continued to support a definition and focus that prioritized treatment of labor animals. Pets and other fauna remained of little concern. Charles Burton Buckley, for example, "did not consider carrying ducks' head downwards" as cruel, while one of the main topics of discussion was on attempts to introduce yokes for bullocks that would not jolt the animal when cargo was suddenly taken off their carts. Under the European administrative leadership of individuals such as S.V.B. Down, who was the Honorary Secretary, colonial understandings of how animals should be treated were promulgated.[66]

The daily activities of this reconfigured SCPA, however, were mainly focused on the work of Inspector Paglar. From his home at 250 Bencoolen Street, where residents were encouraged to report cases of cruelty, he would investigate various stables, docks and houses and issue reports on overloading of carts, improper use of collars and employment of clearly sick animals. He would then liaise with the police on each case. The municipality supported these efforts by providing access to workers, including the assignment of P. Scott Falshaw, the Veterinarian Surgeon, to the SPCA beginning in 1893. Many of the investigations that Paglar and Falshaw conducted resulted in fines, such as "a Chinaman ordered to pay $20 for cruelty to a bullock" in February 1900.[67]

---

[65] Anonymous, "Society for the Prevention of Cruelty to Animals," *ST*, 31 July 1890, p. 3.

[66] Anonymous, "Society for the Prevention of Cruelty to Animals," *ST*, 31 July 1890, p. 3.

[67] While ideal from a British perspective, this system was not perfect. One letter writer complained to the press about trying to report bullock abuse but having difficulties meeting Paglar. U.V., "Cruelty to Animals," *SFP*, 30 Apr. 1900, p. 3; Anonymous, "Society for the Prevention of Cruelty to Animals," *SFP*, 14 Feb. 1900, p. 4; Anonymous, "Saturday, 10th February 1900," *ST*, 10 Feb. 1990, p. 2.

The practice of a voluntary organization pointing the police toward cruelty cases, and then overseeing the prosecution of the accused while keeping the fines as a form of payment to support it, eventually raised questions within the government related to its financing and administration.[68] This resulted in proposals that the government retain any fines awarded if they initiated a case of prosecution for animal cruelty. As the police had numerous officers who could make such claims, in contrast to two employees of the Society, this proposition would cripple the SPCA. Members of the government also began to question the authority that Paglar possessed. In September 1900, Magistrate H.G. Sarwar asked the Inspector what justified his power to arrest and bring cases before the court. The undermining of Paglar's authority implied that such cases should be directly under the jurisdiction of the police.[69]

By late 1900, when S.V.B. Down returned to Europe, the SPCA was on the verge of being shut down. W.E. Hooper, the Registrar of the Hackney Carriage and Jinrickisha Department, advised that the organization "must be re-constituted, if it is to continue to receive support from Government." Members decided to write the parent organization in London, in hope that they could receive information, with the goal of modeling it on the Society in England. It was felt that the Society in Singapore, "whilst good work has been done," was unable to address issues such as cruelties directed at bullocks and horses related to "the common offence committed by Chinese and Natives of abandoning animals to a lingering death."[70] Programs to address a perceived Asian proclivity to cruelty toward animals, therefore, were perceived as limited in their influence. In this atmosphere, in September 1901, the government formally dissolved the SPCA as a

---

[68] This was important as donations only brought in $30 in 1897, while fines produced $1,492. Most of this money went to Paglar's salary, which was $600 per year, with additional outlays for a peon's wages, gharry hire and other miscellaneous fees. CO276/40: "No. 691: Statement of Accounts of the Society for the Prevention of Cruelty to Animals," p. 1475.

[69] Anonymous, "The R.S.P.C.A.," *ST*, 15 June 1990, p. 3; Anonymous, "The R.S.P.C.A.," *ST*, 25 Sep. 1990, p. 2.

[70] CO276/42: "No. 505: SCPA Report for 1900," pp. 621–2; Rimmer, "Hackney Carriage Syces and Rikisha Pullers in Singapore," p. 130.

quasi-independent entity addressing Western notions of cruelty. The elite of Singapore society now believed that such functions could be normalized within the government bureaucracy to provide protection to work animals in a British imperial port in Southeast Asia.

Cruelty toward animals, of course, did not disappear with the arrival of direct colonial rule, or the closure of the SPCA, nor was it limited to the Asian populace of the port. The type of animals and the behavior towards them that were defined as cruelty, however, were considered under different, imperial standards. In 1896, for example, a crowd of Europeans watched as a "poor little live dog," a brown puppy, was placed in the tiger cage in the zoo at the Singapore Botanic Gardens. The spectators had several other puppies nearby in case the tiger was particularly hungry. The first sacrificial dog crouched in a small drain hole, "paralyzed with terror," for over two hours, while passers-by watched the development with glee, condemned the gathered crowd voraciously or fled in disgust. This feeding of live dogs to the tiger had been done, apparently, on the orders of H.N. Ridley, "the European in charge," according to "A Raffles School Boy" who had gone to the Gardens to search for his lost dog, only to find "it in the cage of the tiger, still alive, but very badly mauled, and the tiger sucking up the blood."[71]

The newspapers received letters of protest over this spectacle, although "it is not unusual in British Colonies, or indeed anywhere else where British authority exist to endeavor to please the public by such a specimen of cruelty." Even the editors of the *Singapore Free Press and Mercantile Advertiser* piped in, calling the event "unnecessary in itself" and it "can only have a banefully injurious effect upon the minds and feelings of young children whom the Garden is a favourite afternoon

---

[71] Throughout the 19th century, pariah dogs were used as bait to capture, or even feed, more dangerous animals. The botanists in the Singapore Botanic Gardens had difficulty maintaining large carnivores in the menagerie, as the cost of meat rapidly depleted budgets. Meanwhile, in Penang, pariah dogs were used to capture crocodiles that bothered local fishermen or users of the water. McNair, *Prisoners Their Own Warders*, p. 136; Barnard, *Nature's Colony*, p. 97; A Raffles School Boy, "The Refinement of Cruelty," *SFP*, 19 May 1896, p. 3; Javanese, "Cruelty at the Gardens," *ST*, 18 May 1896, p. 2; A Lover of Dogs, "A Protest," *SFP*, 18 May 1896, p. 3.

resort. Nature may be cruel, but that fact should be inculcated as an object lesson upon the tender and impressionable minds of young people."[72] That is, as long as it followed British standards and definitions.

Defining Cruelty in a New Century

The Society for the Protection of Animals existed as an independent entity in Singapore from 1876 until 1901. Upon the dissolution of the SPCA, the Legislative Council passed an ordinance that transferred $5,918 from the Society's accounts to the municipal government and requested it take over the responsibilities of the organization, on the condition that more inspectors monitor cases of cruelty. This resulted in the creation of the Prevention of Cruelty to Animals (PCA) Department, which was located in the Hackney Carriage Registration Office and under the leadership of Hooper, reflecting the role that treatment of horses and bullocks retained within understandings of humane treatment of animals as well as its placement within colonial bureaucracy and transportation.[73]

This newly formulated department of an old institution was to focus on "combatting cruelty generally" in contrast to the previous focus on individual cases. The ultimate aim, according to announcements during this period, was to address the issue of animal cruelty through the coordination of "governing bodies in the town." Nevertheless, the PCA soon returned to its previous approach to animal cruelty, searching out individual cases and imposing fines related to the treatment of work animals in the daily lives of residents. For example, a carriage owner was fined $25 for using a horse with sores under the collar in November 1902 and two bullock drivers were punished for overloading

---

[72] Ridley also hunted pariah dogs that ventured into the Singapore Botanic Gardens, shooting those that trespassed. He casually discusses one instance from 1908 in his own notebooks. Royal Botanic Gardens Kew Archives [hereafter, RGBK], Henry Nicholas Ridley Papers [hereafter, HNR] 3/2/6: Notebooks, vol. 6, pp. 113–5; Anonymous, "Cruelty at the Botanic Gardens," *The Mid-Day Herald*, 20 May 1896, p. 2; A Lover of Dogs, "A Protest."

[73] Anonymous, "The R.S.P.C.A.," *ST*, 15 June 1900, p. 3; Anonymous, "The S.P.C.A.," *ST*, 13 Aug. 1901, p. 3; Anonymous, "Municipal Commission," *SFP*, 28 Aug. 1926, p. 7; CO273/180/32044: "Ordinance 14, 1902, Prevention of Cruelty to Animals," p. 64; Tan, "The Beastly Business," p. 150.

their carts in February 1903. This pattern continued throughout the first two decades of the 20th century, with hundreds of prosecutions and fines being assessed—with 1915 being a typical year, as 730 cases are listed—while the PCA slowly became an anonymous entity within the colonial bureaucracy. Ultimately, by 1922, it could be reported that, "few people even know of the existence of the PCA Department."[74]

By the early 1920s the PCA Department came under renewed public scrutiny and criticism, as its activities during the previous two decades had done little to prevent cruelty "in any degree that is noticeable to any person of humanitarian inclinations." This state of affairs led one member of the public to posit that there was little "doubt if there is any city in the world where there is daily more general and unchecked cruelty to dumb beasts than in Singapore." "Bullocks, dogs, pigs, and various species of feathered creatures, are subjected to excessive hardship and suffering, very nearly approaching what might be described as torture." Edwin Brown, who was the Chief Commissioner of the Boy Scouts in Singapore, supported these broad declarations when he assumed the post of municipal commissioner in 1924. At that time, he gave a long harangue about how little had changed over the previous quarter century. According to Brown, cattle still faced terrible conditions that bordered on torture, and the treatment of animals in the pet shops along Rochor Road was "inhumane" while "prosecutions have been strangely few." Much of this was blamed on a PCA that was "hopelessly understaffed."[75]

In the context of these criticisms, various representatives of the colonial government, in both the Municipal Commission and the Legislative Council, called for "a systematic campaign to prevent and punish callous cruelty to animals and birds such as may be seen every day of the year." This can best be seen in the public statements of local representatives on the Legislative Council, including Tan Cheng

---

[74] Anonymous, "Singapore Municipality," *MT*, 12 Jul 1916, p. 5; Anonymous, "Untitled," *ST*, 7 Nov. 1902, p. 4; Anonymous, "Untitled," *ST*, 19 Feb. 1903, p. 4; Anonymous, "Cruelty to Animals," *MT*, 14 Aug. 1922, p. 6.

[75] Anonymous, "Cruelty to Animals," *The Malayan Saturday Post*, 13 Sep. 1924, p. 12; Anonymous, "Untitled," *ST*, 17 Feb. 1925, p. 8; Anonymous, "Municipal Commission," *ST*, 14 Oct. 1925, p. 10; Anonymous, "Cruelty to Animals," *MT*, 6 Feb. 1926, p. 15; Anonymous, "Municipal Commission," *SFP*, 28 Aug. 1926, p. 7.

Lock and H.H. Abdoolcader.[76] Among the other leaders calling for a reassessment of animal cruelty, and one that raised the issue two years before Brown became municipal commissioner, was Malay intellectual Eunos Abdullah who, in August 1922, questioned his fellow municipal commissioners with regard to the "inactivity" of the PCA and whether it could monitor birds and other animals kept in shops or as pets. He also requested reforms be instituted in the treatment of stray dogs, with the creation of a place "for keeping until an owner can be found" instead of "shooting them in the public streets." These calls for change reflected a transformation in how residents of Singapore related to animals. Only five years earlier, a representative of the PCA had visited bird shops and produced a favorable report of the institutions that Eunos was criticizing. In this earlier account the author even mentioned that, while "fowls and ducks are overcrowded in baskets" in Market Street and Penang Street it did not merit charges of cruelty.[77] The shifting definition was beginning to encompass the treatment of domestic animals and fowl.

The prominent role of leaders of the Asian community in these debates over the definition of cruelty, and its expansion beyond work animals, in Singapore in the 1920s is of note. In the discourse on the topic up until this time, Asians had been depicted as the perpetrators of much of the violence. It was common to find claims voiced in the press that cruelty was "rife" in Singapore as "the untutored Asiatic mind towards dumb animals" was considered to be unnecessarily brutal. Some considered the situation hopeless, claiming, "It is scarcely possible to succeed in instilling their minds that dumb creatures need, perhaps, far greater protection by man than mankind itself.[78]

---

[76] In addition, and in this context, Isaac Manasseh reminded Boy Scouts that they were required to do good deeds, as the sixth law of scouting was "a scout is a friend to animals," they should become active supporters of the PCA Department in the municipality by reporting cases of abuse and taking stray cats and dogs to the Infirmary. Anonymous, "Scouts and Animals," *MT*, 4 Oct. 1928, p. 10; Tan, "The Beastly Business."

[77] Anonymous, "Municipal Meeting," *ST*, 23 Aug. 1922, p. 9; Anonymous, "Untitled," *ST*, 6 Aug. 1917, p. 8.

[78] This continued for the remainder of the colonial era, with E.G. Pritchard writing in 1930 that, "You cannot expect the natives of the East to take much trouble over animals; that is putting the case mildly. Very often they will not look after a sick beast, and are cruel in their treatment of all animals, if it is the easiest way out of difficulty." H.B.L., "Protection of Animal and Birds," *ST*, 4 Oct. 1923, p. 10; E.G. Pritchard, "Our Animals. An Appeal for Help," *MT*, 6 Jan. 1930, p. 5.

The impetus for a reassessment of what constituted cruelty during this period, however, was mainly coming from Asian members of the Legislative Council, with most British officials only responding to the issue after it was raised, as was the case with Brown when he broached the topic in 1924. This not only represented an incorporation of values and mores among the colonized Asian elite, as they took on and voiced the civilizational discourse that was directed toward the larger society, but also an early effort to find a greater voice for the residents of the island, whether human or animal. The focus on issues related to animal cruelty among Asian leaders within the imperial government structure also may have functioned as the employment of a relatively neutral topic as a subtle critique of the basic treatment of other creatures in the imperial port.

In response to the enquiries from Eunos Abdullah, PCA Inspector Hooper began to visit animal and bird shops twice a week. In addition, the PCA took over responsibility for the "dog nuisance," the destruction of packs of stray dogs that roamed throughout Singapore, from the police. Hooper, however, appeared less than enthusiastic with his new responsibilities, as the PCA had mainly monitored cruelty directed toward only work animals up to this time. He, for example, did not deem the inspection of pet shops a proper use of resources, as the businesses were often small and "willful ill-treatment or intentional cruelty are rare." Ultimately, he argued, "no official supervision of pets seems possible," particularly as his staff consisted of one inspector, three shooters and three coolies who had to spend most of their time killing approximately 250 dogs per month, their main task since the beginning of the century.[79]

To address any potential criticism of his treatment of stray curs, and to appease the critics, Hooper eventually agreed to enact a policy of "one dog, one cartridge" in which the firearm discharge was one that would not merit additional effort on behalf of the shooter nor further suffering on behalf of the victim. While "catching with a noose would be more humane," he reasoned it would not be as effective as shooting strays. After all, "dogs that are obviously well bred" are "caught and taken to the Animal Infirmary," where they are kept until an owner takes the opportunity to claim them. The rest were shot. The main

---

[79] Anonymous, "Cruelty to Animals," *MT*, 14 Aug. 1922, p. 6; Anonymous, "Municipal Commission," *ST*, 26 Aug. 1922, p. 9.

task of the PCA, thus, continued to be oversight of work animals, stray dogs and those headed to the slaughterhouse. This resulted in some commentators describing the department as being filled with "ludicrous, ineffectual half-amateurs."[80]

These calls for new understandings of what constituted cruelty, and what should be the remit of civil servants tasked to prevent it, mirrored changes in the early 20th century in global understandings with regard to the issue. In Britain, scholars have interpreted the first two phases of RSCPA activity as urban attacks on rural culture—with legislation against treatment of work animals and limiting entertainment as well as the protection of rare species that could be hunted—which were manifested in Singapore through the development of the SPCA to defend bullocks and horses as well as ordinances passed in 1884, 1904 and 1923 that limited the hunting of wild animals.[81] When the PCA began overseeing the licensing of dogs, taking over from the police, it began to monitor cruelty directed toward animals that had no utilitarian function. They were pets, essentially. It was at this time that calls to prosecute humans that abused pets came into the public record, as occurred to an unnamed abuser of a cat with broken hind legs discovered along Orchard Road in September 1923.[82]

Following these criticisms, and in line with changing definitions of cruelty, the colonial government reestablished the Society for Prevention of Cruelty to Animals in 1927 with expanded facilities and scope of responsibilities. With "a European veterinary surgeon in charge," the SPCA now operated out of an animal infirmary located on Kampong Java Road. This facility housed a hospital with a staff of inspectors and dressers. Employees also had access to vehicles, including an ambulance and a blue van in which they would roam Singapore fulfilling their increasing and shifting responsibilities.[83]

---

[80] Anonymous, "Are You Esteemed?," *MT*, 1 Oct. 1924, p. 6; Anonymous, "Municipal Commission," *ST*, 26 Aug. 1922, p. 9.

[81] The Wild Birds and Animals Act, 1923, prohibited the killing of particular animals, such as the sambar deer. The lack of any wildlife in Singapore, however, made the legislation more important in the Malay Peninsula compared to the home of the colonial government. Harrison, "Animals and the State in Nineteenth-Century England," pp. 790–2; Lye, "Wildlife Protection Laws in Singapore".

[82] Anonymous, "Municipal Commission," *ST*, 10 Aug. 1923, p. 10; Anonymous, "Untitled," *ST*, 20 Sep. 1923, p. 8.

[83] Anonymous, Singapore S.P.C.A.," *ST*, 4 Sep. 1929, p. 18; Anonymous, "Singapore P.C.A. Society," *ST*, 17 Sep. 1929, p. 17.

The remit of the SPCA was changing, and this can be seen in its annual report for 1928, which focused on three main categories of animals. Bullocks still suffered from being overworked and often appeared "lame and emaciated ... with sores and abscesses under the yoke. Tail twisting, overloads, overworking and keeping for long periods without water" were common. As for cats and dogs, "many, homeless animals" roamed the streets. "They lead miserable existences, living on garbage and maimed by motor-cars."[84] Finally, it was reported, "the chief form of cruelty consists of overcrowding of birds and small animals in cages." Continuing on, "the shooting and trapping of birds is illegal," and finally there was "excessive handling and improper manner of carrying" fowls from the market.[85]

There had been a slow transformation in definition and scope of cruelty, from a focus on work animals to domestic animals, since the turn of the 20th century. This was mainly due to a revolution in transportation in a rapidly modernizing imperial society. Motorized vehicles quickly replaced the labor of animals, resulting in bullock carts and gharries rarely being seen in the municipality by the 1920s. While horses and bullocks remained on the island, they now were mainly found "in the outlying areas, where residential building was proceeding and roads were often bad and hilly." This decline in their use was rapid. There were approximately 4,000 bullocks in Singapore in 1900; in 1929, only 1,500 remained. These numbers halved each of the next two years, with only 701 bullocks in 1930 and 330 in 1931. In a related trend, by 1934, John Laycock led a motion in the Municipal Commission to abolish horse gharries, as there were only 19 left in Singapore, 12 for public hire while the rest were used for private

---

[84] By 1928, the Animal Infirmary began offering to destroy unwanted dogs. This would often occur in the middle of the year, as the date for dog licenses came due, "and owners may feel unable to keep their dogs." Members of the public were urged to bring the unwanted dogs to the Kampong Java Road facility, "where they will be given a painless death or a new home may be found for them. The fee for destruction in the lethal chamber is one dollar, but the Society is willing to pay this sum if the owner cannot afford it." Barbara H.C. Thomas, "Ownerless Dogs, *MT*, 28 June 1928, p. 7; Anonymous, "Cruelty to Animals," *MT*, 2 Apr. 1928, p. 5.

[85] Anonymous, "Cruelty to Animals," *MT*, 2 Apr. 1928, p. 5; Nurfadzilah Yahaya, "The Question of Animal Slaughter in the British Straits Settlements during the Early Twentieth Century," *Indonesia and the Malay World* 43, 126 (2015): 182.

Image 4.5: One of the last remaining horse gharries in Singapore, 1930s. Courtesy of Cambridge University Digital Library.

transportation. By 1935 only eight hackney carriages remained.[86] The main focus of animal cruelty cases for over 50 years was no longer a factor in Singaporean society.

With changes in basic transportation, the notion of mistreatment of an animal, and the type of animals, also had shifted. Accounts in newspapers reflect this trend, with reports highlighting the treatment of work animals becoming increasingly rare. Fines now were being assessed for treatment of domestic animals—with reports of overcrowding animals in cages or pens, or the handling of chickens and ducks in the markets—as officials began paying attention to animal dealers or market stall operators, in contrast to the increasingly rare cart or gharry driver. This resulted in "a Chinese animal dealer carrying on business in Trengganu Street" being charged, in 1928, for keeping

---

[86] Anonymous, "Improving Animal Treatment," *SFP*, 8 Jan. 1930, p. 30; Anonymous, "Singapore S.P.C.A.," *ST*, 25 June 1931, p. 12; Anonymous, "Picturesque Singapore Gharries?," *ST*, 27 Sep. 1934, p. 17 Rimmer, "Hackney Carriage Syces and Rikisha Pullers in Singapore," p. 132; Cocteau, *Round the World Again in 80 Days*, pp. 125–6.

"monkeys, bears, snakes, etc ... in boxes which were so small that they could scarcely move." He was fined $14.50 plus costs. The next year a "Chinese poultry dealer in Serangoon Road was fined $10 by the Second Magistrate (Mr. J.I. Miller) for cruelty to a blind and crippled chicken by throwing it into a dust bin." In the same month, May 1929, William Basapa of 549 Upper Serangoon Road "was charged with aiding and abetting cockfighting at the rear of his premises," making it the first time cockfighting had been charged in court in Singapore.[87]

With the virtual disappearance of work animals in public areas in Singapore, efforts were now mainly focused on the wild animal and bird shops, which "were a reproach to this city." These businesses, where the numerous strands in the human-animal relationship intersected— ranging from the hobby of keeping exotic birds as pets, the wildlife trade, and shifting understandings of what constituted cruelty—became sites of contestation for the remainder of the colonial period. Criticisms that ranged from inadequate accommodation to conditions that were described as "deplorable" and "unsanitary." In this atmosphere the Municipal Council began debating new regulations relating to cruelty to animals. The key proposals were that licenses should be required for shops that sell wild animals and birds.[88] While these suggestions were enacted, pet shops continued to be a focus of debates for several years.

By the early 1930s, following a high-level report on their activities, the Legislative Council continued to discuss the regulation of pet shops in Singapore. Eventually, in 1933, Governor Cecil Clementi appointed

---

[87] The cockfight took place on 7 April. "There were about a dozen cock birds in the compound. Some had feathers missing from the back of their necks, while scars were apparent. There were some feathers lying about." A witness to the proceeding, "saw two cock-birds laid down by Malays and saw them begin to fight." Basapa had already received a warning for hosting cockfights on his property in November 1928. The defendant, "a land owner, and trustee of his father's estate" "employed thirteen servants living at the back, Malays, Chinese and Indians." "He collected wild animals and traded in prize poultry." Anonymous, "Cock-Fighting," *SFP*, 31 May 1929, p. 11; Anonymous, "What Is Cruelty?," *MT*, 8 Dec. 1928, p. 10; Anonymous, "News in Brief," *The Malayan Saturday Post*, 25 May 1929, p. 24; Anonymous, "Cock-Fighting in Singapore," *ST*, 31 May 1929, p. 12.

[88] It also included a provision for licensing bullock cart drivers, and drovers of cattle, although this appears to reflect concerns from a previous era. Anonymous, "Municipal Meeting," *MT*, 29 June 1929, p. 7; Anonymous, "Municipal Meeting," *MT*, 26 Oct. 1929, p. 7.

a committee, whose members included wild life activist T.R. Hubback, Raffles Museum scientist F.N. Chasen and Legislative Council member Tan Cheng Lock, which produced the *Report of the Wild Animals and Wild Birds Committee*. The report recommended that the operation of pet shops be strictly regulated, while a central market for the sale for captured wild animals, principally birds, be established. Following the submission of the report, nothing happened. According to Fiona Tan, there was a "reluctance of public bodies" to enact any legislation due to personality clashes in the Legislative Council, a general laissez-faire attitude with regard to government regulations and the difficulty monitoring the illicit flow of animals in the port.[89] An additional factor, however, may have been that these shops were pushing the line between domestic and wild. The emphasis on cruelty had shifted to that which occurred to domestic animals. These animals had yet to make that transition.

On the centenary of the RSPCA in Britain, in 1936, some residents of Singapore questioned whether its colonial counterpart had any place on their island. Following the failure to enact legislation to regulate pet shops, criticism turned inward, with complaints directed at how the SPCA killed dogs or the state of the Animal Infirmary. Tan Cheng Lock was often the most vocal proponent for the rights of domesticated animals, with the editors of *The Straits Times* supporting his stance. The result was descriptions of the SPCA as "deplorable" institution, and "an indictment of the general public of Singapore" for its inability to effectively address cruelty in the society. The decline in the institution had been swift. By 1934 the Registrar of Societies announced that he had reason to believe that the SPCA had ceased to exist, and asked to see proof of its activities and membership. Ultimately, it was reported that the "society, while never actually disbanded, had fallen to a very low ebb." This state of affairs was held up as proof that "Singapore still lags behind Great Britain and other parts of the English-speaking world in its insistence upon humane treatment of animals." In the waning years of British imperial rule, and alongside the centenary celebrations for the RSPCA, the SPCA did reconstitute

---

[89] Tan, "The Beastly Business," pp. 170–1; Anonymous, "Lost, Stolen or Strayed," *ST*, 13 Sep. 1935, p. 10; Jeyamalar Kathirithamby-Wells, *Nature and Nation: Forests and Development in Peninsular Malaysia* (Singapore: NUS Press, 2005), pp. 198–208.

itself, under the guidance of new committee members including Omar Alsagoff and Seah Eng Tong, who "placed it on a firm footing again." This institution to protect the defenseless in society remained, but was toothless. It was simply a necessary component of life in a British imperial port. As one account reported, "The SPCA is especially useful in a cosmopolitan city like Singapore, for it serves as a rallying-point for members of all communities who are anxious to bring about more enlightened treatment of animals."[90]

This treatment had undergone decades of transformation, much of it rooted in imperial ideology and British notions of the proper treatment of animals. While the vast majority of time and effort had been directed at improving conditions for work animals, developments in the late 19th century had also raised the specter of how to handle domestic pets in the colonial society. It all came to a head in the mid-1880s when Singaporeans grew increasingly concerned with how their favorite domesticated pet was acting. Dogs in Singapore, and how they were perceived and regulated, were going to change.

---

[90] Anonymous, "Cruelty to Animals," *ST*, 14 Sep. 1934, p. 10; Anonymous, "S.P.C.A. and Animal Infirmary," *MT*, 1 Oct. 1934, p. 4; Anonymous, S.P.C.A. Non-Existent?," *ST*, 8 Sep. 1934, p. 12; Anonymous, "A Centenary and a Revival," *ST*, 9 Apr. 1936, p. 10; CO276/133: "No. 2038: Ordinance No. 116 (Societies)," p. 2579.

CHAPTER FIVE

Domestication, Regulation and Control of Dogs, and Other Animals

In early April 1884, the steamship *Oxfordshire* entered the harbor of Singapore. The vessel, having left England several months earlier, was on a journey around the world, transporting goods, people and information. Among the items on board, according to an announcement in *The Straits Times*, were "some twenty or thirty well bred dogs," including terriers, bulldogs, and greyhounds as well as various poodles. The animals were ferried ashore, along with English potatoes, and auctioned off on 7 April in Raffles Place, the focus of European commerce in the port.[1]

Such canines were highly desired in Singapore, as they were fine examples of a revolutionary change in animals over the previous few decades centered in England. This transformation was the development of the modern domestic pet. While dogs had been present in all human societies for millennia, providing companionship and occasionally utilitarian functions, these animals were of a new breed, literally. In

---

[1] It was discovered later that the Captain of the *Oxfordshire* had bought the dogs in London for "a very cheap rate" as most of them had been stolen, although this was of little consequence at the time. Anonymous, "Singapore Debating Society," *The Straits Times Weekly Issue*, 15 Oct. 1889, p. 10; RGBK, HNR3/2/3: Notebooks, Volume 3, p. 123.

contrast to semi-feral mongrels, which had been labeled a nuisance and were normally found throughout Singapore as well as the rest of the world, these imported dogs were the result of breeding and eugenics, the creation of sub-species that expressed desired characteristics and were seen as "pure." They were pets, a status previously limited to a very small percentage of canines that the elite of global societies may have owned. These new breeds of dogs were being cultivated to represent symbols of social divisions and distinctions. To own one characterized its human master as a member of the elite of a rapidly changing and industrializing society.

The development of well-bred dogs was a phenomenon intimately related to imperialism, science and class in the 19th century. The purveyors of pedigree canines enjoyed the cultivation of particular characteristics as "it offered a vision of a stable, hierarchical society, where rank was secure and individual merit, rather than just inherited position, appreciated," as Harriet Ritvo has summarized.[2] Dog fanciers during this period meticulously cultivated the physical characteristics of the animals, eventually developing specific breeds and classes, which were assigned ranks and orders of preference. The result of this anthropogenic selection was the creation of living symbols of prevailing attitudes toward a racial science in which genetic characteristics could be manipulated to achieve desired results.

The development of such breeds in England began with foxhounds in the 18th century, reflecting the transmission of a rural dog to one better suited to an urban environment as well as a glorification of the upper-class pursuit of hunting. By the mid-19th century distinct groups of canines—such as terriers, greyhounds, and spaniels—became systematized, leading to the first official dog show (held in 1859 in Newcastle), where the animals were rewarded for elegance and breeding, characteristics appealing to a genteel and sophisticated urban audience. Integrated within these developments was a distinct culture of class and Victorian ideals.[3] It was this culture that the captain of the *Oxfordshire* was selling to the residents of Singapore. These dogs were living examples of imperial superiority.

The various residents of Singapore who successfully secured a desired companion in April 1884, however, had little idea of what was

---

[2] Ritvo, *The Animal Estate*, p. 84.
[3] Ritvo, *The Animal Estate*, pp. 94–115.

to come. During the journey to Southeast Asia, "one or two of the creatures got 'queer' on the passage, and had to be destroyed." Over the next few years, these "fancy dogs" led to increased restrictions and regulations, as well as further domestication of the common pet in Singapore. Ultimately, they were the origin of changes in how humans regulated, controlled and domesticated other animals that went beyond the concept of class and elitism. After all, some of these well-bred dogs had rabies.[4]

A virus causes rabies. Unlike most viruses, which travel through the bloodstream, *Rabies lyssavirus* moves through the nerves and does so quite slowly. It enters the body through a bite, or breaks in the skin. Once it enters a nerve the virus usually proceeds at a pace of only a few centimeters a day until it reaches the brain. It then begins replicating itself in the brain, causing inflammation of the organ and destroying nerve cells in the process. This infection leads to a warping of normal behavior while stimulating aggression, symptoms which were commonly known in the 19th century. As one letter writer to *The Straits Times* mentioned, dogs might become sullen, "fidgeting," while barking at imaginary objects. Their voice would begin to change, and they would lick cold surfaces while exhibiting "an insatiable thirst." As inhibitions decreased, salivation increased. While lunging and biting, often with a foaming mouth, the infected animal would attack anything around them, often in a demonic manner. If any other mammal was bitten during these periods of aggression, the disease "may be communicated by contact of the dog's saliva with the skin, or mucous membrane." Rabies was one of the most terrifying ailments any one could suffer, as it turned humans into animals.[5]

Rabies has been present for millennia, having been reported in ancient Mesopotamia and India. In an age in which the source of most diseases was thought to result from "bad air," it was one of few that the real origin was understood. It came from the bite of an animal.[6] Although it is most closely associated with dogs, almost all

---

[4] CO275/39: "Report of Committee Appointed to Enquire into the Question of Rabies in Singapore," Papers Laid before the Legislative Council, No. 4 (1890), p. C19; Anonymous, "Sale of English Dogs," *ST*, 5 Apr. 1884, p. 2.

[5] L., "Hydrophobia," *The Straits Times Weekly Issue*, 23 July 1884, p. 13; Bill Wasick and Monica Murphy, *Rabid: A Cultural History of the World's Most Diabolical Virus* (New York: Penguin Books, 2012), pp. 3–5.

[6] Wasick and Murphy, *Rabid*, pp. 17–31.

mammals can catch rabies, which refers to the disease in animals; humans catch "hydrophobia." Meaning the fear of water, hydrophobia refers to a particular symptom, when the victim recoils violently when offered water, although they may be thirsty. After being bitten by a rabid animal, it usually takes one to three months for hydrophobia to appear in a human. In the agonizing wait to learn your fate, the victim could be treated, with the most common form being cauterization of the wound, while knowing that the death rate for those infected was essentially 100 percent. The disease begins to manifest itself with a fever and nerve tingling at the site of the bite. Violent spasms, uncontrolled excitement, paralysis of random limbs, confusion and a loss of consciousness follow. The carrier of the virus will then violently attack others, and these attacks were often followed by periods of lucidity.[7]

Rabies stimulated a tremendous amount of anxiety and fear throughout the world in the 19th century, and the conquest of the disease was a scientific triumph of an era when there were great advances in knowledge of diseases and germ theory.[8] Much of the credit was due to pioneering microbiologist Louis Pasteur, who began experiments to develop a vaccine in 1880. Four years later, Pasteur announced that he had found a treatment that involved a modified rabies virus of reduced virulence, which provided inoculated dogs with protection. He then turned his attention to the development of a treatment for hydrophobia and, in 1885, he used graduated doses of the vaccine to save the life of a young boy named Joseph Meister. The development of the anti-rabies vaccine was a global sensation. By the late 1880s it reduced the mortality rate for infections in humans who had been bitten from 16 percent to less than 1 percent. Patients began flooding the Pasteur Institute seeking treatment, and a new focus could be placed on eradicating the disease in an era in which it could travel to well-connected ports throughout the world.[9]

Singapore and the Straits Settlements were part of this interconnected world in which infected animals were able to travel on steamboats and railroads during the incubation period without suspicion. This was how rabies entered Singapore. The eventual solution to eradicating

---

[7] Wasick and Murphy, *Rabid*, pp. 8–10.

[8] Neil Pemberton and Michael Worboys, *Rabies in Britain: Dogs, Disease and Culture, 1800–2000* (Basingstoke: Palgrave Macmillan, 2007).

[9] CO275/39: "Report on Hydrophobia," pp. C76–9; Pemberton and Worboys, *Rabies in Britain*, pp. 102–32; Wasick and Murphy, *Rabid*, pp. 119–48.

rabies in this colonial port, however, had very little science behind it. Instead, it was rooted in a combined culture of violence and regulation. While colonial authorities under the East India Company had been reluctant to address the issue of the "dog nuisance" with taxation and protocols, and the maintenance of domesticated canines had become increasingly common among the elite of Singaporean society, the presence of rabies would require action. This led to the development of new approaches that would govern the relationship between humans and animals in a British colonial port in Southeast Asia. The dogs that were on board the *Oxfordshire* represented not only an importation of developing British values related to class and pets, but also an integration into networks of disease, monitoring and regulation in an imperial society.

The Mad Dog Scare

In May 1884 rabies appeared in the canine population of Singapore. It began with "a few peculiar cases of mania" among the dogs in the military encampment near the Singapore Botanic Gardens. "A dog in the barracks started off and bit every dog within reach, and many of these died in convulsions a few hours afterwards," it was reported. The owner of the canine was Lieutenant J.L. Armitage; he had purchased the fox terrier from the *Oxfordshire* during the auction on 7 April. Although there was some uncertainty over whether the dog was rabid, the authorities issued alerts. In June, the death of a small Malay boy named Kamis, who was bitten on the face, confirmed suspicions. This was only the beginning. Three Europeans then died of hydrophobia in quick succession. The first was George Gardiner, who succumbed while working on the *Telegraph Hulk*, the ship used to lay communication cables throughout the Empire; William Marsh of Bencoolen Street and a military officer named A.J. Lawford followed soon afterward, all victims of the virus. "The mad dog scare" continued throughout June and July 1884. One collector of tales from the period recounted that "A panic arose and other men who had been bitten died of fright or drank themselves to death."[10]

---

[10] CO275/39: "Report of Committee Appointed to Enquire into the Question of Rabies in Singapore," p. C19; Anonymous, "Untitled," *ST*, 10 Feb. 1885, p. 2; RGBK, HNR3/2/3: Notebooks, Vol. 3, p. 123.

Although initial suspicion was directed toward the mongrels that roamed the streets and had been a persistent menace for decades, it was soon pointed out that it was only present "in certain districts of the settlement which might reasonably be supposed to be exempt from disease dogs." As one report announced, "no less than fourteen mad dogs have been killed at Tanglin in or about the military barracks there, and a large number have been bludgeoned in Orchard Road." That this occurred in Tanglin was important, as the area was considered to be "the European quarter of the town," with one visitor reporting that it had "a great number of large and beautiful bungalows standing in large compounds with all sorts of tropical plants and palm trees." The presence of rabies in the elite environs of Singapore was verified further in late July, when a rabid dog rushed the son of Edmund W. Wells of the Telegraph Company, "a little boy, about five years of age," who was playing in the compound of his house. The dog bit the child on the chin and along the jaw.[11]

The rabies outbreak of 1884 probably was not the first appearance of the disease in Singapore, although previous instances had been contained quickly. In April 1847, a twelve-year-old boy died after a dog bit him, making it the second case that month. Nothing else was reported on the matter. Five years later, in 1852, the Superintendent of Police, Thomas Dunman, "killed a mad dog" in Tanjong Katong before "any damage was done." Throughout the 1840s and 1850s, the authorities raised the possibility that the disease had appeared among the stray dog population during periods of active culling related to the "dog nuisance," making rabies a simple addendum justifying the periodic slaughter of the animal.[12] If rabies was present, the rate of infection was not high; it was not of much concern.

---

[11] Anonymous, "Miscellaneous Items," *The Straits Times Weekly Issue*, 10 May 1884, p. 2; Anonymous, "Hydrophobia," *The Straits Times Weekly Issue*, 25 June 1884, p. 2; Anonymous, "A Lady on Singapore," *The Straits Times Weekly Issue*, 5 Oct. 1892, p. 7; Anonymous, "Summary of the Week," *The Straits Times Weekly Issue*, 2 July 1884, p. 1; Anonymous, "News of the Week," *ST*, 6 Aug. 1884, p. 2; Anonymous, "Summary of the Week," *The Straits Times Weekly Issue*, 13 Aug. 1884, p. 1.

[12] CO275/39: "Report of Committee Appointed to Enquire into the Question of Rabies in Singapore," p. C19; Anonymous, "Untitled," *SFP*, 8 Apr 1847, p. 2; Anonymous, Advertisements column 1," *SFP*, 3 Feb. 1848, p. 1.

Under such conditions the presence of rabies in previous decades was quickly forgotten, which attests to the infrequent presence of the disease in Singapore. Much of this denial was based in the belief that it was a disorder rooted in temperate regions. In 1881, for example, "W" opined in a letter to the press that "fortunately this fearful disease is unknown in the [Straits] Settlements," while another anonymous contributor argued in *The Straits Times* that it was "not native to these parts; it cannot originate here; climatic conditions are against it."[13] Although observers were certain that rabies had been absent from Singapore prior to the 1880s, it now had clearly arrived and it needed to be addressed. The initial problem, however, was getting the authorities to accept that it originated from England, not the local pariah dog population, despite evidence that it was predominant in animals kept as pets. The reaction to this conundrum was a familiar one.

The response to the rabies outbreak in 1884 was increased attention on an activity that had been practiced for decades in Singapore: the culling of mongrels. Although authority in the port had transferred from the East India Company to the Straits Settlements Government, the organized and focused hunting of dogs had continued and, by the 1880s, took place over four days during the months of January, April, July and October. The appearance of rabies in the canine community simply led to an intensification of these activities, with the police announcing that open culling would take place throughout the entire month of July, "without exception," although it would lead to the death of "many valuable domestic pets." This one-month killing spree did not eradicate the problem. In mid-August, the authorities proclaimed another month of dog killing would occur beginning 25 August. "All dogs at large and not wearing either a collar and chain or a muzzle" would be shot or destroyed.[14] Despite these month-long culling exercises, mongrels continued to roam the streets of Singapore, with one account describing

---

[13] W, "Cure for Hydrophobia," *The Straits Times Overland Journal*, 16 June 1881, p. 7; Canis, "Hydrophobia," *The Straits Times Weekly Issue*, 2 July 1884, p. 10.

[14] These efforts to expand the destruction of dogs did not merit a response from the SPCA in Singapore. The organization, after all, was a government entity representing elite views while the victims would be the mongrels that had plagued Singapore for decades. Their focus remained on the treatment of cattle and horses during this period. Anonymous, "Hydrophobia," *The Straits Times Weekly Issue*, 30 July 1884, p. 6; Ritvo, *Animal Estate*.

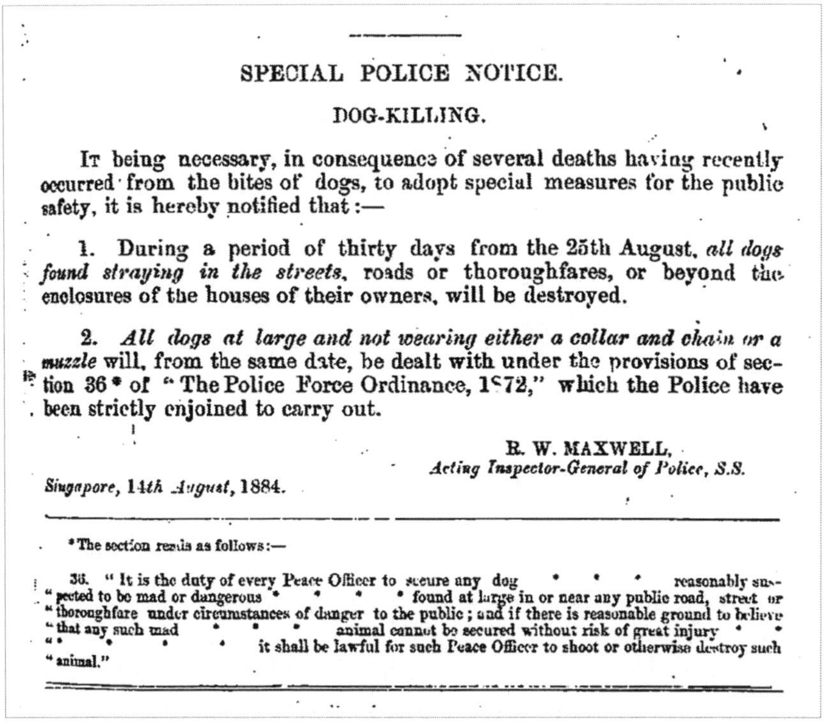

SPECIAL POLICE NOTICE.

DOG-KILLING.

It being necessary, in consequence of several deaths having recently occurred from the bites of dogs, to adopt special measures for the public safety, it is hereby notified that:—

1. During a period of thirty days from the 25th August, *all dogs found straying in the streets,* roads or thoroughfares, or beyond the enclosures of the houses of their owners, will be destroyed.

2. *All dogs at large and not wearing either a collar and chain or a muzzle* will, from the same date, be dealt with under the provisions of section 36 * of "The Police Force Ordinance, 1872," which the Police have been strictly enjoined to carry out.

R. W. MAXWELL,
Acting Inspector-General of Police, S.S.

Singapore, 14th August, 1884.

* The section reads as follows:—

36. " It is the duty of every Peace Officer to secure any dog * * * reasonably suspected to be mad or dangerous * * * found at large in or near any public road, street or thoroughfare under circumstances of danger to the public; and if there is reasonable ground to believe that any such mad * * * animal cannot be secured without risk of great injury * * it shall be lawful for such Peace Officer to shoot or otherwise destroy such animal."

Image 5.1: Dog killing notice from the *Government Gazette*, 14 August 1884. CO276/15: "Government Notification, No. 345," p. 871.

"ten pariah dogs disporting themselves at one time on that patch of ground behind the Chinese Free School in Cross Street."[15]

A report written at the end of the century recalled the state of the stray dog population in the municipality of Singapore during the 1880s.

> These dogs were not seen to any great extent by day, as they frequented and took up their abode in and about waste land, grave yards and the hills surrounding the Town densely covered with undergrowth. They however trooped out by thousands at dusk and during the night went their rounds in search of food, returning to their retreats in the undergrowth at daylight. In addition to these many hundreds of dogs were owned by natives and Europeans and were well housed and cared for.[16]

---

[15] Senex, "The Dog Nuisance," *ST*, 8 Jan. 1885, p. 3.
[16] CO273/246/4381: "Report on the Suppression of Rabies," (1899), p. 225.

Under such circumstances, culling would take a considerable amount of effort before it would have an impact on the overall canine population, particularly one in which rabies was beginning to take root. Furthermore, as the periodic month-long dog culling exercises in 1884 had little impact on the number of mongrels, the program was expanded further in 1885. For example, the entire month of March was dedicated to killing strays in Singapore. These efforts, nevertheless, did not prevent rabies from becoming endemic within the domesticated pet population.[17]

Government authorities began to realize that the rabies problem was not dissipating, as it had in earlier decades with quick culls of dogs being the solution. To address this issue, in mid-1885, they finally decided to pass amendments to the Quarantine and Prevention of Disease Ordinance XIX of 1868. While this earlier law had not addressed issues related to diseased animals, it now allowed for the right to quarantine any imported animal and formalized dog culling exercises. This resulted in a series of important changes to how animals would be treated in Singapore. As a start, the government now prohibited the direct importation of any dogs. All ship captains had to declare any canine onboard their vessels, and no dog was allowed on shore without direct consent of a health officer, after undergoing a quarantine of one month. In addition to these restrictions, the authorities announced further limitations on the movement of all canines after a European resident named Robert Klassen was bitten in Trafalgar Estate in early 1885, and died in June of that year. The Governor and Legislative Council, using the amendments to the original 1868 ordinance, enacted orders to monitor "public thoroughfares and for destroying dogs" in the Straits Settlements, which resulted in a recommendation from the police that all domesticated dogs be restrained within houses or at least compounds while orders were issued "to kill all dogs, day and night."[18]

The elite of Singapore, who desired the type of dogs that had to be imported, however, expressed concern over these new regulations,

---

[17] CO276/15: "Government Notification, No. 295," 1884, p. 750; CO276/16: "Government Notification, No. 131," 1885, p. 265.
[18] CO273/246/4381: "Report on the Suppression of Rabies," (1899), p. 224; Anonymous, "Prevention of Disease," *ST*, 13 Nov. 1886, p. 2; CO276/17: "Ordinance No. XIX of 1886," (1886), pp. 2139–42; CO276/16: "Government Notification, No. 341," 1885, pp. 1048–9.

describing them as being of "doubtful legality," as they signaled a reduction in the supply of desired breeds and increased costs as well as delays in obtaining a pet. In such circumstances, one European complained, "the breed of English dogs will soon become extinct, and the householders will be driven to keep yelping Pariahs as watch dogs." In addition, leading residents chafed at the restrictions placed on the movement of their dogs. The answer to the question of blame remained elusive among many of these well-to-do residents of the island.[19]

Despite resistance from elite dog owners, Samuel Dunlop, the Inspector-General of Police for the Straits Settlements, pressed on. He announced in the face of criticism that, "All dogs found straying in the streets, roads, or public thoroughfares, or beyond the enclosures of the houses of the owners ... may be destroyed." Large-scale culling programs continued into 1886. During the exercise in September of that year the police were particularly active, which elicited complaints about the restrictions that were now being placed on domestic pets.[20]

One incident highlighted these tensions. On 28 September a child was playing with his pet—"an old and favorite dog"—at the gate of the family compound on Victoria Street. "A Policeman and a Kling cooly" came on the scene and, according to the house owner, "at once began battering the poor dog about in a most inhuman and brutal manner and split open its head in presence of my wife, who was standing on the verandah and who remonstrated with them for such barbarous conduct." The dog killers left after fulfilling their duty and the child "wept bitterly at the loss of his only pet." When a family servant went to retrieve the carcass and bury it, the policeman and the coolie returned and an argument ensued. They had left earlier to find a buyer for the carcass and had "sold it to a Chinaman for 30 cents." The scene descended into further chaos when the coolie and the policeman argued about their share of the bounty. The coolie shoved the policeman, and two other officers came and arrested him. This led the house owner to question the entire program to eradicate rabies

---

[19] Anonymous, "Untitled," *ST*, 4 June 1885, p. 2.
[20] Quarantine, "Correspondence," *ST*, 8 June 1885, p. 3; CO273/246/4381: "Report on the Suppression of Rabies," (1899), p. 224; CO276/16: "Government Notification, No. 478," 1885, p. 1340; CO276/17: "Government Notification, No. 133," 1886, p. 374; CO276/17: "Government Notification, No. 399," 1886, p. 1293.

and restrict the movement of susceptible animals on the island.[21] Dog culling and restrictions, which were promulgated to protect the human population, had descended into a parody of violence, bureaucracy and prejudices.

In this context, a different approach to the problem was needed. As one contributor to the newspapers put it, "Now that the periodical dog killing season is coming round again, the powers that be might surely case about for some better means to gain the object in view than that of barbarously killing dogs by clubbing them." The requirement to restrain dogs was also leading to exasperation among the public. As another letter writer proclaimed, "Those who have dogs are obliged to chain them, and it is not at all pleasant at night to hear your and your neighbor's dogs howl all night long and make it impossible for any one to sleep." He went on to add that, "For a month we must put up with this infernal nuisance, or else lose our dogs."[22]

Registering Responsibility

Rabies persisted in Singapore for the remainder of the 1880s despite quarantine provisions and increased efforts to destroy curs. This was because the disease had become endemic among the pet dog population already on the island, and these precious animals were under the protection of elite residents who wanted to own a symbol of their status, and were reluctant to address the root of the issue. A reminder of this dichotomy occurred in December 1886 when a Chinese resident went to the Central Police Station and requested that he be sent to the hospital. He died shortly thereafter from hydrophobia. Several weeks earlier "a small dog belonging to one of the European police" had bitten the man.[23]

In an environment in which public dog killing was the norm, and rabies remained ensconced among elite pets, the public began proposing solutions to help regulate the canine community. The result was renewed calls for a dog tax, and its associated licensing and

---

[21] W, "Dog Killing," *ST*, 1 Oct. 1886, p. 3.

[22] Anonymous, "Dog Killing," *The Straits Times Weekly Issue*, 2 Sep 1886, p. 8; Toby, "Dog Killing," *ST*, 27 Feb. 1885, p. 35.

[23] Occasional reports of a similar nature appeared periodically in the newspapers. Anonymous, "Notes," *SFP*, 4 Dec. 1886, p. 331; CO276/18: "Government Notification, No. 69," 1887, p. 186.

registration, particularly after other colonial cities began imposing such fees.[24] In a letter to the editor of *The Straits Times*, Saladin called dog culling an "insane and cruel institution" that usually results in "the occasional disappearance of some lady's much prized pet, or a valuable housedog." In the meantime, "it is almost impossible to walk through any of the native streets in either the town or suburbs of Singapore without meeting with a pack of snarling, mangy pariahs, any one of which may, for aught we know, be mad." If these animals could be identified, and isolated from the domesticated canine population, they could be "wholly exterminated." To separate them, Saladin called for a dog license to be imposed."[25]

Such taxes had been proposed for decades, with it being a subject of public debate during the 1860s. By 1865 the editors of *The Straits Times*—after "most serious and uncomfortable reflection"—called upon the Municipal Commission to levy a "dog tax" against anyone who wanted to shelter a dog with the hope that this would quickly expose any owner while the rest could be culled more vigorously. Without such a tax, residents were "subjecting ourselves to discomfort and danger." The main goal of the tax was to force dog owners to declare their responsibilities. Collars and tags would identify the registered animals, while all other dogs would be destroyed. "Indeed, the amount of the Tax would probably be such as to render the keeping of one dog an indulgence within the reach of all, but to render the keeping of a dozen a matter for consideration." In the decade leading up to the Mad Dog Scare, these proposals never went beyond a periodic debate.[26]

---

[24] For example, Dutch authorities introduced such a tax in Batavia in 1887 following an outbreak of hydrophobia. Anonymous, "A Dog Tax," *ST*, 12 Nov. 1887, p. 2; CO276/18: "Government Notification, No. 69," 1887, p. 186; Anonymous, "Notes," *SFP*, 4 Dec. 1886, p. 331.

[25] The funds raised could be used to pay for dog culling efforts and eventually "some such laudable and merciful purpose as the building of shelters for horses. Saladin, "Dog License," *ST*, 20 Sep. 1886, p. 3; Anonymous, "Dog Licensing," *ST*, 23 Sep. 1886, p. 2; Anonymous, "Untitled," *SFP*, 25 Sep. 1886, p. 182; Anonymous, "News of the Week," *The Straits Times Weekly Issue*, 6 Aug. 1884, p. 2.

[26] For example, the possibility a dog tax entered the public forum in 1881, when the Straits Settlements Government contacted the Municipal Commission over the issue. At that time, the commissioners replied that it "should be as moderate as possible" and only applicable within a 5-kilometer (3 miles) radius of the town center, along with a program "where all stray dogs might be impounded and

Despite such long-standing reluctance, a dog-licensing regulation for Singapore was finally passed in October 1888. It came into effect in December of that year. Under these new directives, every dog in Singapore had to be "registered by the Commissioners of the Municipality within which the dog is kept." For the annual fee of $1 within the municipality and 50 cents in rural areas, residents received a "metal label bearing the registered number of the dog in respect of which the tax is paid." The government would also keep a register containing the name of the owner, along with other information that identified the animal. Any dog found without a collar and identification number would be "destroyed, impounded or dealt with," and non-compliance with the new regulation resulted in a fine of $5 for any dog owner. If a dog needed to be quarantined the charge for upkeep was 15 cents per day. During the first month 201 dogs were registered, and in 1889 the total reached 3,664.[27]

Along with these new regulations, the system of dog culling also transformed. The official policy now was to capture unlicensed dogs with "long tongs or nippers" and then put them in a cage on wheels. The cage had two compartments, "one for dogs likely to be claimed, the other for those which from their appearance had no owner." Once they reached the pound, "good dogs" were taken aside and placed in

---

destroyed." Neither the Straits Settlements government, nor municipal officials would take responsibility for the matter. In the meantime, each side appealed to the other to enact measures, with each attempting to pass responsibility—in Singaporean parlance, to *tai chi*—to the other. In 1884, for example, the commissioners issued a statement that "under the existing circumstances," following the outbreak of rabies, it was "high desirable that some action should be taken in the matter," and then promptly did little for four years. Much of this would be resolved following the passage of rules laying out the responsibilities of the Municipal Commission in 1887. National Archives of Singapore 425: MPMC, 8 Dec. 1881, pp. 146–7, 155–6; 18 July 1884, p. 890; Anonymous, "The Dog Nuisance," *ST*, 1 July 1865, p. 1; Anonymous, "Friday, 12th May, 1865," *ST*, 13 May 1865, p. 2.

[27] It appears that registration was required, or at least enforced, in the municipality. Outside of the municipality, efforts at dog licensing were much more laissez faire at this time. CO276/19: "Government Notification, No. 582" (1888), p. 2023; CO276/19: "Government Notification, No. 583" (1888), p. 2024; CO276/19: "Government Notification, No. 280" (1888), pp. 953–4; CO273/246/4381: "Report on the Suppression of Rabies," (1899), p. 225; CO276/19: "Government Notification, No. 752" (1888), p. 2539; NA425: MPMC: 6 Jan. 1888, p. 1411; 1 Aug. 1888, p. 1491.

enclosures in case their owners came searching for them. "The cage with the other dogs was lifted by a crane and dropped into the river and the dogs drowned; the carcasses afterwards being buried." A dog inspector, as well as four peons, were hired to oversee this system. There were 29 applicants for the position of dog inspector, before the municipal commissioners decided to hire a former prison warden, A. Cheeseman.[28]

These new efforts to control the canine population came after another spike in rabies cases in Singapore in early 1888. Governor Cecil Clementi Smith, who had become concerned after "four or five cases of hydrophobia admitted to Singapore General Hospital," which was "far in excess of those in any other place in the British Dominions," wrote to the Colonial Office seeking assistance. Following this appeal, Lord Knutsford—the Secretary of State for the Colonies—approved the attachment of Dr. F.K. Hampshire, the Colonial Surgeon in Penang who was in England on home leave, to Paris to enquire whether the techniques Pasteur had developed could be applied in the tropics. If this was not possible, it appeared that "drastic" action would be needed.[29]

The limitations in the strategies to fight rabies in Singapore became apparent in the second half of 1889, when several more people were bitten. In early September 1889, a Chinese resident was found on the sidewalk—the five-foot way—along Victoria Street. He was "vomiting, and frothing at the mouth, and exhibiting all of the symptoms of hydrophobia." He was placed in a rickshaw and taken to the Pauper Hospital. His friends told the authorities that it originated two months earlier when a poodle bit the man. "The injury was so slight a nature that scarcely any notice was taken of it" until symptoms began to appear. The reluctance to seek treatment also occurred when another dog bit a blacksmith and his son at Pekin Street several days later. The rabid dog

---

[28] In the past officials would pile up the carcasses of the dogs on the corners of public thoroughfares, and their "rapidly decomposing bodies tainted the air with poisonous emanations." In addition, the dog inspector was initially paid $50 per month, while each peon received $8 per month. NA425: MPMC: 6 Jan. 1888, p. 1605; Anonymous, "Friday, 26th May, 1876," *The Straits Observer*, 26 May 1876, p. 2; CO276/19: "Government Notification, No. 598" (1888), p. 2042; CO273/246/4381: "Report on the Suppression of Rabies," (1899), p. 226.

[29] CO273/158/2761: "Hydrophobia," pp. 27–30; Anonymous, "Meeting of the Legislative Council," *ST*, 5 April 1889, p. 3; Pemberton and Worboys, *Rabies in Britain*, pp. 102–32; Anonymous, "Miss Blackmore in Paris," *The Straits Times Weekly Issue*, 6 May 1891, p. 11.

initially went after the child, biting "pieces out of the little fellow's legs." While fighting off the dog, the boy fell into a sewer drain. The dog landed on the child "and again started to worry and bite." The father came to help, and the dog "flew at the Chinaman's face and fastened its teeth on to his nose, ultimately pulling a portion of the flesh." Another passer-by arrived, and killed the dog with "a chopper."[30]

The rabid dog that attacked the father and son on Pekin Street was not a pariah, despite initial newspaper reports. The canine was registered—No. 183—and the owner was Tah Wah Liang, who lived at 148, Kampong Bugis. Both victims received treatment at the hospital, but refused to remain under observation.[31] Within weeks the boy was ill, and the last hours for the child were "simply agonizing to witness." According to a newspaper report, "he was attacked with periodical convulsions, when he would call for water, but on water being brought to him, he would draw back and bark after the fashion of a dog, and so his agony continued until death put an end to his sufferings." An Indian barber also died of rabies in September, while a young Indian boy living on Orchard Road suffered an attack from "a black and white terrier dog."[32] This was the beginning of the greatest hydrophobia outbreak in Singaporean history and, because preventive measures had not addressed the core issue—the presence of the disease in the elite dog population—concern and panic began to seep into the society.

In the midst of what came to be known as the Hydrophobia Scare of 1889, A. Griffin visited Singapore, providing a picture of the atmosphere in the port and the unease that enveloped much of the island. Griffin spent most of his time with an old school friend, Conrad P. Thierschlaer, a German resident of Singapore who "talks English like a native, and Malay like an Englishman."[33] Thierschlaer lived along Orchard Road, which was "suggestive of the leafy lanes of England." On the journey to the Thierschlaer residence after his arrival, Griffin took note of the distance been colonizer and colonized in the

---

[30] Anonymous, "A Mad Dog in Singapore," *The Straits Times Weekly Issue*, 9 Sep. 1889, p. 2; Anonymous, "Hydrophobia in Singapore," *ST*, 7 Sep. 1889, p. 2.

[31] Anonymous, "Municipal Commissioners," *ST*, 26 Sep. 1889, p. 2.

[32] Anonymous, "The Prevention of Hydrophobia," *ST*, 23 Sep. 1889, p. 1; Anonymous, "Hydrophobia in Singapore," *ST*, 30 Sep. 1889, p. 2; Anonymous, "More Hydrophobia," *The Straits Times Weekly Issue*, 17 Sep. 1889, p. 1.

[33] A. Griffin, "Jottings from the Diary of a Globe-trotter in Singapore," *The Straits Times Weekly Issue*, 23 Sep. 1889, pp. 3, 8.

port. He observed that "the resident European ignores his brother the heathen" in most daily interaction, particularly after Thierschlaer sent three rickshaw drivers tumbling into a ditch with his carriage on their journey from the port. Following a night of restful sleep, and attempts to avoid rats and lizards in the bathing area of the compound, Griffin joined his old school friend for breakfast. They discussed "the prevalence of hydrophobia" while being surrounded by "a whole menagerie of dogs round the breakfast table, in various expectant attitudes." Thierschlaer lamented that, "pariah dogs are largely infected and have a nasty habit of biting other dogs." The presence of so many dogs made Griffin nervous, which was further exacerbated when a mongrel wandered into the compound, and one of Thierschlaer's hounds, a yellow one, went out to interact with the cur. Seeing the unwanted visitor, Thierschlaer ordered his "Chinese boy" to bring his revolver. Thierschlaer shot at the pariah, but killed the "yellow dog." The unwanted intruder fled the scene.[34]

The attitude Thierschlaer displayed toward dogs represented one of the key issues related to rabies in Singapore in the 1880s. The elite remained reluctant to admit that their pets were the primary hosts of the disease and continued to insist that the solution was to increase dog culling. Such arguments continued in the press, with "Anging Gila" (a pseudonym meaning "Mad Dog" in Malay) suggesting "the horde of pariah dogs should be at once crushed out." The anonymous letter writer even argued that the new registration system was of limited effectiveness as, "no one ought to acquire for one dollar the right to keep a dangerous animal at large; and at present all dogs are dangerous."[35]

Despite the admonitions of "Anging Gila," the ground was beginning to shift. With the rise in the number of cases, and each case beginning with a bite from a domesticated dog as occurred with the attack on Pekin Street, the demonization of pariah dogs came under scrutiny and blame slowly began to shift toward high breeds. As one letter writer to *The Straits Times* asked, "Is the case so thoroughly proved against the Singapore pariah after all?" Another resident sought a compromise in apportioning blame when he stated, "hydrophobia may be lurking both in high bred animals and curs of low degree."[36]

---

[34] Griffin, "Jottings from the Diary of a Globe-trotter in Singapore."

[35] Anging Gila, "Hydrophobia," *ST*, 10 Sep. 1889, p. 3.

[36] Hound, "Hydrophobia," *ST*, 13 Sep. 1889, p. 3; Pariah Dog, "The Prevention of Hydrophobia," *ST*, 23 Sep. 1889, p. 3.

The presence of the disease among well-bred dogs in Singapore became even more apparent when C.E. Crane, one of the leading residents of Singapore and a municipal commissioner, had to put down five of his seven dogs in September 1889 after they became infected with rabies, although he claimed the infection had originated when his dogs were bitten by pariah dogs. In the same month the entire canine population at two different residences in Tanglin had to be destroyed. Although rabies had spread to such an extent that it was not "prevalent in any one district more than in another," it remained a very real presence among the elite community. This led to the realization that it had "reached proportions so alarming, and is of so serious a nature, that all the merely sentimental consideration that come into the relations between man and dog should be ignored." The elite needed to accept that they, and their pets, were the problem. After all, as one anonymous letter writer posited, "so long as the sufferers from hydrophobia are only a few poor Asiatics, there is always the possibility of the greatness of the danger overlooked."[37]

A Combination of Drastic Measures

In an atmosphere in which rabid dogs continued to be present in elite areas of town, the editor of *The Straits Times*, Arnot Reid, "started raising a panic," particularly after "a missionary's child had been bitten by a mad dog."[38] Reid began advocating a drastic response, calling for all dogs in Singapore to be quarantined on St. John's Island for six months or killed. If the Legislative Council would support such action with an

---

[37] Anonymous, "The Prevalence of Hydrophobia," *The Straits Times Weekly Issue*, 17 Sep. 1889, p. 1; Anonymous, "The Prevention of Hydrophobia," *ST*, 1 Oct. 1889, p. 3; CO275/39: "Report of Committee Appointed to Enquire into the Question of Rabies in Singapore," p. C20.

[38] The child was an "ill bred little urchin," who had punched a "little harmless white dog" in the nose as it was running around the courtyard of a hotel. The dog subsequently bit the child, who screamed, and led to the waiters from the hotel chasing the dog down and killing it. Only afterwards was the dog labeled as "mad." "This kind of thing increased the panic, till at last it got forgotten." This depiction of the young, human victim, and the atmosphere in Singapore at the time, is from the Director of the Singapore Botanic Gardens, H.N. Ridley, who believed most cases in Singapore were "false hydrophobia," brought on by sensationalism and irrational responses. RGBK, HNR 3/2/3: Notebooks, Vol. 3, pp. 125–31.

ordinance, he reasoned, in "six months the island of Singapore shall be cleared of dogs." Reid went on to explain how this was to be done:

> Owners of dogs ought, under such an Ordinance, to be required either to kill them or to hand them over to a Government department to be killed; or, alternatively, they may hand them over to the same department to be kept separately in quarantine for six months on one of the neighboring islands at the owner's cost. Meanwhile stray dogs would be vigorously hunted down, not merely by officials appointed for that end, but by natives who would be incited to action by a reward for each dog they might kill.

After six months, the quarantined dogs would return, theoretically, to a rabies-free Singapore, with the additional advantage of finally solving the dog nuisance. Anticipating the passage of such an ordinance, the commander of the military barracks ordered every dog in Tanglin quarantined or destroyed.[39]

The appeals for quarantine reflected continuing class issues as elite members of colonial society, who maintained pet dogs as a demonstration of their status, could afford to isolate their precious companions. Even though many of these residents had multiple dogs, such as the Thierschlaer household near Orchard Road, some of which had a utilitarian purpose such as the pulling of dogcarts, they could afford any fees that would be charged for the service. They could also bear the absence of their dogs for half a year as a symbol of their willingness to sacrifice for the larger good. The solution seemed simple, for the well-to-do. Their pets would be certified as acceptable for residence in Singapore after six months.[40]

---

[39] Anonymous, "The Prevention of Hydrophobia," *ST*, 13 Sep. 1889, p. 2; Anonymous, "The Prevention of Hydrophobia," *ST*, 20 Sep. 1889, p. 2.

[40] In a tellingly racist commentary, reflecting colonial attitudes with regard to the use of such dogs, one resident questioned the call for quarantine not based on the cost but on the possible absence of his utilitarian canines that kept Asian marauders at bay. As he questioned, "Are we to be left defenceless against the light-fingered Chinée who enter our compounds appropriating door mats, lamps, or anything portable, or the nimble goat, who nibbles on all our shrubs and flowers?" He went on to add, "When they are gone to execution or St. John's, good-bye to my fowls." Pariah Dog, "The Prevention of Hydrophobia," *ST*, 23 Sep. 1889, p. 3; A. Griffin, "Jottings from the Diary of a Globe-trotter in Singapore," *The Straits Times Weekly Issue*, 23 Sep. 1889, p. 1; Anonymous, "The Police Regulation of Traffic," *ST*, 26 May 1892, p. 2.

Resistance to quarantine proposals, based mainly on utilitarian purposes, however, appeared "from Chinese and other Asiatics," which reflects different understandings of how dogs interacted with humans in the communities of colonial Singapore. The ownership of dogs was not based in race, although that is how it was addressed in the contemporary accounts. For much of society, dogs were an integral part of the household and they had a purpose, usually the protection of owners and property. As one report in *The Straits Times Weekly* summarized when reporting on an unrelated incident related to a Chinese resident named Soh Ah Bey, he had "as usual with his class, one or two dogs of the pariah type, which in way kept off intruders into the garden."[41]

Despite such resistance from easily ignored owners of less well-bred dogs, the proposal to quarantine all canines, and to destroy any that were not registered, began to gain traction, with one anonymous contributor to the discussion proclaiming, "Utter destruction and quarantine commend themselves on the ground that boldness means safety." The next month, at a meeting of the Singapore Debating Society in October, the subject under consideration was whether "it is desirable that all dogs in Singapore be destroyed or placed in quarantine for 6 months." The proposal, however, did not pass. Many of those in attendance supported the basic goals of such proposals, but felt it was unrealistic to expect all stray dogs in Singapore to be culled. The task was too formidable.[42]

The Legislative Council met soon afterward to discuss whether increased regulation was the best method of handling rabies. The main proposal under consideration called for a reminder that all dogs be registered, while there was a request to enact, "compulsory muzzling under a penalty of non-compliance." At the same time, in October 1889, the municipal commissioners formed a Hydrophobia Committee, consisting of five members, including Tan Jiak Kim and the Colonial Engineer, Henry Edward McCallum.[43]

In the midst of this debate, in October 1889, F.K. Hampshire returned from his visit to the Pasteur Institute. He submitted a report,

---

[41] Anonymous, "Fatal Shooting Case at Serangoon," *The Straits Times Weekly*, 3 Dec. 1890, p. 9; Anonymous, "The Prevention of Hydrophobia," *ST*, 19 Nov. 1889, p. 2.

[42] Anonymous, "Prevention of Hydrophobia," *ST* 24 Sep. 1889, p. 2; Anonymous, "The Singapore Debating Society."

[43] Anonymous, The Prevention of Hydrophobia," *ST*, 13 Nov. 1889, p. 2; Anonymous, "The Prevention of Hydrophobia," *ST*, 5 Oct. 1889, p. 3.

which arrived in mid-November from Penang, to the Legislative Council in Singapore. Based on his time at the center of rabies research, Hampshire summarized what was known about the disease at that time,[44] and raised two serious issues for the Straits Settlements government to consider. The first revolved around concerns related to adapting the required laboratory equipment to the tropics. The development of the vaccine required the rearing of rabbits and the harvesting of their spinal cords, which subsequently had to be stored at a temperature between 20° and 25° Celsius. In Singapore "rabbits of sufficient weight and size to give satisfactory results" were rare and expensive in the markets. This concern led into the second issue, which involved costs. Hampshire estimated that the development of a hydrophobia treatment center for the Straits Settlements would require an annual expenditure of $633, of which more than half would go to the purchase of bunnies. Facing such obstacles, he argued that, while possible, such efforts would not be cost effective, and the authorities were unlikely to fund such an initiative.[45]

As the treatment of rabies and hydrophobia at the time was considered too expensive and problematic, Hampshire advocated an approach to stamping out the disease that had been adopted in numerous communities worldwide. The main precepts were fourfold. All stray dogs should be destroyed; "the keeping of useless dogs should be discouraged" through taxation; importation of dogs should be outlawed, or those imported subject to quarantine; and, in districts where rabies is prevalent, muzzling should be compulsory. He reasoned, however, that much of this was doomed to failure, because both the European and Asian communities were too obstinate with regard to their animals. "There is no

---

[44] For example, children appeared to be more susceptible, and bites to the head had a greater chance of leading to death than if they limbs were the site of infection, as the brain and spinal cord are "now recognized as the essential seat of the virus." If bitten, "caustics and cutting out the bitten parts have proved useful as preventives against the virus getting a foothold." To treat the disease, Pasteur had developed a series of inoculations, which required intricate laboratory procedures and precise administration to the victim. Anonymous, "Hydrophobia," *The Straits Times Weekly Issue*, 30 July 1884, p. 6; CO275/39: "Report on Hydrophobia," pp. C73–4.

[45] The difficulties with funding and operating such facilities is covered in a series of letters requesting the purchase of equipment, and rabbits, which can be found in a series of files held in CO273/164; CO275/39: "Report on Hydrophobia," pp. C79–80.

possibility of European owners of dogs confining dogs to their premises, or enforcing the use of a muzzle when the dog is beyond the owner's premises. In regard to native dogs, there is, I think no probability of enforcing effectual muzzling." As a newspaper account of the report summarized, it was believed that any approach that required self-discipline among humans would fail, "on the ground of the impossibility of enforcing it among our mixed and ignorant population." Ultimately, Hampshire believed that the only solution was "the destruction of all dogs in Singapore."[46] The Legislative Council now waited for the report of the Hydrophobia Committee.

In January 1890 the Hydrophobia Committee released its report. Although the committee supported a combination of "extirpation and quarantine," they were reluctant to adopt both measures. As a compromise they advocated a combination of drastic measures, including the continual culling of stray dogs and the muzzling of owned dogs, as well as registration, higher taxation, strict control, and a restriction on the number of dogs allowed in each residence. The recommended period of muzzling of all dogs on the island was to be "six months after the complete extirpation of the stray dogs." As it was believed that it would take six months to kill all of the pariah dogs in Singapore, the total period of muzzling would be for a year. In addition, an outright ban on the importation of dogs would be enforced over the twelve-month period of quarantine and extirpation. It was also recommended that all imported dogs from countries where rabies was prevalent be subject to a one-month quarantine, and then monthly inspections for the next six months.[47]

These recommendations echoed attempts to control rabies in the 1860s and 1870s in Great Britain. An important figure in the development of provisions to cull all stray dogs and enact dog-licensing schemes was George Fleming, who published a book entitled *Rabies and Hydrophobia* in 1872. Fleming was a veterinarian and his goal was to promote an increased appreciation among his colleagues for dogs, which

---

[46] CO275/39: "Report on Hydrophobia," pp. C73–80; Anonymous, "The Prevention of Hydrophobia," *ST*, 15 Nov. 1889, p. 2.

[47] The use of muzzles, the committee noted, had been effective in ridding Berlin and Scandinavia of rabies. Anonymous, "Report on Rabies," *ST*, 25 Jan. 1890, p. 2; CO275/39: "Report of Committee Appointed to Enquire into the Question of Rabies in Singapore," pp. C24–5.

were often overlooked in a time when the focus was more clearly placed on work animals. To limit rabies, Fleming recommended the culling of "useless curs," vigorous dog taxes, and active muzzling in areas where the disease was prevalent. These protocols came into force in England in the 1880s, when there was an epizootic outbreak of rabies, and subsequently were transferred to the colony, where the government of the Straits Settlements adopted an active and regulatory bureaucracy with regard to canines. Such regulations also reflected cultural, geographical and power relationships prevalent in Singapore.[48]

Behind these basic provisions lay a transformation of the human-animal relationship in Singapore, and how the island was governed. One of the major proposals of the Hydrophobia Committee was to treat the island of Singapore as one entity. "We strongly recommend that steps be taken by the Government in the country identical with those which we advise be adopted in the Municipality within their limits, the whole island being subject to the same procedure."[49] With the arrival of direct colonial rule, Singapore had been divided into a municipality—constituting the port and its immediate environs—and a rural area outside of the core. The municipality had its own government and bureaucracy, while the rest of the island fell under the Straits Settlements administration. The vast majority of people in Singapore lived in the municipality, while the remainder mainly contained scattered plantations growing a range of products such as gambier, pepper, coffee and pineapples. In these rural areas most residents were Chinese agriculturalists over which the government had minimal influence, and it was these residents that were depicted as providing the greatest resistance to any measures introduced to address rabies.[50]

The differences between town and country in late 19th-century Singapore can be seen through dog registration. Although the government required dog owners to register their domestic pets beginning in the late 1880s, the legislation was rarely enforced in rural Singapore. In the municipality, however, residents were required to purchase

---

[48] George Fleming, *Rabies and Hydrophobia: Their History, Nature, Causes, Symptoms, and Prevention* (London: Chapman and Hall, 1872); Pemberton and Worboys, *Rabies in Britain*, pp. 84–90, 133–47.

[49] CO275/39: "Report of Committee Appointed to Enquire into the Question of Rabies in Singapore," p. C22.

[50] Tony O'Dempsey, "Singapore's Changing Landscape since c. 1800," pp. 21–2.

metal plates into which numbers were etched. These plates were then affixed to "pieces of rattan, string or anything that comes to mind." The Hydrophobia Committee recommended that this system be rationalized further. Instead of allowing owners to purchase numbers, and then randomly using them on any dog they chose, they now required each canine to be registered individually, along with their address as well as a description of each dog, including its sex. The number plate would come with "a proper collar to which the number will be riveted." This would also prevent theft, which seems to have been a problem with some owners trying to avoid the regulations. No such system existed in rural areas. This led members of the committee to advocate, "that licenses should be issued in the country as well, and that in principle the system which will be brought into operation in the town should be strictly followed there also." During "the period of repression," the Hydrophobia Committee thus recommended that all of these numbers should be riveted to the muzzle that all dogs would be required to wear throughout the island.[51]

The Hydrophobia Committee also proposed limits to the number of dogs that could be registered at each residence. Their ideal quantity was two dogs per household. "This number is in most cases sufficient for protection purposes, and if any additional dog be licensed it should be on special conditions." In addition, the licensing fee for a dog was raised to $1.50 per year in the municipal limits, and 75 cents elsewhere.[52] The Municipal Commission arranged for the registration of all dogs on the island to take place at police stations and the main Municipal Office. In May 1890, extra officers were posted to the Wayang Satu, Alexandra Road, Geylang and Teluk Blangah police stations, as they "comprised the principal districts of the town in which dogs were kept." In addition, during the "muzzling period," all registered dogs were to be inspected monthly "by a properly qualified

---

[51] CO275/39: "Report of Committee Appointed to Enquire into the Question of Rabies in Singapore," p. C22.

[52] This was a rise from $1 and 50 cents respectively. Any additional dog, beyond the two allowed, would be taxed at $5 per year. Exceptions were "made in favour of packs of dogs kept properly under control for sporting purposes," which reflects the elitist nature of many of these provisions. CO275/39: "Report of Committee Appointed to Enquire into the Question of Rabies in Singapore," p. C23; NA425: MPMC: 26 Mar. 1890, p. 1682.

man, not necessarily a Veterinary Surgeon." Finally, based on the recommendations of the Hydrophobia Committee, the government was given the right to enter private property "for the purpose of killing unregistered dogs and detecting any which may be kept without the necessary license." This was a shift in how the authorities dealt with matters in Singapore. During the culling of dogs in previous decades, any animal within the confines of a residence was safe. The government now regulated all aspects of dog ownership, including the right to enter into private spaces to inspect the animals.[53]

With the passage of these new regulations in 1890, the system of capturing unlicensed dogs and taking them to a pound and drowning them was discontinued. To rid the island of curs, promoters of the new policy argued that "it is generally agreed that the best way of killing stray unregistered dogs is by the use of buck-shot." In rural areas, traps were also to be used. The person overseeing these new provisions was Cheeseman, who was "properly licensed and provided with necessary badges," along with "3 native dog shooters." The Hydrophobia Committee also recommended that rewards not be offered to the dog killers, as "with the class of men which will have to be employed," and rewards would "result in their drawing little or no distinction between registered and unregistered dogs, the muzzles being easily removed and thrown away after the death of the animal." Finally, the Committee recommended that the island be divided into districts for monitoring and enforcement.[54] The key aspect of all of these recommendations was one that was not included. Exile of registered canines to an offshore island was not being considered, at least not at this time.

The patchwork of measures to address the hydrophobia scare was rooted in different understandings of the role of animals in society. As *The Straits Times* decried, "The lion on the path seems to be the inconvenience to the Chinese planter and gardener class, who set great store upon watchdogs as protection against robbers and predatory wild

---

[53] NA425: MPMC: 23 April 1890, p. 1691; 14 May 1890, p. 1698; CO275/39: "Report of Committee Appointed to Enquire into the Question of Rabies in Singapore," pp. C23–4.

[54] In addition, it was recommended that convicts be employed to make the muzzles, which would make them more cost effective. CO273/246/4381: "Report on the Suppression of Rabies," (1899), p. 226; CO275/39: "Report of Committee Appointed to Enquire into the Question of Rabies in Singapore," pp. C24–7.

animals." Opponents to quarantining argued that it would discourage agricultural cultivation and endanger the food supply of Singapore. Even the muzzling of all dogs in Singapore would negate their protective role "from two-legged and four-legged foes." Reid continued his criticism of what he considered to be a shortsighted compromise to appease "our mixed multitude of fatalist and suspicious Asiatics." As he argued, "The short supply of garden produce sinks into insignificance compared with the safety from risk of terrible death which extirpation only confers."[55]

These proposals were seen to be the easiest method of dealing with a difficult situation. As one government official argued, "We believe that by these means rabies can be stamped out with the least hardship and inconvenience to the community in general." Owners could retain their dogs, or at least two of them, during the "period of repression," and with the rise in registration fees, owners "shall be induced to give greater attention to the animal than he has hitherto been in the habit of doing, and to keep down the useless number of dogs about his premises." In April 1890 the Legislative Council approved the various proposals of the Hydrophobia Committee and, as such, regulations related to rabies were added to the "Quarantine and Prevention of Disease Ordinance, 1886."[56]

By mid-1890, legal processes related to dogs with the goal of extinguishing rabies in Singapore were in full force. Dog Inspector Cheeseman reported in the initial months that "no fewer than about 4,000 of the canine race have fallen victims to his prowess," although the number of staff assigned to dog culling and monitoring on the island was limited to two people. During the next year, Cheeseman and his staff continued with their work, killing on average, 60 to 70 dogs per month in the municipality and between 150 and 200 in the rural Singapore.[57]

---

[55] Anonymous, "Report on Rabies," *ST*, 25 Jan. 1890, p. 2.

[56] CO275/39: "Report of Committee Appointed to Enquire into the Question of Rabies in Singapore," p. C22; CO275/39: "The Quarantine and Prevention of Disease Ordinance, 1886," Papers Laid before the Legislative Council, No. 13 (1890), p. C69; CO276/21: "Government Notification, No. 214," (1890), p. 710.

[57] In November 1890, the claim for the number of dogs destroyed was lowered to between 2,000 and 3,000 at an official municipal commissioners meeting. Anonymous, "The Races," *The Daily Advertiser*, 27 Oct. 1890, p. 2; Anonymous, "Divorce," *The Daily Advertiser*, 6 Nov. 1890, p. 3

This raises the question, however, of how serious a health problem rabies actually was in late 19th-century Singapore. In his Annual Report for 1889, Max F. Simon, the surgeon, declared that only three cases of hydrophobia had been fatal. In contrast, 76 people died of cholera during the same period. Over the entire period of rabies suppression in Singapore, from 1884 until 1892, only 21 people sought treatment for hydrophobia in hospitals in Singapore. Even in 1884, during the height of concern related to the disease, more than 14 people died of smallpox while 681 passed away due to "bowel complaints." This meant that the effect, and necessity, of these regulations was exaggerated, which led one report in 1890 to claim, "the inspector of the dog department has cleared the town very considerably, but work remains to be done. Rabies has not been heard of for some time, but this does not mean it is stamped out."[58]

Table 1: Treatment of Hydrophobia at Singaporean Hospitals, 1884–1892.[59]

	General Hospital		Native Police	Pauper Hospital	Total
	Europeans	Natives		Natives	
1884	–	3	–	–	3
1885	–	–	–	–	–
1886	1	2	–	–	3
1887	–	3	–	–	3
1888	–	4	–	–	4
1889	–	1	–	1	2
1890	–	1	–	1	2
1891	–	2	1	1	4
1892	–	–	–	–	–
	1	16	1	3	21

[58] Anonymous, "The Public Health in 1889," *The Straits Times Weekly Issue*, 11 Jun 1890, p. 11; CO275/39: "Report of Committee Appointed to Enquire into the Question of Rabies in Singapore," p. C19; CO276/16: "Government Notification, No. 97" (1885), p. 165; Anonymous, "Medical Report 1888," *ST*, 13 Apr. 1889, p. 5; Anonymous, "The Singapore Debating Society"; Anonymous, Untitled," *The Daily Advertiser*, 23 Oct. 1890, p. 3.

[59] Some of the supposed victims, of course, did not seek treatment at the hospitals, such as the few Europeans who died in the initial outbreak in 1884. The Pauper Hospital was later renamed Tan Tock Seng Hospital. Numbers taken from CO273/246/4381: "Report on the Suppression of Rabies," p. 232.

H.N. Ridley, the Director of the Singapore Botanic Gardens, dismissed many of the accounts of rabies in Singapore during this period. He had witnessed rabid dogs in Oxford and London as a youth and, in a letter he wrote to *The Straits Times* some 15 years after events, claimed that "I have never seen a case in Singapore even during the hydrophobia scare some years ago and am doubtful if there were really any cases of then." Ridley suspected that cases in the 1880s and early 1890s were "false hydrophobia, or death from scare of hydrophobia," and although he was not in a mood to enter a debate best left to "the medical man," he wanted "to say that to raise a hydrophobia scare in a town whether the disease occurs there or not is to my thinking one of the wickedest crimes that any one can commit."[60] This meant that, while there were cases of rabies, the regulations had an influence on the society that went beyond the extirpation of a disease.

"In a Spirit of Oppression and Vulgar Insolence"

Whether it was a disease that was rampant in the society, or a publicly induced mania of "false hydrophobia," reports of the return of rabies to Singapore appeared by the end of 1890, when mad dogs bit "several persons" in December of that year. One fatality was "a Chinese lad living in Neil Road, who was a scholar in the Anglo-Chinese School, and a prize-winner at the recent examination." This rise in cases led Arnot Reid to revive his call for a joint policy of quarantine and extirpation of all dogs, and for further enhanced efforts to rid the island of rabies.[61] The issue now came to be one at the heart of the rural-urban dichotomy on the island.

Reid traced the problem with the new regulations to their applicability only in the municipality, leading him to continue criticizing the government over these issues:

> And even if the Municipality had been able to keep several men at work, the circumstances of life in Singapore, where each house has its compound, would have prevented any thorough work. And even if the municipal officers had been thorough in such work, the fact

---

[60] H.N. Ridley, "The Rabies Scare," *ST*, 20 July 1905, p. 5.

[61] Anonymous, "Hydrophobia Again," *ST*, 28 Apr. 1890, p. 2; Anonymous, "Death from Hydrophobia," *The Daily Advertiser*, 15 Dec. 1890, p. 3; Anonymous, "The Stamping Out of Hydrophobia," *ST*, 15 Dec. 1890, p. 2.

that the Government has neglected the work beyond the municipal area would have rendered the municipal efforts of no avail; for dogs do not recognize the municipal boundaries.

His solution was to re-enact the quarantine—this time for only three months—and "during that period to induce scores of Asiatics to engage in dog-hunting as an easy means of earning money."[62]

The subject of dogs dominated the municipal commissioners meeting on 18 February 1891. The President of the Commissioners, Alexander Gentle, spent much of the time replying to the queries of Thomas Shelford, the President of the Chamber of Commerce. Gentle explained that there had recently been an expansion of dog hunters from the budgeted two men to eight, who roamed the municipality searching for unregistered dogs with "the cheapest and safest guns" available. Coolies armed with shovels to bury the dogs killed accompanied these canine hunters. The discussion then turned to the possibility of enacting a rewards system, which led to a debate over how to provide evidence, with the two main proposals offered being the presentation of the carcass or just the tail of the dead dog. Gentle also reminded Shelford of the limits of enforcement throughout the island of Singapore, as the rural areas were beyond the purview of the Municipal Commission. McCallum recommended that this issue be brought before a meeting of the Executive Council of the Straits Settlement Government.[63]

The next day "an influential deputation" visited Governor Cecil Clementi Smith "in regard to the necessity which is said to exist for taking steps to prevent the spread of hydrophobia in Singapore." At the meeting it was decided

> to enforce muzzling of all dogs throughout the settlement for a period of twelve months, and that all dogs found abroad without muzzles shall be shot, that one muzzle shall be supplied free to each householder outside the Municipality and that any more required must be paid for, that the staff recommended by the Committee of 1889 for carrying out regulation in the country, and that the Legislative Council be asked to vote for the necessary funds, viz. $6000 for half a year.

---

[62] Anonymous, "The Stamping Out of Hydrophobia," *ST*, 15 Dec. 1890, p. 2.
[63] NA425: MPMC: 18 Feb. 1891, pp. 1827–30; Anonymous, "Municipal Commissioners," *ST*, 19 Feb 1891, p. 3.

All agreed to these steps, with Shelford claiming that "his Chinese colleagues" and members of the Chinese Advisory Board were in full support.[64]

In March 1891, the Legislative Council met to finalize this agreement, although the main issue on the agenda that day was the need to raise taxes and monies that the Colonial Office wanted for the upkeep of the military in Singapore. This tax came to be known as the Military Contribution, and it would influence governance and financing in the Straits Settlements for the next several decades. This important topic, however, was pushed to the side due to the agitation of the audience. They wanted the Legislative Council to take part in a discussion on hydrophobia, and how to properly deal with it.[65]

With the passage of "The Singapore Dog Ordinance of 1891" all regulations and rules related to dogs became enforceable throughout the island. Every canine in Singapore was to be registered, and muzzled when outdoors. Owners were required to bring their dogs to the Municipal Office to obtain the license. If they were not able to do so, they had to provide a full description of the dog "written in English" and it "must be handed to the registering officer." The officer then would "properly affix" the badge "bearing the registered number for the current year" to the collar. Each owner would then receive a printed receipt and license "in which shall be entered a description of the dog." Any individual harboring an unregistered dog was subject to a fine of $10. Finally, and most importantly, there was to be a ban on the importation of all dogs into Singapore—"From Johore too?" "Yes, from everywhere"—for a year, beginning 1 June.[66]

The solution after several years of rabies outbreaks, thus, was to register, muzzle, destroy and ban. The decision to muzzle dogs was

---

[64] CO275/43: "Thursday, 19th February, 1891," pp. 17–8; CO273/246/4381: "Report on the Suppression of Rabies," (1899), p. 226; Anonymous, "The Prevention of Hydrophobia," *ST*, 17 Feb. 1891, p. 2; Anonymous, "Municipal Commissioners," *ST*, 19 Feb 1891, p. 3; Anonymous, "The Proposed Legislation to Prevent Hydrophobia," *The Straits Times Weekly Issue*, 18 Feb. 1891, p. 7; NA425: MPMC: 18 Feb. 1891, p. 1829.

[65] Anonymous, "The Legislative Council," *The Straits Times Weekly*, 25 Feb. 1891, p. 4

[66] CO276/22: "Government Notification, No. 120," pp. 360–1; Anonymous, "The Legislative Council," *The Straits Times Weekly*, 25 Feb. 1891, p. 4; NA425: MPMC: 1 Apr. 1891, pp. 1853–4.

seen as a compromise, as quarantining the animals would put dog ownership beyond the reach of many. "On the other hand, muzzling does not cost much, and every man, be he rich or poor, if he so desires, can save his dog." In addition, the government would provide the first muzzle for free. Before the muzzles could arrive, however, a new wave of government-approved dog killing commenced, under the leadership of three more dog inspectors who were hired to help Cheeseman with his responsibilities. It was a period in which, "the Dog exterminators seem to breathe vengeance against the canine tribe. No mercy is shown to poor doggie, and not the ghost of a chance is ever given him to escape the deadly missile."[67]

During this period, in mid-1891, the dog killing free-for-all led to discomfort in society, and had the potential to expose rifts between the ruler and the ruled. In June, a resident was taken to court for threatening the Dog Inspector after the government official entered a compound on Serangoon Road to enquire about dogs that were inside the wall, but not muzzled. The owner of the canines, Victor Charles Valtriny, threatened Cheeseman with a shotgun, and the case dragged through the courts and even became a formal complaint discussed before the municipal commissioners, who quickly grew exasperated with Valtriny's contrariness, labeling him "absurd."[68]

Ridley continued to doubt the necessity for these efforts and was horrified at the behavior of the inspectors, as well as the arrogance of the municipal commissioners. As he recorded in his journals, it was a period in which government officials dismissed any criticism of the system, and even threatened prosecution against anyone who protested. In addition, Ridley claimed that there was a well-known, but never recorded, quota of victims that the dog cullers had to supply or face dismissal. One man who later worked for Ridley told the botanist that during the

---

[67] The new dog inspectors were W. Gombarte, J.C. Neubronner, and C.R. Seiger. NA425: MPMC: 24 June 1891, p. 1884; Anonymous, "Government Action Re Hydrophobia," *The Daily Advertiser*, 10 Mar 1891, p. 2; Anonymous, "Random Notes," *The Daily Advertiser*, 4 July 1891, p. 2; Anonymous, "Dog Statistics," *The Straits Times Weekly Issue*, 10 Nov. 1891, p. 2.

[68] Valtriny was an alcohol merchant who had lived in Singapore since 1854. Maxime Pilon and Danièle Weiler, *The French in Singapore: An Illustrated History (1819–Today)* (Singapore: Editions Didier Millet, 2011), pp. 96–7; Anonymous, "The New Dog Regulations," *ST*, 23 June 1891, p. 2; Anonymous, "Municipal Commissioners," *ST*, 3 Sep. 1891, p. 3; NA425: MPMC: 2 Sep. 1891, p. 1909.

early 1890s, they would "shoot the Chinese's dogs any-how, take the badges and muzzles away, and count that dog into their daily work."[69]

The case of an elderly woman who raised poultry and had three dogs reflects the tenor of the time. It was reported that she traveled into the municipality to register her dogs and get muzzles for them. When informed that all muzzles had been given out, she returned home. "Two hours afterwards it is alleged a dog inspector entered her compound and shot two of her dogs." During this same period, a rumor spread that a Malay boy "was accidentally shot in the forehead by one of the dog killers in firing at a dog." There were also reports that "Chinese out in the Country Districts" would "stand between the gun and the dog at the risk of losing their own lives."[70]

The disquiet over the liberties the dog killers were taking reached an apex in September 1891 when the municipal commissioners received complaints from three dog owners, named Elphick, Thomson and Sahat. The dogs that Elphick and Thomson owned had been muzzled and collared but were without the metal registration tags, which apparently had dropped off. The dogs were shot. While unsavory, the commissioners accepted the explanation that the Dog Inspector offered, and considered a request that H. Starling—in the newly created position of Superintendent of Rabies—be allowed to replace lost badges at his own discretion.[71]

The case of Sahat's dog, which was killed on 24 August 1891, however, was the straw that broke the camel's back. As summarized in the press:

> A dog having been shot, while it was attached by a very short chain to the verandah pillar of a compound house; and while a woman and children were weeping within a few feet of it; and while the woman was praying for her favourite's life, and offering to muzzle the dog, with the muzzle that they had removed to feed it.[72]

---

[69] RGBK, HNR 3/2/3: Notebooks, Vol. 3, p. 127.

[70] There were also reports that many of the muzzles were defective. Owners could remove the "front strap," which would allow the "dogs liberty to bite." NA425: MPMC: 14 Oct. 1891, p. 1927; Anonymous, "Local and General," *The Daily Advertiser*, 9 March 1891, p. 3; Anonymous, "Local and General," 16 Mar. 1891, p. 3; Anonymous, "A Hard Case," *ST*, 30 June 1891, p. 3; Anonymous, "Local and General," *The Daily Advertiser*, 21 Mar. 1892, p. 3.

[71] NA425: MPMC: 16 Sep. 1891, pp. 1914–5.

[72] Anonymous, "The Municipal Dog-Killing," *The Straits Times Weekly Issue*, 7 Oct. 1891, p. 8.

According to reports, Cheeseman had approached the house on Serangoon Road while Sahat was absent. He saw a dog on the verandah, and entered the compound. Despite protests from the lady of the house and her children, he shot the dog, "and blood was shed over the verandah giving the children such a fright they could not get over it for days." Even W.E. Hooper, of the Municipal Commission, condemned the killing of Sahat's dog. Eventually, members of the public raised $25 to help Sahat buy a new dog, and people began to openly criticize a system in which "the net sum of the whole is that the government of Singapore is allowed to be conducted in a spirit of cruel oppression and vulgar insolence."[73]

Facing criticism at the brutality in the dog killing, the commissioners reiterated that the dog inspectors were carrying out their orders, handling a difficult situation, and continued to receive the support of the colonial authorities. At this meeting, however, Cheeseman resigned, which was "accepted without remark."[74] In addition, G.P. Owen replaced Starling as the "Superintendent of Rabies." As a leading member of the community and sportsman, Owen could act as a more sophisticated face of the "Dog Department," which then proceeded to expand its scope and influence. Under his leadership, the staff increased from one inspector and three dog shooters, to one superintendent, five inspectors, ten native dog shooters, and five buriers. These employees were then sent into a newly reorganized space, in which the island was divided into five wards, each having an Inspector, two dog shooters and one burier.[75]

By late 1891 most stray dogs had been cleared from the town. When a mongrel was killed in the urban core it was usually "near the boundary limits and had apparently strayed into the Municipal bounds from the districts beyond." While efforts in the municipality appeared to be successful, there were still "a large number of what are called

---

[73] Anonymous, "Dog Inspector," *ST*, 17 Sep. 1891, p. 2; Anonymous, "Municipal Commissioners," *ST*, 17 Sep. 1891, p. 3; Anonymous, "Municipal Commissioners," *ST*, 1 Oct. 1891, p. 3; Anonymous, "Monday, January 4, 1892," *SFP*, 4 Jan. 1892, p. 2; Anonymous, "The Dog Case," *ST*, 1 Oct. 1891, p. 2.

[74] Within the power structures of the government and elite, the resignation of Cheeseman was considered to be "of little consequence." Cheeseman left Singapore, and died of cholera in Bangkok in 1900. Anonymous, "The Dog Department," *The Daily Advertiser*, 30 Sep. 1891, p. 2; Anonymous, "The Dog Case," *ST*, 1 Oct. 1891, p. 2 NA425: MPMC: 30 Sep. 1891, p. 1921; Anonymous, "Untitled," *ST*, 15 May 1990, p. 2.

[75] CO273/246/4381: "Report on the Suppression of Rabies," (1899), p. 227.

'anjing utan'"—literally "jungle dogs," but meaning those without owners—"that lived in deserted lands and grave yards." This led the usually sardonic Ridley to comment on the change with the aside that, "there were at these times a large number of feral and ownerless dogs about the place and these were mostly destroyed, which was a good thing."[76]

One of the key factors in this change of attitude was a new flexibility displayed among the dog killers following the Sahat case. The commissioners had urged Owen to "see that the regulations were enforced with as little harshness as is compatible with their object," and this advice was put into practice. In addition, as one of the key problems related to enforcement of the new rules had been a limited stock of free muzzles, the arrival of a new supply in November 1891 meant that the killing could be resumed, and domesticated dogs could be properly separated from curs. As one report summarized, "After that every un-muzzled dog could be shot, which simplified matters considerably." During this active period of culling, from September 1891 until May 1892, 13,895 dogs were destroyed.[77]

By March 1892, according to a newspaper report, "it is positively a wonder that there are any more dogs left to kill" in Singapore, which led government officials to begin considering whether the restrictions related to muzzling, registration and importation of canines were still necessary.[78] After meeting with the Executive Council, it was decided to extend the dog regulations for another year, although the issuance of free muzzles was discontinued in April 1892, and the number of personnel in the Rabies Suppression Unit was reduced to one super-intendent and two persons for each post of inspector, native shooter,

---

[76] During the year 1891, 18 dogs "either known to be or supposed to be suffering from rabies" were destroyed. CO273/246/4381: "Report on the Suppression of Rabies," (1899), p. 229; RGBK, HNR 3/2/3: Notebooks, Vol. 3, p. 131; Anonymous, "Municipal Progress in October," *ST*, 26 Nov. 1891, p. 3.

[77] The government had issued 609 free muzzles, while 1,006 were purchased at police stations. CO273/246/4381: "Report on the Suppression of Rabies," (1899), p. 229; CO276/26: "Report on the Work of Suppression of Rabies Outside Municipal Limits, from Commencement to Date," 20 Jan. 1893.

[78] Outside of the municipality culling continued until it reached the outer islands of Singapore by mid-1892, when inspectors landed on Pulau Tekong and Pulau Ubin, and exterminated "no fewer than 86 of the canine tribe." Anonymous, "Local and General," *The Daily Advertiser*, 8 Aug. 1892, p. 3.

and burier by September of that year. The town was also reduced into two districts. Enforcement in the municipality now shifted to regulation and monitoring, with dog inspectors issuing 94 summonses in 1892, of which 77 were required to pay fines.[79]

By early 1893 it appeared that Singapore was escaping from the fog of rabies and the violence used to contain it. In January the government published an assessment of the system that trumpeted its effectiveness. There had not been a reported case of hydrophobia for the entire year of 1892, and the last case had been the death of Chua Kim Soon in October 1891. Much of the credit was given to Owen, who oversaw the inspectors and used his sportsman status to become the symbolic hunter who rid Singapore of dogs. Owen had also supported the dog killers during periods when their actions were under scrutiny and open to criticism—particularly during the Sahat case in which he was the only commissioner to endorse Cheeseman—and reaped the benefits of an enhanced status among the European elite of Singapore. He was the one who "had been able to deal with this pest of rabies so successfully," and now had time for other duties in society, such as a return to the position of secretary of the Cricket Club.[80]

This absence of rabies for two years resulted in the promulgation of "The Singapore Dogs Orders 1893." These new regulations revoked the need for a muzzle within the municipality, although all dogs still needed to be registered and wear a collar with an identifying tag,

---

[79] CO276/26: "Report on the Work of Suppression of Rabies"; CO276/24: "Government Notification, No. 159" (1892), p. 1043; Anonymous, "The Municipal Commission," *SFP*, 31 Mar. 1892, p. 3; Anonymous, "The Dog Regulations," *The Daily Advertiser*, 4 Apr. 1892, p. 3; Anonymous, "Suppression of Rabies," *The Daily Advertiser*, 21 Mar. 1892, p. 3; Anonymous, "The Municipal Commission," *SFP*, 4 Mar. 1892, p. 2; CO273/246/4381: "Report on the Suppression of Rabies," (1899), p. 228.

[80] Although he could now take part in more leisurely pursuits, Owen would remain the Superintendent of the Department for the Suppression of Rabies (as well as the Fire Brigade) for the remainder of the decade. Anonymous, "Municipal Commission," *SFP*, 1 Sep. 1892, p. 2; Gilbert E. Brooke, "Medical Work and Institutions," in *One Hundred Years of Singapore, Being an Account of the Capital of the Straits Settlements from its Foundation by Sir Stamford Raffles on the 6th February 1819 to the 6th February 1919*, vol. I, ed. Walter Makepeace, Gilbert E. Brooke, and Roland St. J. Braddell (London: John Murray, 1921), p. 513; CO276/26: "Report on the Work of Suppression of Rabies"; Anonymous, "Rabies Suppression," *SFP*, 23 Jan. 1893, p. 3.

and the importation of any dog continued to be banned. Any dog without such a collar could be destroyed.[81] The next year, funding for the "The Rabies Department" was eliminated from the budget. The police assumed responsibility for licensing and other related activities, particularly outside the municipality. By mid-1896 the authorities were ready to ease some of the other restrictions even further, as there had not been a report of rabies in Singapore since 1891. Owen announced that there was "no danger of the disease again shewing itself," and proclaimed that throughout the island, "with the exception of an occasional unhealthly looking dog, the present classes of native dogs on the Island are strong and healthy looking and cared for."[82]

As the fear of rabies dissipated among the residents of Singapore, new annoyances related to the system arose. These ranged from thieves stealing badges and collars to elite residents complaining when their dog was killed, although they had no collar and were wandering outside the owner's compound. Due to the presence of rabies in the Netherlands East Indies and the Malay Peninsula, however, Owen advocated a continuation of the ban on importation of dogs "from any Eastern country." He went on to add, however, that "dogs might be imported from Europe under strict quarantine regulations," which "would be a modification appreciated by many who would like to import thorough-bred dogs into the Island." This compromise was rejected. The importation of dogs would be banned for the remainder of the decade.[83]

The suppression of rabies was a triumph for the Municipal Commission, as well as the Straits Settlements government. Official programs had rid the island of a scourge, and brought under control the dog

---

[81] The withdrawal of muzzling restrictions was contrary to the recommendation of the Municipal Commissioners. Governor Smith vetoed the provision, as it "proved irritating and harassing." Anonymous, "H.E.'s Veto in Municipal Affairs," *The Straits Times Weekly Issue*, 28 Mar. 1893, p. 2; CO276/24: "Government Notification, No. 163" (1893), pp. 578–9; CO273/246/4381: "Report on the Suppression of Rabies," (1899), p. 228; NA 426: MPMC: 15 Feb. 1893, p. 2158; 15 Mar. 1893, pp. 2169–70.

[82] Anonymous, "Unlicensed Dogs," *The Mid-Day Herald*, 8 Jan. 1895, p. 2; CO276/28: "Government Notification, No. 275" (1894), pp. 734; Anonymous, "Official Report of the Legislative Council Meeting," *The Mid-Day Herald*, 24 Apr. 1896, p. 2.

[83] Anonymous, "Mr. Owen's Rabies Report," *ST*, 9 May 1896, p. 2; CO273/246/4381: "Report on the Suppression of Rabies," (1899), pp. 228–9; NA426: MPMC: 12 Oct. 1898, p. 3329.

nuisance that had plagued the residents for decades. During the 1890s over 22,000 dogs were killed in Singapore, according to government records, while the number of registered dogs in the municipality was less then 3,000. The only drawback, according to the official government report, was that dogs—such as fox terriers, spaniels and setters—had "greatly degenerated from lack of new stock and hardly a pure bred dog is now to be met with." By 1899, however, the Chief Medical Officer proclaimed that, "Rabies has been completely stamped out of the Island of Singapore." This occurred three years before rabies was eradicated in another island on the other side of the world: Britain in 1902.[84]

To start the new century, Owen, the Superintendent of Rabies Suppression, wanted to return on home leave to England. Government officials approved his sabbatical request and used his absence to ease many of the strict regulations related to dogs. Beginning in August 1900, dog owners could now attach the registration badge to their pet's collar outside the presence of a government official. More importantly, canines were now allowed ashore from ships, as long as they went directly to the quarantine station for animals that the municipality had established on St. John's Island. The owner of the dog would then pay any fees for the period of upkeep and inspections.[85] This established the quarantine and importation rules for dogs that were in place for the remainder of the colonial period in Singapore. Canines were to be allowed, but only if they were monitored, registered and controlled, as well as approved by colonial society.

Disease, Animals and Imperial Control

While Singaporean authorities were monitoring the movement of dogs on the island in the last decade of the 19th century due to an outbreak of rabies, another disease began to spread throughout Asia that would test the limits of science and regulation, all-important components of imperial rule. This disease was bubonic plague, which had devastated much of Eurasia in the 14th century, killing at least a third of the

---

[84] Similar anti-rabies regulations, including licensing, were also enacted in Hong Kong after Singapore had successfully done so. Poon, "Dogs and British Colonialism," p. 316; Pemberton and Worboys, *Rabies in Britain*, p. 1; CO273/246/4381: "Report on the Suppression of Rabies," (1899), pp. 230–1.

[85] NA427: MPMC: 20 June 1900, p. 3885; 15 Aug. pp. 3931–3.

global population. While it never again reached such levels of morbidity, the plague remained present for centuries, occasionally bursting into epidemics that would devastate societies, as happened in southwestern China in the mid-19th century. By early 1894, bubonic plague reached Guangzhou, where it killed 80,000 people in six months and spread to the nearby city of Hong Kong. By 1896 it had reached Singapore and Bombay, where it led to riots. In what came to be known as the third pandemic of black plague, the disease eventually spread throughout the world, entering ports ranging from Honolulu and Sydney to Glasgow and Buenos Aires. The response, in the words of historian David Arnold, was "a new interventionism" on behalf of colonial governments, which were becoming adept at studying, regulating and enforcing the interaction of humans and animals to prevent the further spread of diseases.[86]

Following the outbreak in southern China, the British government commissioned Alexandre Yersin—a doctor at the Pasteur Institute in Vietnam—to travel to Hong Kong to help with the study and treatment of victims. During this period, alongside Japanese colleague Kitasato Shibasaburo, Yersin identified the bacillus for the first time. Following this breakthrough, imperial nations throughout the world gathered at international conferences and diplomatic meetings to establish measures to address the disease. At an international conference held in Venice in 1897, many of these governments adopted quarantine and diplomatic procedures in preparation for another potential plague outbreak. These measures reflect that, although the causal agent of the disease had been identified, an actual treatment was yet to be developed. The cornerstone of the advocated approach was the isolation of the infected and destruction of carriers, all of which had been used to counter rabies during the previous decade. This became necessary when the plague bacillus re-entered global trade networks in the early 20th century, along with its tremendous potential to wreak havoc.[87]

---

[86] David Arnold, *Colonizing the Body: State Medicine and Epidemic Disease in Nineteenth-Century India* (Berkeley, CA: University of California Press, 1993), p. 203; Myron Echenberg, "Pestis Redux: The Initial Years of the Third Bubonic Plague Pandemic, 1894–1901," *Journal of World History* 13, 2 (2002): 429–49.

[87] Philip Ziegler, *The Black Death* (Harmondsworth: Penguin, 1970); Echenberg, "Pestis Redux"; E.G. Pryor, "The Great Plague of Hong Kong," *Journal of the Royal Asiatic Society of Great Britain and Ireland-Hong Kong Branch* 15, 69 (1975): 61–70.

Such havoc threatened Singapore in early 1901, when bubonic plague reappeared in the British imperial city. This first came to the attention of the authorities after a coolie in Tanjong Pagar named Permal died from the disease. A good friend of the deceased, Sammy, reported the death to the Municipal Health Officer and led him back to their quarters on Tapah Street. The authorities transferred the body to the morgue. Although none of the outward symptoms could be seen, an autopsy of Permal's spleen produced evidence of plague bacilli in abundance. Permal had worked at 89 Market Street, and one of his colleagues had contracted the disease the previous month, resulting in his quarantine at St. John's Island. When another Indian coolie died on 16 February, and tested positive for the bacillus, all of his housemates were removed and placed under a similar quarantine. The government subsequently announced that all passengers scheduled to leave Singapore were now required to undergo a health check at the dock before embarkation. Six residents of Singapore, four Tamil and two Chinese, died of the plague that month. All were coolies.[88]

Beyond quarantining coolies who may have been infected, the government sprang into action. The authorities had been prepared for such an event. Reports from Calcutta and Hong Kong on the situation were prominently featured in the press, and were often the subject of discussions in the Executive Council of the Straits Settlements every time they met in the first six months of 1901. Two years earlier, with the passage of The Plague Ordinance 1899, a direct result of the international meetings, officials could take a variety of measures during an outbreak, including quarantine and disinfecting places, people and items thought to house the bacillus. With the death of six residents in 1901, and based in this earlier legislation and concerns, the government announced a prohibition against the importation of rags, sacks, used carpets, and raw animal hides as well as hoofs, horns and animal hair. Each of these items was appealing to rats, which often found refuge in them on ships and in warehouses and were the traditional carriers of the disease. When no further deaths from bubonic plague followed, Governor Frank Swettenham ordered the enforcement of the ordinance suspended two weeks later.[89]

---

[88] CO276/42: "Notice No. 160," p. 243; "Notice No. 239 and No. 240," p. 338; "Notice No. 301," p. 381.

[89] CO276/39: "Notice 1127," pp. 2346–7; CO275/62: Executive Council Meeting Minutes, p. 39; CO276/42: "Notice No. 305," p. 401; "Proclamation," p. 477.

This earlier legislation had also spurred the government to work on preventative measures to limit the spread of disease in Singapore in the year leading up to the death of Permal from an isolated outbreak. In anticipation of such an event, the Government authorized the Sanitary Board to offer a reward of 2 cents for every dead rat brought to their offices beginning in early 1900. Initially, the program was not very successful, with only 759 rats surrendered in the first few months. The municipal commissioners then raised the bounty to 3 cents, and promoted police stations as collection points for the animals, "dead or alive," which resulted in "scavengers" bringing in 35–40 rats per day by April.[90]

By June 1900, the rat collection program took off, averaging 325 rats a day, which rose to 445 per day by August. A system soon developed in which dead rats were taken to rickshaw depots, where they were placed in carts for removal to an incinerator. The carts would often remain for days, gathering carcasses. When this led to many rickshaw coolies falling sick at the Kreta Ayer depot, the authorities placed the blame on this underclass, as they had awaited collection "too long." While the program was to end in December 1900, the first victim of the plague died in Tan Tock Seng Hospital and Permal soon followed, necessitating a continuation of the program into the next year. Eventually, an estimated 161,000 rats were destroyed in the first year of the exercise.[91]

By the early 20th century Singapore was a vibrant, modern port that played a key role in British interests. It was the capital of the Straits Settlements, and effectively all of Malaya, the home of

---

[90] In May 1900, a Chinese scavenger entered the Kreta Ayer Depot with four rats nailed to a board, the traditional method of presenting them for a reward. Instead, he was arrested for cruelty to animals, as one of the rats with a metal spike through its body was still alive. Anonymous, "That Rat, "*SFP*, 25 Jan. 1900, p. 3; Anonymous, "Municipal Commission," *SFP*, 12 Apr. 1900, p. 3; Anonymous, "Municipal Commission, *SFP*, 25 May 1990, p. 3; Anonymous, "Untitled," *SFP*, 26 May 1990, p. 2; Anonymous, "Cruelty to Rats," *ST*, 31 May 1900, p. 3. I would like to thank Lock Hui Qi for initially drawing my attention to this material.

[91] Anonymous, "Rats!," *ST*, 20 June 1900, p. 3; Anonymous, "Municipal Commission," *ST*, 5 July 1900, p. 3; Anonymous, "Municipal Commission," *SFP*, 30 Aug. 1900, p. 3; Anonymous, "Untitled, *ST*, 27 Dec. 1900, p. 2; Anonymous, Municipal Commission," *ST*, 11 Apr. 1901, p. 3.

government and commerce in the region. It was an imperial city, one of dozens scattered throughout the world through which goods, humans and animals passed, and sometimes stayed. These urban spaces developed, and rule and regulations concerning the interaction of all of its creatures came to encompass a variety of activities that assisted the authorities in controlling and protecting the residents of the port to ensure the smooth operation of the economy and society. These efforts to control the plague through quarantines, control, and animal destruction were considered to be a success, as the number of deaths in Singapore was limited and the disease was kept at bay. It reflected the benefits of regulation that imperial rule had brought to the region, and an application of the lessons learned during the Mad Dog Scare of the 1880s and 1890s. Humans and other animals continued to inhabit the space of Singapore, while the various institutions that had been created to monitor and oversee this interaction continued. Whether it was shifting understandings of how to define cruelty or even keep and register a pet, the relationships would continue to develop within a colonial society, setting standards of governance for all of the inhabitants that lived on a small island in Southeast Asia.

The regulation and monitoring of animals, and its relationship to disease prevention, continued throughout the remainder of the colonial era in Singapore. Occasionally, these efforts would gain the attention of the government, such as in 1909, when it received reports of outbreaks of rabies in Java and Penang. As a preventative measure, there was a sustained anti-rabies and dog culling exercise that resulted in a drop in the number of registered dogs from 4,840 to 2,594 following the destruction of 3,200 canines.[92] Dog culling and quarantining remained constants on the island, representing the thin line between pet and stray, civilized and savage, control and chaos.

The registration of domestic pets, and their inclusion in the household, continued throughout the colonial era, thus setting a standard for which animals were acceptable to the society. Any animal that breached accepted norms was subject to violence. This can be seen in 1935 when there were 8,572 registered dogs in Singapore, while "9,698 others were destroyed either by guns or by lethal means." Four Tamil dog shooters, who roamed "the districts every day between six in the morning and six in the evening" carried out these campaigns. They were "the equal of

---

[92] Anonymous, "Singapore in 1909," *ST*, 5 July 1910, p. 7.

any shot gun expert in Malaya" and "seldom use two cartridges to kill." Dogs killed outside the municipality were buried, while those in the town were brought on carts to an incinerator in Geylang. Their efforts led J.T. Forbes, the Municipal Veterinary Surgeon, to proclaim that "Singapore is remarkably free from unlicensed dogs as compared with any other town in the East," before adding "the average dog here is fairly healthy." Due to continuing restrictions on the importation of "foreign dogs" and the dog shooting campaigns, rabies had been kept at bay since the 1890s. In addition, "it may not be generally known that a householder owning a licensed gun is empowered to shoot, or otherwise destroy, any unlicensed or ownerless dog he finds in his garden."[93]

Alongside the efforts to limit and regulate the canine population of Singapore was a corresponding celebration of spectacles that catered to the economic, social and political elite of the colonial port, setting an ideal for the human-animal relationship. Much of this can be seen in dog shows that were held on an annual basis in the late colonial era. The one for 1936 serves as an illustration. In January of that year, The Malayan Kennel Club, which was affiliated with The Kennel Club, London, held their third annual gathering in which well-to-do residents of Singapore could display their dogs at the new racetrack on Bukit Timah Road. With 73 different classes of dogs, and 106 entries, it was a celebration of breeding and class with the most popular dogs being smooth fox terriers (22 entries), followed by Alsatians and cocker spaniels (16 entries, each), reflecting the popularity of these canines in elite Singaporean society. The vast majority of these dogs were European owned, with the prominent exception being those under the care of Sultan Ibrahim of Johor, who owned at least 13 animals in the competition.[94] At the end of the proceedings Lady Thomas, the wife of the Governor, presented to E.C. Stevens, the wife of a leading police

---

[93] In the first half of 1937, there was an outbreak of distemper, which authorities believed was rooted in the stray dog population, leading to curs being shot in public at a rate of 40 per day at the height of the campaign. As ten dogs were registered every day that year, there was a 4:1 ratio of killing to pet ownership during this brief period. Anonymous, "Gunfire Slaughters Singapore's Night-Yowling Dogs," *ST*, 9 July 1936, p. 12.

[94] Other prominent Asian or local participants included Tan Chin Tuan, Tan Chong Chew, Seet Sian Tuan and E.S. Manasseh. Anonymous, *Catalogue of the Singapore Dog Show*.

administrator, The Malayan Kennel Club Association Singapore Cup for a blue roan cocker spaniel that she cherished. The dog, however, had been bred outside of Malaya. The prize for best locally bred dog went to "Brutus," an Alsatian under the care of L. Carrard.[95]

The dichotomy between domesticated and diseased, imported and elite, as well as efforts to control and regulate their presence—including efforts to limit stray dogs, and even kill potentially plague-ridden rats—came to the fore in 1937. In April of that year a dog arrived in Singapore from Zamboanga in the Philippines. Although the owner had a variety of official certificates proclaiming the health of the canine, and proof of anti-rabies vaccination, it was placed in quarantine for two months until a final certificate arrived from the Philippines stating that no rabies had been present on Mindanao Island for six months. The dog, however, was harboring the virus. On 20 August, it bit a European man and a Chinese woman, and was taken to the animal infirmary. This was the first case of rabies and hydrophobia in Singapore in over 30 years. As advances had been made in vaccines and cures, the authorities had a store of treatments available to them. The man and woman immediately received the "anti-rabic Pasteur treatment"; the dog died on 25 August.[96]

The government sprang into action, and the approach the authorities took was familiar, as it ranged from "mass shootings, to muzzling and to inoculation." The government announced that no dog was permitted "out of doors ... unless it is led by a chain or lead of strong cord or leather so as to be at all times in effective control or wears a muzzle in such a manner as to render it impossible for the dog to inflict a bite." Any canine in Singapore found otherwise, "may be destroyed by any person whomsoever." There were also orders to inoculate all dogs with the anti-rabies vaccine, and owners were required to take their pets to the old Racecourse Road buildings along Kampong Java Road for this specific purpose. Meanwhile, 36 individuals—ranging from Atan bin Ahmat to Max Pereira—were conferred powers to destroy

---

[95] Anonymous, "Singapore Dog Show Results," *MT*, 20 Jan. 1936, p. 15; Anonymous, *Catalogue of the Singapore Dog Show*.
[96] CO275/149: "Report on the Veterinary Department, Malaya, for the Year 1937," p. 937; Anonymous, "A Happy Day in Store for Singapore's Dogs," *ST*, 20 Mar. 1938, p. 5.

dogs and enter private houses to enforce the rules. Dogs in Singapore, in the words of a newspaper article, were "having a bad time" in late 1937 and early 1938.[97]

During this period, which was in force until May 1938 when Singapore was declared rabies free, some residents objected to the "drastic measures" enacted, particular muzzling and the right of inspectors to enter compounds, much like their predecessors a half a century earlier. This led to calls to revive the SPCA, which had been "active and moribund at intervals during the past few years."[98] In this context, "A Real Dog Lover," began to ask some very pointed questions that provide a picture of domestic pets and their relationship to larger society in late colonial Singapore. Among his queries were, "Why are poor dumb animals made to pander to the whims and fancies of wealthy cranks and exploiters?"; and why are dog breeds that are suited to cold climates allowed to be imported into tropical Singapore? His ultimate conclusion was that "so-called dog fanciers and profiteers with imported pedigreed dogs are usually the people to blame!"[99]

The role that "so-called dog fanciers and profiteers" played in society was one that had marked the development of domestic pets and the regulations placed over them for over five decades. The same people who had purchased "fancy dogs" from the *Oxfordshire* in 1884 and those that owned animals ill-suited to the tropical climate of the

---

[97] While 12,125 canines were vaccinated, another 7,938 were destroyed. CO276/145: No. 2483: The Quarantine and Prevention of Disease Ordinance (Chapter 186), p. 2465; CO276/145: No. 2782: The Quarantine and Prevention of Disease Ordinance (Chapter 186), p. 2783–4; CO276/145: No. 2783: The Quarantine and Prevention of Disease Ordinance (Chapter 186) and the Quarantine (Veterinary) Rules, 1936, p. 2785; Anonymous, "Rabies Case in Singapore," *SFP*, 28 Aug. 1937, p. 9 CO275/151: "Report on the Veterinary Department, Malaya, for the Year 1938," p. 485.

[98] R. Onraet, the Inspector-General of the Police, was the president of the Society, reflecting the intersection of policing, monitoring and cruelty in colonial society. Anonymous, "S.P.C.A. Revival Planned," *ST*, 26 Sep. 1937, p. 4; Frederick Jones-Davies, "Much Animal Cruelty Could Be Avoided," *ST*, 1 Oct. 1937, p. 12; Animal Lover, "Dog-Shooting," *ST*, 5 Oct. 1937, p. 12; A Dog Lover, "Objection to Rabies Rules," *ST*, 16 Sep. 1937, p. 16; Anonymous, "New Leash of a Dog's Life: No More Muzzles," *MT*, 3 May 1938, p. 12; CO276/148: No. 1299: The Quarantine and Prevention of Disease Ordinance (Chapter 186), p. 1293.

[99] A Real Dog Lover and Once a Member of the S.P.C.A. Committee, "Are Cold-Climate Dogs Suited to Singapore," *SFP*, 3 Sep. 1937, p. 7.

city in the late 1930s were participating in the public display of control and wealth, and imperial control. They were able to afford animals that had been genetically manipulated to have characteristics their owners desired, and they were chosen to be part of the colonial society. While they may have carried disease with them was but a distraction. Through monitoring, control and destruction of those without desired characteristics, canines and humans could continue to interact in a society that had boundaries, rules and regulations that reinforced class, power, wealth and science.

CHAPTER SIX

Markets, Proteins and the Public Abattoirs

Isabella Bird, a popular travel writer in the late 19th century, visited Singapore in 1879. Bird spent a few days in the main hub of the Straits Settlements, mainly resting at the bungalow of the Colonial Secretary and marveling at the vibrant life in the streets, particularly the clothing on display. Beyond the small number of Europeans who dressed in a manner that left her exasperated, the rest of population dazzled her with "every Oriental costume from the Levant to China." Parsees wore "spotless white," Jews and Arabs were in "dark rich silks," and Indians had clothes of "red and white" with the merchants standing out in their "great white turbans, full trousers, and draperies, all white, with crimson silk girdles." Finally, Malays in red sarongs and Chinese "of all classes, from the coolie in his blue and brown cotton, to the wealthy merchant in his frothy silk crepe and rich brocade" caught her eye. For the visitor used to the "ugly, graceless clothes" of her "dim, pale" home island of Britain, Singaporean fashion was "an irresistibly fascinating medley."[1]

The diverse proteins found in the markets, restaurants, kitchens and streets of this British-controlled port also echoed this fascinating

---

[1] When viewing the dress of passers-by in Singapore in 1936, Jean Cocteau remarked, "In the East all eccentricities of dress are subject to a code." Cocteau, *Round the World Again*, p. 115; Bird, *The Golden Chersonese*, pp. 144–5.

medley. The variety of meat available in colonial Singapore was of such a range that it often startled visitors, such as one American who expressed his astonishment with the poultry found in the market because "it includes a great deal more here than at home; as we found not only chickens, ducks, geese and other familiar things, but a great variety of pigeons, quails, pheasants, and other edible birds from the forest." In addition to such birds, visitors could also partake in the flesh of pigs, fish, turtles, and even the occasional tiger. This assortment of protein led John Thomson to use it as an encapsulation of the vibrant makeup of Singapore, as "the pork-hating Jew of Persia embraces the pork-loving Chinese of Chinchew. The cow-adoring Hindoo of Benares hugs the cow-slaying Arab of Juddah."[2]

Ruling over the cosmopolitan mix of residents, and their dietary preferences, was a highly influential European community, which regulated the society in a manner that applied British understandings of proper governance and civilization to the colony. A remarkable aspect of those who exercised imperial power and determined policy was their low population numbers, as Europeans never made up more than a thousand residents in Singapore throughout the 19th century.[3] Thus was the power of imperialism and the right to determine societal standards and rules. In this society Britons were able to enact regulations that would influence the basic lives of everyone, including the diet, which centered on a few key proteins, mainly fish, pork and beef.[4]

For the British community in Singapore, beef was central to their diet and national identity. This was based in the belief that consumption of the meat was intimately related to an increased vigor and corresponding moral authority, leading Britons to consider their nation to be the "greatest beef-eating country in the world" by the late 19th

---

[2] Knox, *The Boy Travellers in the Far East*, pp. 302–3; Bird, *The Golden Chersonese*, p. 139; Thomson, *Some Glimpses into Life in the Far East*, p. 16.

[3] This meant that, "the presence of one Her Majesty's frigates might double that number." Thomson, *Some Glimpses into Life in the Far East*, p. 206.

[4] John Crawfurd, *Journal of an Embassy from the Governor-General of India to the Courts of Siam and Cochin-China: Exhibiting a View of the Actual State of Those Kingdoms* (London: H. Colburn, 1828), p. 554; Frank Vincent, *The Land of the White Elephant: Sights and Scenes in South-Eastern Asia: A Personal Narrative of Travel and Adventure in Farther India, Embracing the Countries of Burma, Siam, Cambodia, and Cochin-China, 1871–2* (London: S. Low, Marston, Low and Searle, 1873), p. 109.

century.[5] Combined with a love for mutton, most likely arising out of their longer and deeper connections to India, British observers were flustered when they surveyed the culinary landscape of Singapore in search of their comfort protein. As Charles Walter Kinoch complained in the 1850s, "no good beef or mutton is to be had on the island." W.H. Read issued a similar grievance when he recounted a story of a British sea captain in Singapore who faced a mutinous crew, as "beef can not be had in this country" and had attempted to substitute turtle meat to satiate the desire for protein among his sailors. Henry Keppel summarized the problem as one of climate and landscape, as "the countries of the Archipelago are generally not suited to pasture, and it is only in a few of them that the ox and buffalo are abundant.... Cattle, therefore, must be imported."[6]

While beef was an obsession among Europeans, fish—both fresh and salted—was the main protein in the Southeast Asian diet. As historian Anthony Reid has written, "a meal of rice was not complete without at least some fish." As Singapore was not only a British imperial port but also a Southeast Asian entrepôt, this also was true. There are accounts that many of the fishermen of Melaka followed William Farquhar to the new East India Company trading post soon after its establishment in 1819. They initially used handlines some 200 meters from the shore to catch their prey, although this quickly changed. According to Munshi Abdullah, "when the Singapore Settlement was a year old there came a certain Malacca man named Haji Mata-mata. He constructed large fish-traps with rows of stakes called *belat* and *kelong*." The first *kelong* (an offshore platform and fish trap) was

---

[5] Thomas Walley, *A Practical Guide to Meat Inspection* (Edinburgh: Young J. Pentland, 1890), p. 3; Chris Otter, "Civilizing Slaughter: The Development of the British Public Abattoir, 1850–1910," in *Meat, Modernity, and the Rise of the Modern Slaughterhouse*, ed. Paula Young Lee (Durham, NH: University of New Hampshire Press, 2008), p. 89.

[6] Among the first items William Farquhar ordered be brought to Singapore from Melaka were "supplies of buffalo and other live stock as you can conveniently carry," IOR/L10: Singapore: Letters to Bencoolen: "Letter to Captain Harris," 19 Feb. 1819, p. 21; 'Bengal Civilian,' *Rambles in Java and the Straits in 1852* (Singapore: Oxford University Press, 1987), p. 17; Henry Keppel, *The Expedition to Borneo of H.M.S. Dido for the Suppression of Piracy: with Extracts from the Journal of James Brooke, Esq., of Sarawak*, vol. 2 (London: Chapman and Hall, 1846), p. 220; An Old Resident, *Play and Politics*, p. 175.

constructed opposite Teluk Ayer, near Tanjong Malang. It became well known as place where many mackerel (*tengirri*) were caught, and Abdullah describes the fish traps as often full. "In fact, such vast surfeit that the fish could not be eaten and had to be thrown away. Their roes were taken out, put in barrels containing salt, and sold as a regular commodity to ships." This continued under John Crawfurd, the second Resident of Singapore, who wrote that "the greatest plenty of fish, and also the best quality," was found in the shallow seas near the island. A variety of methods were employed to gather these fish, ranging from hooks and lines to weirs and traps. Eventually, two methods prevailed, and they were based on community preferences. Malay residents usually employed permanent stakes, while Chinese fisherman more commonly used nets.[7]

While Britons preferred beef and Southeast Asians enjoyed fish, Chinese residents were the main consumers of pork in Singapore. The meat was so associated with the community that one survey described it as "almost exclusively enjoyed by the Oriental." Europeans, meanwhile, considered it to be a protein best consumed in colder climates. As Chinese migrants made up some 80 percent of the population throughout the colonial era, pork dominated the protein landscape with a similar percentage of pigs being slaughtered for meat in Singapore by the late 19th century. To ensure a steady supply in the early years of colonial rule, John Crawfurd issued an appeal for the development of a pork farm in November 1823, when the population reached 10,000 residents. Under the early Company-led government this was a farm in the sense that it allowed the owner of the license the right to sell pork, but in this instance also allowed the holder to raise pigs on the island. This early initiative provided "the most numerous and industrious of our population" with "one of the principal necessities of life."[8]

---

[7] Anthony Reid, *Southeast Asia in the Age of Commerce, Volume 1*, p. 29; Cameron, *Our Tropical Possessions in Malayan India*, pp. 134–5; Abdullah, *The Hikayat Abdullah*, pp. 142–3; Reeves and Reeves, "Port-City Development and Singapore's Inshore and Culture Fisheries," pp. 123–4.

[8] By the 1830s the revenue the pork farm produced was used to support a basic public hospital along Stamford Road. Anonymous, "Singapore Pork Farm," *Singapore Chronicle and Commercial Register*, 17 Mar. 1831, p. 2; Buckley, *An Anecdotal History of Singapore*, pp. 78, 150; Anonymous, "The Food Supply: Chinese and Their Exclusive Delicacy," *ST*, 27 Apr. 1907, p. 7.

Image 6.1: Market scene, 1890s. Courtesy of National Archives of Singapore.

Residents purchased pork from butchers scattered throughout the town, as well as at a market the government quickly established at Teluk Ayer, where fish and poultry were also readily available. This market opened in 1825, replacing an earlier fish market that was located along the Singapore River, and became the only centralized place to purchase meat and vegetables in Singapore for the next 20 years.[9] In 1845, Ellenborough Market began to provide similar services. As it was located next to the Singapore River, this new market specialized in fish and other products from the sea. To supplement these two markets, the newly established municipal government created Clyde Terrace Market and Rochor Market in the 1870s, followed by Orchard Road Market in 1894.[10]

---

[9] At the time Teluk Ayer Market was on the sea, allowing boats to transfer their goods directly to the stalls and stallholders. An octagonal structure was originally constructed in 1836, and further expanded in 1894. Nicole Tarulevicz, *Eating Her Curries and Kway: A Cultural History of Food in Singapore* (Urbana, Ill: University of Illinois Press, 2013), p. 12–3; Leong Foke Meng, "Early Land Transactions in Singapore: The Real Estates of William Farquhar (1774–1839), John Crawfurd (1783–1868), and Their Families," *JMBRAS* 77, 1 (2004): 29.
[10] Crawfurd, *Journal of an Embassy*, p. 556; Hallifax, "Municipal Government," p. 333.

Anna Brassey, a travel writer, visited one of these markets (most likely Teluk Ayer Market) in the 1870s, and described it as being divided into sections based on the type of meat for sale. The fish were sold in an area that was "the cleanest, and best arranged, and sweetest smelling that I ever went through. It is situated on a sort of open platform, under a thick thatched roof, built out over the sea, so that all the refuse is easily disposed of and washed away by the tide." Two jetties ran out from the platform so fishing boats could offload their cargo directly into the market. The poultry section, on the other hand, was a chaotic and "curious place." It was "alive with birds in baskets, cages, and coops, or tied by the leg and thrown down anyhow," while the air was filled with "quacking, cackling, gobbling, and crowing." Brassey described it as "marvelous."[11]

The five markets of 19th-century Singapore provided access to a variety of foods and goods for the residents of the island with limited government oversight for the first seven decades of colonial rule. Fish were sold fresh and fowls were usually alive, as "the heat is so great at Singapore ... it would begin to decay in a very short time after being slaughtered." Visitors, thus, found "most of the chickens were in coops, or tied together by the legs; and the same was the case with the geese and ducks." Larger animals, such as pigs, were slaughtered at private butcheries, and the meat sold from the front of these establishments or in the markets. As long as the populace had access to the basic components of their diet, little attention was paid to these sites, and they did not appear to be a problem for most of the century. As one observer noted in the 1850s, "there is always a supply ... of good fish in the market, and with that and Chinese pork, the residents are content."[12]

Although most residents seemed content to consume fish, turtle and pork they purchased at these markets, it did not satiate the British obsession with beef. In addition, unlike chickens and pigs, which were reared in Singapore, and fish caught along its shores, beef and other staples had to be imported, arriving through vast shipping networks

---

[11] Anna Brassey, *A Voyage in the 'Sunbeam,'* p. 411.

[12] Another common protein found at the butcheries and markets in the 19th century was turtle meat, which was so plentiful that "turtle-soup is anything but a luxury" and the flesh was "ordinarily sold." "Bengal Civilian," *Rambles in Java and the Straits in 1852*, pp. 17–8; Hallifax, "Municipal Government," p. 334.

Image 6.2: Poultry in baskets. Courtesy of the New York Public Library.

into a functioning and efficient port.[13] The consumption of these proteins thus became a nexus for a variety of issues, ranging from cruelty to regulation, which reflects imperial concerns and the role of animals in the colony. Ultimately, the industrialization of this process in Singapore, through the development of public abattoirs to replace the scores of private butcheries in the municipality, would symbolize the introduction of the benefits of an imperial presence through the creation of a sanitary regime.

The imposition of this sanitary regime was rooted in global efforts to regulate, control and create societies that were healthier, and more governable. As Lynn Hollen Lees has identified, such regulation was "the mainspring of municipal action," particularly in the Straits Settlements, and it would come to represent a triumph of Western civilization in Southeast Asia.[14] Through a Sanitary Board and various government departments that focused on areas such as health and the development of infrastructure, a disciplining and control of the society proceeded. In Singapore, scholars such as Brenda Yeoh and Goh Chor Boon have

---

[13] As Thomson wrote, with regard to foodstuffs, Singapore had "always been dependent on Java, Siam, and Bengal," particularly for rice. Thomson, *Sequel to Some Glimpses into Life*, p. 239; Otter, "Civilizing Slaughter."
[14] Lynn Hollen Lees, "Discipline and Delegation: Colonial Government in Malayan Towns, 1880–1930," *Urban History* 38, 1 (2011): 48–64.

brought attention to these efforts at sanitary reform in the municipality, particularly with regard to housing, public sewerage and water systems.[15] Attempts to monitor dogs and other animals in the household, and prevent the spread of infectious diseases, ran parallel to such efforts. Permutations in this sanitary regime also influenced the management and delivery of animal proteins to a colonial populace. With regard to animal husbandry and slaughterhouses, after all, the distancing of the act of killing, as well as making it more rational and efficient, not only provided protein to a colonial populace, but also reduced the spread of disease and allowed for monitoring of consumption. This process began with rationalization of the trade that brought these animals into the port, and maintained them prior to slaughter.

Regulating Animal Husbandry

Beginning with the transfer of authority from the East India Company to the Colonial Office in 1867, the government began a new phase in the rearing and treatment of animals in Singapore, particularly those that were to be consumed. In this regard, the maintenance of spaces in which they were kept, and their relationship to sanitation, quickly came under scrutiny. For instance, in December 1874, the municipal commissioners rejected an appeal from bullock cart owners along Macao Street (now Hongkong Street) to keep ten bullocks in "their pent-up stables," as it "would materially improve the sanitary condition of the neighborhood where they now congregate, and where, not long ago, the cholera found numerous victims owing to the accumulated filth." While this case focused on work animals, and fed into the need for a Society for the Prevention of Cruelty to Animals (SPCA, after 1900 the PCA), over the next two decades such concerns shifted to the food supply, as government authorities promulgated legislation that regulated the rearing of animals that were to be consumed, with fines often used to punish purveyors of tainted meat. An example of such efforts includes the imposition of a $50 fine on a "Kling salesman" in 1886 "for selling beef unfit for human food."[16]

---

[15] Yeoh, *Contesting Space*; Goh, *Technology and Entrepôt Colonialism in Singapore*, pp. 120–42; Lynn Hollen Lees, *Planting Empire, Cultivating Subjects: British Malaya, 1786–1941* (Cambridge: Cambridge University Press, 2017), pp. 121–5.

[16] Anonymous, "Municipal Commissioners," *ST*, 16 Jan. 1875, p. 2; Anonymous, "The Municipality," *The Straits Times Weekly Issue*, 10 June 1886, p. 6.

These rules and regulations were part of a system that transformed living animals into food relatively quickly. Beef cattle and other mammals imported as food, after all, were not expected to live for long in Singapore due to the lack of pasture. Upon arrival in the harbor these animals were sent to pens or sheds, where they recovered from the sea journey, and awaited slaughter. The transfer of cattle between the port and pens often resulted in chaotic traffic on roads and footpaths in the 19th century, which was exacerbated when pigs were sent toward the town prior to meeting their end. In 1882, for instance, the municipal commissioners received complaints about pigs that "roam at large on the public thoroughfares in the town and country," which led the police to shoot 99 stray pigs, "which were found rooting at roadsides."[17]

Animal pens and cowsheds were licensed under the Indian Act XIV of 1854, and they were commonly found scattered throughout the municipality, which led to complaints about the smell, noise and sanitation issues in the increasingly overcrowded town as the society developed.[18] In 1885, prominent residents of Tanglin—including W.H. Read and Thomas Shelford—began to grumble about "numerous piggeries and duck farms" in their neighborhood, describing them as a "serious and increasing nuisance," and requested their removal beyond the "town limits." Similar complaints were received for the Tanjong Pagar district. The municipal commissioners quickly scrutinized animal husbandry, particularly in commercial areas or European enclaves, and began to refuse to renew licenses and issue demands that animals be transferred to new facilities. When the owner of piggeries "in the district between Grange and Orchard Roads" requested more time to move in November 1885, they were turned down. The next year, the municipal commissioners shifted their attention to other areas in Singapore, including Chinatown, as piggeries located along Amoy Street were ordered closed as they were "highly objectionable" on sanitary grounds.[19]

---

[17] NA425: MPMC: 25 Aug. 1882, p. 252; 7 Dec. 1882, p. 298.

[18] The rate in the early 1880s was $5/year to keep pigs, while cattle were 50 cents/head. NA425, MPMC, p. 102; A Ratepayer, "Correspondence," *The Straits Advocate*, 5 Jan. 1889, p. 6.

[19] NA425: MPMC: 10 June 1885, pp. 1007–8; 11 Nov. 1885, p. 1075; 22 Sep. 1886, pp. 1217–8.

While piggeries and duck farms gained the initial attention of the authorities, their focus soon turned to the issue of cattle sheds. In February 1889 *The Straits Times* received a letter complaining about "fierce" cattle roaming public paths on Pulau Saigon, an island in the Singapore River near Robertson Quay. "Little Kling boys" tended these cattle, but their "savage" nature, which caused them "to chase persons passing by," led to a call for seizure and impoundment of the offensive creatures.[20] The area that fell under the most intense scrutiny, however, was along the appropriately named Kerbau (Buffalo) Road in Kampong Kapor. The key problem was that "dung and such like filth" accumulated and inundated the drains in the area, resulting in complaints that the cowherds were "quite ignorant of those hygienic principles which it is the duty of the Municipality to impress on the natives in a practical manner."[21]

These cases led to further calls to regulate animal husbandry in the municipality, with the ultimate goal being either forcing them out of town or locating animal pens in "two or three Campongs where the sheds could be effectually supervised." This was due to health concerns, according to the Active Health Officer in June 1889, as he argued that the owners of these sheds, "as a rule are most obstinate in carrying out any improvements," particularly related to drainage. One cowshed under question located on Prinsep Street, "in the midst of the populous quarter of town," was the focus of particular ire from officials and became a symbol of what the commissioner hoped to discourage. Although the owner was following all rules and regulations, it was considered to be an intolerable nuisance as it affected "a large number of worthy people living in the vicinity."[22]

By late 1889 the municipal commissioners began drafting new by-laws for cowsheds, dairies, piggeries and poultry yards, which came into effect in February 1890, to deal with these complaints in a rapidly

---

[20] A.B., "Dangerous Cattle," *ST*, 23 Feb. 1889, p. 3.

[21] Much of this was related to claims that typhoid fever had visited the neighborhood recently, and "it is not surprising that the atmosphere around is poisoned and produces disease and death." Anonymous, "Public Nuisances," *The Straits Advocate*, 12 Jan. 1889, p. 4.

[22] Anonymous, "Untitled," *The Straits Advocate*, 14 June 1889, p. 4; Anonymous, "The Municipal President's Progress Report for June 1889"; Anonymous, "Public Nuisances," *The Straits Advocate*, 12 Jan. 1889, p. 4.

expanding urban space. While animal husbandry would remain in the municipality, the animals now "must be kept in places constructed and drained to the satisfaction of the Commissioners, and also substantially fenced in." The space allotted was also regulated; it was to be "not less than 5½ feet [1.67 meters] broad" for each cow, bullock or buffalo, while each horse had 7 feet (2.13 meters). With regard to sanitation, "any stable, cattle-shed or other place for keeping sheep, goats, swine or poultry" should be "thoroughly cleansed daily," while they should also have a central collection point for "all dung, soil or other manure produced or accumulated" so that it could be "kept in an inoffensive condition and so as not to be productive of any nuisance." All of this waste was to be removed once a week. With these new by-laws, government authorities hoped, "the evils complained of should soon be things of the past."[23]

Once regulations overseeing animal husbandry had been promulgated, officials turned their focus to the shipping networks that brought animals to Singapore. These networks had been expanding since the mid-19th century, which was necessary to feed the growing population and also reflected developing state control over commerce throughout the colonial era, as John Butcher has argued. One of the results of these policies was a growth in the fish catch as trawling vessels moved beyond the immediate shores of Singapore into the protein-rich fishing grounds of the South China Sea and Straits of Melaka to meet the needs of a population that expanded from 60,000 residents in 1850 to 220,000 residents in 1900.[24]

---

[23] Despite the new regulations, and the administration of fines, problems related to animals and sanitation continued to persist, mostly related to sanitation and hygiene. Particular attention was given to cattle stables off Tanjong Pagar Road, opposite Craig Road, which were "in a bad an unwholesome condition." They were "dirty, ill-ventilated, and draining all their filth into the street surface drain." Anonymous, "Extracts form the Municipal President's Progress Report for March," *The Straits Times Weekly Issue*, 6 May 1891, p. 3; CO276/21: "Government Notification–No. 110: By-Laws for the Control and Supervision of Stables and Cattle-shed and Places for Keeping Sheep, Goats, Swine and Poultry," pp. 329–30; NA425: MPMC: 10 Oct. 1889, p. 1631; Anonymous, "An Abattoir," *ST*, 22 Nov. 1889, p. 2; Anonymous, "A Long-Needed Bye-Law," *The Straits Times Weekly Issue*, 25 Feb. 1990, p. 12.

[24] John G. Butcher, *The Closing of the Frontier: A History of Maritime Fisheries of Southeast Asia, c. 1850–2000* (Singapore: ISEAS, 2004).

Fish, as well as poultry, however, did not merit close monitoring for issues related to cruelty and sanitation during most of the colonial period in Singapore as they were not high enough on the evolutionary scale to merit concern in contrast to mammals.[25] This meant that the primary consideration with regard to the fish trade for colonial authorities was to ensure that it provided sufficient protein to the populace and was readily accessible, thus making the trade in this protein similar to an agricultural commodity like rice. This also held true for poultry, which were kept live in the markets and then slaughtered upon purchase. The key issue was availability, not how they were raised and slaughtered.[26] Monitoring of food animals concentrated on mammals, as they were the focus of the European diet, and for which religious proscriptions had regulated consumption for centuries. In addition, mammals that humans consumed for food were associated with problems related to the spread of disease and sanitation, particularly cattle.

Just as quarantine laws addressed the importation of dogs during the mid-1880s, there were also concerns over the health of food animals that entered via the port. As early as 1876 there was a discussion of banning the import of cattle from Bangkok due to disease, which would have had a serious impact on their numbers in the Straits Settlements, as Siam was their main site of origin.[27] This anxiety among colonial officials continued into the early 1880s and 1890s, particularly after the Netherlands East Indies government informed their Straits Settlements counterpart that cattle infected with foot and mouth disease had been exported to Sumatra from Singapore. In order to prevent further

---

[25] It was only in 1935 that the notion of ill treatment of fish was first raised. "Eden" wrote to the papers claiming that live fish in Singapore markets were kept in insufficient water and when sold "their gills and mouths are pierced by a gunny bag needle, and they are strung together and carried home," while also often having the fins chopped off while still alive. Eden, "Sale of Live Fish," *ST*, 25 Feb. 1935, p. 7; Felicity A. Huntingford and Sunil Kadri, "Welfare and Fish," in *Fish Welfare*, ed. Edward J. Branson (Oxford: Blackwell Publishing, 2008), pp. 19–31.

[26] Once the public abattoirs opened in the 1890s, some members of the public expected the municipal commissioners to direct their attention to regulating the slaughter of chickens. This did not occur. The issue quickly died down and only reappeared in the 1920s, when it became a serious issue of debate. Only a Sparrow, "Notes by the Way," *The Daily Advertiser*, 3 Jan. 1893, p. 2; Yahaya, "The Question of Animal Slaughter."

[27] CO273/89: "Possible Prohibition of Cattle Export from Bangkok" (1876).

diplomatic, veterinarian and trade disputes, the Legislative Council amended the Quarantine and Prevention of Disease Ordinance in 1894 to address this issue. While it had "elaborate provisions for preventing the introduction of infectious and contagious diseases into the Colony and their spreading within the colony" and had been used to prevent further rabies outbreaks during the same period, it now required the monitoring of all livestock imported and exported.[28]

As part of these concerns, the government issued several reports on the cattle trade, which provide a picture of how the Straits Settlements obtained a commodity that was dear to the British heart: beef. While cattle arrived from India, Java, Bali, and Australia, 23,000 of the more than 28,000 head of cattle imported into Singapore in 1890 were from Siam. The cultivation and export of cattle was a major industry in the Thai kingdom, providing beef to consumers throughout Southeast Asia. There were 22 steamships with facilities that supplied Singapore with cattle, and eight of them solely plied the route to Bangkok while "occasional vessels and native craft also take up the trade."[29]

The various reports describe a trip from Siam to Singapore that was filled with dangers for the bovine passengers. A commentary in *The Singapore Free Press and Mercantile Advertiser* from 1894 serves as an illustration of this issue as it questioned the necessity of such a trade, positing that the journey raised the specter of cruelty, and exposed the hypocrisy of Britons engaged in the civilizational rhetoric of Asian backwardness that had led to the establishment of the SPCA in Singapore. The anonymous critic argued that, while most of the cattle had been stolen in Siam, following local traditions related to trade, the "savage bandit" treated the cattle better than "the more civilized British subject who imports him into the Straits."[30]

He went on to add,

> the bad treatment of the ox begins when he encounters civilization. First when he is shoved on board the steamer, belaboured with a thick stick (or sometimes many thick sticks) and his tail properly

---

[28] CO273/199/1122: "Ordinance 20 of '94, Diseased Cattle (Prevention of Export)."
[29] Anonymous, "The Singapore Import Cattle Trade," *The Straits Times Weekly Issue*, 10 Nov. 1891, p. 6; Anonymous, "The Trade of Bangkok in 1888," *The Straits Times Weekly Issue*, 7 Oct. 1889, p. 5.
[30] Anonymous, "The Bangkok-Singapore Cattle Trade," *SFP*, 5 Mar. 1894, p. 3.

twisted so as to give the animal a strong sensation of pain. When on deck, he is often lashed by the nose by a piece of twine attached to a thick rope, and then he is destined to stand for four days in this position until he reaches Singapore.... For three days, sometimes four, the animal is allowed no food nor water to drink, the system being to starve the beast until near the port of disembarkation, when hunger and thirst are so great that it will eat and drink to great excess, and thereby appear plump and round, to as to deceive the purchaser.[31]

The observer of this practice went on to add, "if his nose is torn and bleeding, he must just abide by it, or if he breaks his lead he has to be tied down to the deck and kept alive until he reaches Singapore."[32]

One advocate for better treatment of the cattle, J.B.M. Leech, travelled on the steamship *Patani* between Bangkok and Singapore in 1901, and equated the journey the cattle ships made to the Middle Passage, which had brought slaves to the New World prior to the 19th century. "The unfortunate animals suffer during the voyage ... particularly during the North-East Monsoon, when the rolling of the vessel under the influence of a beam sea converts the cattle deck into a pandemonium of mutilation and agony, ended only by the death of the great majority of helpless victims." According to Leech, there were 130 cattle on board, "all on deck. Most of the cattle were in stalls of the most flimsy description, but some of them were merely tethered by the nose on deck." The steamship company received $5 for each live head of cattle delivered to Singapore, and the captain told Leech that proper accommodation would reduce the carrying load by two-thirds. During the five-day voyage to Singapore they encountered strong winds and rough seas, and the cattle suffered broken legs while others had their horns ripped off in the melee. The result was 100 cows being "killed and thrown overboard, simply smashed to pieces by the rolling

---

[31] Anonymous, "The Bangkok-Singapore Cattle Trade," *SFP*, 5 Mar. 1894, p. 3.

[32] These comments merited a retort in *The Daily Advertiser* a few days later, which dismissed much of the account as blatant exaggeration if not misrepresentation. The author, "Observer," was a frequent passenger of the cattle ships, and believed it was not in the interest of anyone involved in the trade to mistreat the cattle, and any imported to Singapore were subject to inspection from the Veterinary Surgeon upon landing. Observer, "The Bangkok-Singapore Cattle Trade," *The Daily Advertiser*, 10 Mar. 1894, p. 2; Anonymous, "The Bangkok-Singapore Cattle Trade."

of the vessel." Leech continued with his description when he told of one "poor beast" that was outside his cabin door with a broken back. Although he wished to shoot it, to put it out of its misery, the Captain prevented him from doing so because "he could get it into Singapore alive."[33]

This account was one of several that attempted to highlight abuses in the cattle trade between Bangkok and Singapore. Each described a system in which the ill treatment of animals on the journey was universal, and had been a persistent issue for several decades. Little was done to improve these conditions, however, as it mostly fell outside the reach of imperial authority. Only upon entering the port of Singapore, according to a British resident, could tales that were "shocking to one's ideas of humanity" possibly cease, as only then could their state of being and interaction with humans finally be monitored and controlled.[34] Despite all of the focus brought to the cattle trade, concerns over its process and civilizational status continued throughout the colonial era, never truly resolved, with the lack of sovereignty over the ships outside of Singaporean and Malayan waters being the primary reason given.

Interconnected with debates over the cattle trade to Singapore and the state of animal pens and sheds on the island were concerns over the quality of butchered meat that was consumed in the colonial society, which led to proposals to develop a public abattoir. The goal was to establish licensed premises where officers could monitor the slaughtering process, echoing developments in Britain over the previous three decades. As was explained in a meeting of the municipal commissioners, "the evils of unchecked free trade in the butchering line to the danger of the public are so glaring that there is no need for enlarging further upon the point raised." To emphasize their point, the authorities recounted how typhoid fever swept through "a large number of pigs" in Singapore in 1886. Although officials investigated the deaths, no carcasses were produced, which "led to the inference that the probability was that they had been 'muchly' disposed of as food among the lower classes." A public slaughterhouse, which government officials supervised, would help monitor and control such cases, and help phase out the 89

---

[33] Anonymous, "The Singapore Import Cattle Trade"; Anonymous, "Wednesday, February 13, 1901," *SFP*, 13 Feb. 1901, p. 2; W.E.S. Hooper, "The Cruelty of the Cattle Trade," *SFP*, 13 Feb. 1901, p. 3; J.S.M. Leech, "Letter to Hooper," *SFP*, 13 Feb. 1901, p. 3.

[34] Old Timer, "The Cruelty of the Cattle Trade," *SFP*. 14 Feb. 1901, p. 3.

private slaughterhouses that were operating in Singapore town in the late 1880s.[35]

The Public Abattoirs

Public abattoirs were new phenomena in Europe during the 19th century and, much like the introduction of the pet dog, reflected a changing relationship between humans and animals in rapidly urbanizing and industrializing societies. As historian Chris Otter has argued, public abattoirs became de rigueur as the quick and clean killing of animals by experts played into perceptions of a more humane treatment of animals, as the general populace would not live alongside and witness the slaughter of other creatures. Emerging understandings of disease and sanitation further reinforced such notions as modern construction methods and mechanization ensured that blood, entrails and even odor could be disposed of or limited, while also allowing for inspection and monitoring. While sanitation and hygiene are rooted in science, the focus on them was a cultural construct, one in which the British colonial authorities created a problem that needed to be solved. Their solutions led to increased regulations over the members of society, both human and animal, and influenced how food was to be consumed. The public abattoir was to become a shining emblem of the benefits of rational and efficient systems for the processing of protein in a modern society. Through "sanitary discipline" the public abattoir was ultimately a symbol of Civilization.[36]

British colonial officials transferred these concepts to the colonies, with Singapore becoming a model for the ideas throughout the Empire, particularly in Asia, with much of it revolving around the processing of beef. This occurred during a period in which the processing and presentation of protein throughout the world also transformed, and it allowed for the authorities to introduce regulations and standards that

---

[35] Anonymous, "The Municipality," *The Straits Times Weekly Issue*, 10 June 1886, p. 6; Anonymous, "Singapore, 25th September, 1886," *SFP*, 25 Sep. 1886, pp. 181–2; NA425: MPCM: 23 Feb. 1887, p. 1287; Anonymous, "The Health of Singapore," *ST*, 14 Nov. 1889, p. 2.

[36] Otter, "Civilizing Slaughter," pp. 89–106; Nicole Tarulevicz, "'I Had No Time to Pick Out the Worms': Food Adulteration in Singapore, 1900–1973," *Journal of Colonialism and Colonial History* 16, 3 (2015). *Project MUSE*, doi:10.1353/cch.2015.0037.

had only been recently developed in Britain. It changed how meat was to be consumed, and began with new approaches to the trade and husbandry of animals in the colonial port. To be a modern, imperial city, Singapore needed a public abattoir.

Despite being mentioned in official documents as "urgently required," the process of approving, constructing and operating a public abattoir in Singapore took more than eight years to complete due to constant bureaucratic dysfunction, budgetary woes, and concerns over the location of the slaughterhouse. The delay even resulted in one resident, Chua Peng Bee, approaching the government in August 1890 to request the "exclusive right of slaughtering pigs within the Municipality." Municipal officials turned down his application. They would only approve the development of a public abattoir that would allow for British-appointed and trained monitoring of the process of slaughter, thus ensuring that sanitation and hygiene standards as they were understood in the West were followed.[37]

The initial plan, first promulgated in 1886, was to construct an abattoir on River Valley Road at the base of Fort Canning Hill. This proposal, however, led to a number of questions about the suitability of the location. As one commentator opined, "In a climate, such as this, unless it is kept faultlessly clean, the smell from it, and the flies, which are sure to abound, will prove annoying to the neighbourhood, and especially tenants of Fort Canning, whilst the only outlet for the blood, garbage, and washings will be the river, already foul enough in all conscience." Due to these objections, alternative sites came under consideration, with Kampong Kapor and Pulau Saigon being mentioned the most frequently.[38]

In the midst of these discussions, the editor of *The Free Press and Mercantile Advertiser* summarized many of the issues that government decision makers faced. "The hot climate requires much forethought and should be adapted from such as are found efficient in Europe, where

---

[37] CO273/152/12670: Building a Wall at Pulau Saigon, p. 58; NA425: MPMC: 5 Aug. 1890, p. 1731; 24 June 1891, p. 1885.

[38] Part of the appeal of these two sites is that they were where the underclasses lived. Solomon, *A Subaltern History of the Indian Diaspora in Singapore*, p. 84; Anonymous, "Extract from the Minutes of Proceedings of the Municipal Commissioners on Wednesday, the 19th May, 1886," *SFP*, 12 June 1886, p. 9; Anonymous, "Notes from the Kampong," *SFP*, 26 June 1886, p. 380; Anonymous, "The Municipality," *ST*, 17 July 1886, p. 2.

atmospheric influences are so vastly different." The alternative sites also faced the problem of drainage, much like the original proposal for Fort Canning Hill, as they would channel waste into either the Singapore River or the Kallang River. "The banks of these streams, which are always exposed at half tide, are already sufficiently offensive, and to add to the nauseous emanations by the outscourings of an abattoir would be an outrage to the public." The debate and discussion on where to locate the slaughterhouse lasted for another 18 months. In June 1888, the municipal commissioners announced that they had chosen to build the abattoir in Pulau Saigon.[39]

Located in the Singapore River between Clarke Quay and Robertson Quay, Pulau Saigon was a triangular island containing a small village with the same name located on it. Prior to the late 1880s, the village was described as "filthy and offensive," as it was "covered with huts upon piles occupied by some of the worst characters in Singapore." Following the proposal that it house the public abattoir, most of the residents were forced to relocate, and engineers raised the island "several feet with town refuse and mud from the river," and surrounded it with a "neat river wall on a novel and economical plan." At the same time workers were transforming the island, James MacRitchie, the Colonial Engineer, researched "the principal of abattoirs and meat markets" while on home leave in 1888, and returned an even stronger advocate for the development of a modern slaughterhouse.[40]

During this period there was a constant back and forth between the Legislative Council and the Municipal Commission over the costs of such a facility in the growing port, which created further delays in its construction. W. Gilmore Ellis, the Acting Health Commissioner, used this delay to plead for a ban on all private butcheries, as they were "prejudicial to the health of the population." This led to complaints among the commissioners over the delays in construction of the abattoir, as the scores of slaughterhouses that continued operating were

---

[39] Anonymous, "Singapore, 25th September, 1886," p. 182; Anonymous, "Local and General," *The Straits Eurasian Advocate*, 23 June 1888, p. 5.

[40] Anonymous, "The Municipal President's Progress Report for June 1889," *ST*, 11 July 1889, p. 3; Anonymous, "The Municipal President's Progress Report for May 1889," *The Straits Times Weekly Issue*, 11 July 1889, p. 3; Anonymous, "Death of Mr. MacRitchie," *ST*, 27 Apr. 1895, p. 3; CO273/152/12670: Building a Wall at Pulau Saigon; Anonymous, "Singapore," *The Daily Advertiser*, 27 Aug. 1891, p. 2.

constantly violating health standards "for allowing animal matter to flow into the public drains, which thus contained pigs' feces, blood clots, and pieces of flesh." In November 1889 the municipal commissioners even temporarily abandoned any plans to build a public abattoir due to the lack of funds. Ultimately, the Straits Settlements government granted the municipality a 67,000 square-foot (0.62 hectares) plot of land, the majority of it reclaimed, for the construction of such a facility. In exchange, the municipality constructed two bridges connecting Pulau Saigon to the mainland. By mid-1890, many of the concerns had been addressed and construction commenced.[41]

At a meeting of the municipal commissioners in August 1890, however, Thomas Shelford promoted a bold addition to the efforts to construct a public abattoir. He requested a second one be built in the Rochor area, as the distance to Pulau Saigon for most pig farmers was considered particularly burdensome. By early 1891, the proposal to construct a "branch abattoir" on Jalan Besar in Kampong Kapor was approved, and "excavation, brick and carpentry work and erection of iron roofing" began. The two abattoirs were to handle the processing of all beef, pork and mutton in Singapore, with the space in square meters dedicated to the slaughter of specific animals set at 167 for cattle, 125 for sheep and 209 for pigs.[42] Construction of these facilities took another two years.

The original plan was to begin slaughtering cattle at the new municipal abattoir on Jalan Besar in January 1893, while the Pulau Saigon abattoir would commence operating soon thereafter. Private abattoirs would be allowed to offer their services during this transitional phase. This move was based on fears over the potential that the public abattoirs held to "create hardship on honest and respectable butchers" as well as "prove highly inconvenient to a great many European residents

---

[41] Anonymous, "The Municipal President's Progress Report for June 1889," *ST*, 11 July 1889, p. 3; Anonymous, "The Health of Singapore," *ST*, 14 Nov. 1889, p. 2; NA425, MPMC, 12 Apr. 1882, p. 196; 24 June 1891, p. 1885; Anonymous, "Municipal Commission," *SFP*, 3 Sep. 1891, p. 3; Anonymous, "Untitled," *SFP*, 4 Apr. 1892, p. 2; Anonymous, "Thursday, 1st October," *The Straits Times Weekly Issue*, 7 Oct. 1891, p. 4

[42] Anonymous, "Abattoir Agitation," *SFP*, 28 Feb. 1894, p. 3; Anonymous, "Municipal Commissioners," *ST*, 19 Aug. 1890, p. 3; Anonymous, "Municipal Notice," *ST* 11 June 1891, p. 2; Anonymous, "Municipal Commissioners," *The Straits Times Weekly Issue*, 14 Apr. 1891, p. 4.

of the place from whom there is generally a demand for an early supply or for extra supplies for picnicking purposes." In addition, the price of meat had begun to rise prior to the opening of the abattoirs with reports of a 30 percent increase mentioned in the press. This created doubt among the public, leading one newspaper editor to opine, "the benefit to be derived from the abattoirs will hardly be compensated for the increased cost of living."[43]

The opening of the abattoirs was delayed into 1894, as the authorities finalized budgets and completed the hiring of personnel who could oversee the hygienic slaughter of animals. Among these new hires was Frank Holley, the proprietor of a livery business on Armenian Street, who was engaged as the Superintendent of the Abattoirs in September 1893. Although the Municipal Commission considered Holley to be "a desirable person for such a post," and sent him to Hong Kong to study the system of slaughterhouse management in that British colony before taking up his position in Singapore, there was little public faith in his ability to oversee such a complex, modern undertaking. As one letter writer to *The Daily Advertiser* opined, "What knowledge, it is asked, could a man whose training has apparently been that of a jockey, have as to sound or diseased meat?" His salary of $175 a month, the author went on to argue, was a waste of public funds when a "native butcher would be a better judge and could be had for $10 or $15 a month."[44]

Many of the issues that delayed the opening of the new abattoirs focused around the difficulty in transitioning from the use of numerous private butchers to two central facilities, as this required a high level of coordination and planning, as well as the abolition of a system that

---

[43] Such an argument had been in the press since 1892, when the editor of the same newspaper—*The Daily Advertiser*—wrote that the new abattoirs "will have to keep a complete staff ... and ... on this account it must be taken as a foregone conclusion that the butchers, like the rickshaw owners, will be properly squeezed in order to meet the expenditure. Unfortunately, however, this will necessitate a heavy rise in the prices of meat." Jingo, "Tit-Bits," *The Daily Advertiser*, 30 Dec. 1892, p. 3; Anonymous, "Local and General," *The Daily Advertiser*, 22 Dec. 1892, p. 3.

[44] Anonymous, "The Municipal Commission," *SFP*, 5 Sep. 1893, p. 9; Hawk, "The Abattoirs," *The Daily Advertiser*, 10 Jan. 1894, p. 2; Anonymous, "Local and General," *The Daily Advertiser*, 2 Sep. 1893, p. 3; Anonymous, "The Municipality," *ST*, 11 Nov. 1893, p. 3; Anonymous, "Advertisements", *SFP*, 22 June 1894, p. 4; NA426: MPMC: 25 Oct. 1893, p. 2261.

had worked for decades. One observer summarized the problem as one in which, "there are in Singapore town about 100 private abattoirs, situated from a half-mile to one-and-a-half miles distance from the two municipal abattoirs. The usual time for beginning each day's work is 3 a.m., and the carcasses should be ready for sale by 5 a.m., each private abattoir killing ten pigs daily." Chinese butchers, who focused almost exclusively on pork, were skeptical that the new facilities could handle all of their needs simultaneously. As the work would have to be done in batches, and plans were to operate it on a "first come, first served" basis, it opened "a door for bribes and extortion."[45] In addition, there would also be a need for time to transport the meat back to their shops, with those living far from Pulau Saigon and Jalan Besar being at a particular disadvantage. Combined with inspections of the living animals, as well as limited quarters for slaughtering and dressing the carcasses, the new abattoirs seemed to be a recipe for inconvenience.

All of these aggravations led to butchers and farmers becoming livid with how the situation was being handled. As the editors of the *The Daily Advertiser* piped in, "the scheme had been entered into in the usual off-hand John Bull fashion without properly consulting those who were expected to use them." By the end of February 1894—facing such issues—butchers throughout Singapore decided to go on strike, despite the offer of free use of the facilities during the transition period.[46]

The official response to this strike was to dismiss the concern of Chinese butchers, whose "dislike of change and their invariable hatred of innovation no matter how necessary" led them to oppose the new regulations and facilities. The intentions of the government, which "the intelligent portion of the Chinese community" supported, was "to improve the quality of the animals killed and also to prevent the rearing of pigs in the more populous portions of the town." Under these circumstances the Commissioner of Chinese Affairs, G.C. Wray, "summoned before him three butchers whom he considered were inclined to give trouble and he intimated to them that they had the choice to obey the new mandate of the Commissioners and slaughter in the new abattoirs or consider their 'occupation gone'." To compensate for the various postponements and chaos, the municipality also

---

[45] Anonymous, "The Municipal Abattoirs," *The Daily Advertiser*, 28 Feb. 1894, p. 2.
[46] NA426: MPMC: 31 Jan. 1894, p. 2307; Anonymous, "The Municipal Abattoirs."

temporarily renewed licenses for private slaughterhouses and announced that the use of the two new abattoirs would be free for an additional two months.[47]

On 28 February 1894, between 3.30 and 4.30 in the morning, 32 pigs, 6 sheep, 6 goats and 2 bulls were slaughtered at Jalan Besar, while on Kampong Saigon 46 pigs and 4 sheep suffered the same fate. The meat from these animals, it was reported, provided approximately one-third of the daily needs of Singapore for these proteins, and government officials believed it represented an end to the disgruntlement that private butchers had expressed. "Porcine mortality" rose over the following days, when, for example, on 8 March 1894 over 140 pigs passed through the two abattoirs. By the end of the month 5,669 animals had been slaughtered in the newly designated facilities.[48] The authorities believed that the strike had fizzled out.

Following this period of transition, however, there were reports that "only cattle and sheep butchers" were patronizing the new abattoirs. Chinese butchers continued their boycott. By October 1894, no pigs were being processed at either designated site, and the price of pork skyrocketed. This led to long discussions among the municipal commissioners regarding rules and regulations, with much of the time dedicated to blaming the issue on "true Asiatic conservatism, stuck to their old ways and time-honoured methods," which would not allow for "new fangled institutions."[49]

To counter resistance to the abattoirs, the commissioners sought compulsory powers from the government of the Straits Settlements. After a long session of debate, the Legislative Council agreed, and passed an ordinance giving the municipality the power to compel all butchers to use the new facilities, as well as outlawing the slaughter of

---

[47] In addition, a third abattoir—to be located at Bukit Chermin Creek—was proposed, although this was not pursued. Anonymous, "Municipal Progress," *ST*, 27 Feb. 1893, p. 3; Anonymous, "Abattoir Agitation," *SFP*, 28 Feb. 1894, p. 3; Baba, "The Commissioners and the Butchers," *The Daily Advertiser*, 1 Mar. 1894, p. 2.

[48] Anonymous, "The Abattoir Agitation," *SFP*, 1 Mar. 1894, p. 3; Anonymous, "Untitled, *SFP*, 8 Mar. 1894, p. 2; Anonymous, "The Municipality," *ST*, 26 Apr. 1894, p. 3.

[49] By mid-March 1894, pork was 24 cents a catty (600 grams), an increase of 85 percent over the previous month when the meat was going for 13 cents. Anonymous, "The Abattoirs Fix," *ST*, 23 June 1894, p. 2; NA426: MPMC: 6 June 1894, p. 2349; 1 August, p. 2377.

Image 6.3: The abattoir at Jalan Besar. Arshauk C. Galstaun Collection, courtesy of National Archives of Singapore.

animals at private sites. It was now "an offence to kill for food or offer for sale the flesh of any cattle, sheep, goat or pig within Municipal limits unless killed at a public slaughterhouse." In addition, using the discovery of tapeworms in pork being sold in Clyde Terrace Market in March 1894 as a justification, the construction of new markets with the latest in sanitation standards and monitoring were announced—the first being Orchard Road Market along with the renovation of existing markets, such as the Teluk Ayer Market under the supervision of MacRitchie—signaling the development of modern wet markets in Singapore. While some slaughtering continued in rural areas, most of the meat supply for Singapore had now been brought under government regulation. As the editor of *The Straits Times* described the situation, "the abattoir experiment has now reached an interesting phase."[50]

---

[50] This is an example of implementing such policy in the colonies long before the metropole. Chris Otter reports that private slaughterhouses continued to be operated well into the 20th century in many parts of England. Otter, "Civilizing Slaughter," p. 103; Anonymous, "The Municipal Abattoirs," *ST*, 24 Nov. 1894, p. 2; Anonymous, "The Food Supply: Some Secrets of Singapore's Menu," *ST*, 25 Apr. 1907, p. 7; Anonymous, "The New Market and Slaughter Houses," *ST*, 1 Mar. 1894, p. 2; NAS426: MPMC: 14 March 1894, p. 2319; Tarulevicz, *Eating Her Curries and Kway*, p. 13.

The first court case following the passage of the new ordinance outlawing the sale of any meat slaughtered outside the abattoirs did not involve a pig butcher. Instead, it was "a Kling man living at 82 Neil Road," who was prosecuted in December 1894 for slaughtering a goat. The next month a Chinese butcher was fined $50 "for exposing for sale, meat that had not passed through the public abattoirs." To emphasize the promotion of these new regulations, the editor of the *Mid-Day Herald* argued that, "this may seem excessive, but the law must be obeyed at any cost," while highlighting that some farmers were taking two or three pigs to the abattoir and then mixing the meat with others that they had butchered at their own premises. "When the meat is cut up and mixed it is not very easy to say which is which." In late 1895 employees of the municipality continued their efforts to enforce the new regulations, when several butchers on Kim Seng Road were served notices. After they "shewed signs of opposition," W.R.C. Middleton, the Municipal Health Officer, gave instructions to have "a quantity of baskets and bullock carts in readiness" to transport all of the pigs directly to the abattoir. Efforts to locate illegal butcheries continued throughout the decade.[51]

In 1899 new instructions were promulgated requiring the Master Attendant and Government Veterinary Surgeon approve the import of any animals into the port, as well as the construction of sanitary facilities on land where they were to be kept. Upon arrival, officials now had to use "a book of notice forms, the pages of which should be consecutively numbered." On the forms they would record the name of the vessel, a description of the animals, their number, and how many were to be landed in Singapore. The Veterinary Surgeon and his assistant were to monitor any animal brought ashore.[52]

While there had been a Veterinary Surgeon in Singapore for decades, these new rules represented a new era in the nexus of human-animal interaction, as it established the main task of the Veterinary

---

[51] In 1899, for example, Wong Kee of 158 South Bridge Road was convicted of "illicit slaughtering" and received a $25 fine. NAS426: MPMC: 15 Feb. 1899, p. 3442; Anonymous, "Untitled," *SFP* 6 Dec. 1894, p. 2; Anonymous, "Jottings," *The Mid-Day Herald*, 5 Jan. 1895, p. 3; Anonymous, "Local and General," *The Mid-Day Herald*, 27 Nov. 1895, p. 3.

[52] CO273/247/17060: "Instructions for the Guidance of the Master Attendant and the Government Veterinary Surgeon in Connection with the Importation of Animals."

Department for the remainder of the colonial era. Stated plainly in their own reports, the officers assigned to this unit were "concerned primarily with the administration and enforcement of animal quarantine laws which are framed with the object of preventing the introduction and dissemination of such destructive infectious diseases as may occur among domesticated livestock and with the investigation of problems relative to introduced or endemic diseases of economic importance." These tasks began at the harbor, as well as the quarantine stations, such as one located at Teluk Ayer. Once on Singapore Island, there were also new rules to regulate "stable, cattle sheds, cow houses or places for keeping sheep or goats except for private use."[53] This meant that all animals, including pets and livestock, in Singapore would now be fully scrutinized and regulated.

Municipal health officials thus began a new phase in providing sanitary proteins for Singaporeans by thoroughly inspecting the delivery of food from the ship to the kitchen. Stables and markets were monitored closely, and reports of unsanitary facilities—such as a "filthy" cattle pen on New Market Road in April 1901—were widely circulated. In May, new regulations focusing on "general conservancy, cleansing of the streets and prevention of nuisances" required that any dead animal had to be removed and buried "within fours hours after daylight," which supplemented rules that addressed the overloading of bullock carts and gharries, ensuring that the animals were well treated.[54]

With the abattoirs operating in an acceptable manner, and private slaughter and the movement of animals from ship to shore scrutinized, the authorities began to focus on transferring all farm animals outside the town limits. Although laws had been passed outlawing their presence, many farmers argued that such facilities were necessary as temporary holding sites near the abattoirs. In light of the transforming animal

---

[53] Veterinary Surgeons originated in military detachments, as they cared for the animals—particularly horses—assigned to the units. The government appointed A.H. Batchelor the first official Veterinary Surgeon in 1884, following outbreaks of cattle diseases on trade networks connecting Singapore with Java and Siam. Anonymous, "Singapore, 25th October, 1884," *SFP*, 25 Oct. 1884, p. 55; Anonymous, "Preliminary Report by Mr. A.H. Batchelor, Veterinary Surgeon," *ST*, 28 Mar. 1885, p. 3; CO275/149: "Report on the Veterinary Department, Malaya, for the Year 1937," p. 877; NAS426: MPMC: 2 Nov. 1898, p. 3357.

[54] NAS427: MPMC: 10 Apr. 1901, p. 4152; 22 May 1901, p. 4193.

husbandry industry in Singapore, the Municipal Commission held a special meeting to discuss "the control and supervision of places for keeping swines and ducks" within the municipal limits. They passed new regulations that required facilities for farm animals be located more than 150 yards (137 meters) "from any public street" or neighbor. The only exception was to be if the animals had been brought in for less than 48 hours and, even then, they had to be kept in specially designated zones that followed strict sanitation standards, ensuring they were distant from water supplies. With the passage of this legislation, it became illegal to keep swine in the municipality without a special license after 1 January 1902.[55]

As usually happened in such endeavors, enforcement of regulations began in the elite Tanglin district, where over 100 pig sties had led to complaints from the residents. Pork farmers protested these closures, and appealed to the authorities for some lenience, all of which were quickly dismissed. After Tanglin, municipal officials expanded their reach to other parts of the town. One of the areas targeted was between Thomson Road and Serangoon Road. Owners of these piggeries, much like their counterparts in Tanglin, maintained that they needed to keep their facilities, as they were relatively near the Jalan Besar abattoir. The Health Officer also denied these appeals.[56] The commissioners then ordered engineers to "prepare plans for pens for the storage of pigs awaiting slaughter" next to the slaughterhouses. The processing and slaughtering of animals in an administrative and bureaucratic manner— in the name of health, sanitation and modernity—had been accomplished. The food supply in Singapore had been secured, and even extended to new laws focusing on maintaining a sanitary space.[57]

By the early 20th century, the use of the public abattoirs and the monitoring of animal husbandry had been normalized, with any news or information related to its operations rarely appearing in the press or

---

[55] NAS427: MPMC: 14 Aug. 1901, pp. 4272–5; 4 Dec. 1901, pp. 4378–9.

[56] A rare exception to these rejections was for one piggery on Alexandra Road, as it was "close to the limits of the area in which the keeping of pigs is prohibited." Even then, the allowance was only temporary. Anonymous, "Municipal Commission," *ST*, 27 Sep. 1902, p. 5; NAS427: MPMC: 12 Sep. 1902, p. 4570; 27 Mar. 1903, p. 4700; 14 Aug. 1903, pp. 4783.

[57] NAS427: MPMC: 26 Sep. 1902, pp. 4574–5; 11 Sep. 1903, p. 4799; Tarulevicz, "'I Had No Time to Pick Out the Worms'."

even government reports.[58] The only exceptions were when there was a petition for an exemption, which Eng Yong Siang requested in early 1896 for the processing of Australian cattle meant for the military. He argued that the animals were simply kept too far from the abattoirs, and were "so wild they could not safely be led through the streets." The compromise was to allow for the butchering of the animals off site, but to require that the meat be brought to the slaughterhouses afterwards for inspection. Another instance is a report that a record number of pigs—1,589 "innocents"—were slaughtered on the eve of Chinese New Year in 1899 to cater for the celebrations, or another that reported that 141,784 animals met their fate in the abattoirs in the previous year.[59]

A Modern Food Supply

During the first few decades of the 20th century, the public abattoirs continued to process meat for the population of Singapore. The entire practice of animal slaughter became routine to the point that little attention was paid to the process in government records or the newspapers, with the most prominent reminder of the presence of abattoirs in the colonial society coming from the stench that emanated from the facilities. The smell from the abattoir on Jalan Besar was so pungent, it led the Municipal Commission to issue sanitary regulations prohibiting the use of night soil in vegetable gardens in the vicinity, although this

---

[58] The streets along which they were located even came to be known in Hokkien as "the slaughter pig depot in Kampong Kapor" (*kam kong ka poh thai tu long*) for Jalan Besar, and "slaughter pig compartment" (*thai tu long kahu*) for Pulau Saigon. H.W. Firmstone, "Chinese Names of Streets and Places in Singapore and the Malay Peninsula (Continued)," *Journal of the Straits Branch of the Royal Asiatic Society* 42, (1905): 96–7, 120–1.

[59] Occasionally crimes did occur, such as when a former gatekeeper at the Pulau Saigon abattoir named Ibrahim threw acid in the face of Assistant Superintendent C. Moore in January 1902 after the latter had reported Ibrahim for "matters of misbehaviour" that had led to his dismissal. The attack resulted in blindness, and Ibrahim was sentenced to "penal servitude for life." Anonymous, "Vitriol-Throwing Case," *ST*, 27 May 1902, p. 5; Anonymous, "Mr. C. Moore's Case," *ST*, 29 May 1902, p. 5; Anonymous, "Friday, July 11, 1902," *SFP*, 11 July 1902, p. 2; Anonymous, "Municipal Commission," *SFP*, 17 Mar. 1896, p. 9; Anonymous, "Untitled," *SFP*, 9 Feb. 1899, p. 2; Anonymous, "Singapore Municipality," *SFP*, 26 Apr. 1899, p. 3.

did little to address the issue. Beyond these aromas, the authorities continued to enforce rules disallowing private slaughter, often quite harshly, which occasionally led to a public outcry. An example occurred in 1904 when an Indian resident named Dollah was fined $40 for killing a goat. Dollah owned the goat, which strayed onto Queen Street and a passing gharry ran over it. The animal was "mortally hurt," so he killed it to put it out of its misery. As he began to skin the carcass and prepare it for cooking, Dollah "was arrested, tried, and convicted" for doing so outside of a publicly designated slaughterhouse.[60]

In 1907 *The Straits Times* published a series of articles focusing on "The Food Supply," which provided a detailed account into a largely hidden part of colonial society on a variety of issues ranging from milk to the abattoirs. The series explained how animals made their way to the plates, or banana leaves, of the diverse population of the port, with a particular focus on the policies and regulations the government enforced "to ensure the cleanliness of Singapore's food, and its freedom from disease." Reflecting the role that regulation and discipline over animals as well as sanitation played within the system, the articles touted how it was an investigation into how a population of some 275,000 residents "with so many religious beliefs in regard to what they eat, live from day to day with scarcely the slightest risk to health from disease."[61]

As had been true throughout the colonial era, butchers imported animals for consumption using the vast transport networks that flowed through Singapore. Beef cattle still mainly came from Siam, while those from India were used for transport purposes or—at most—milk. Other regions, such as Kelantan and Bali, also supplied cattle, but the beef was "exceedingly coarse," resembling buffalo meat, thus making it less desired among consumers. India supplied most of the mutton consumed in Singapore, with smaller contributions from Java and

---

[60] Public appeals for donations to pay for his fine were successful. Anonymous, "The Oppressed Kling," *ST*, 27 Apr. 1904, p. 5; Anonymous, "Follow Your Nose," *SFP*, 16 July 1915, p. 1; Anonymous, "Untitled," *ST*, 12 Dec. 1903, p. 4; Victor R. Savage and Brenda S.A. Yeoh, *Toponymics: A Study of Singapore Street Names* (Singapore: Eastern Universities Press, 2003), p. 231.

[61] Anonymous, "The Food Supply: Some Secrets of Singapore's Menu," *ST*, 25 Apr. 1907, p. 7. This article was part of a reply to a long running dispute, and fears, over adulterated food being served to the public, which Nicole Tarulevicz has discussed. Tarulevicz, "'I Had No Time to Pick Out the Worms'."

Australia, while goat came from India and China. Most pigs were not imported; instead they were bred and raised on farms in rural areas.[62]

Upon arrival in the harbor, the Government Veterinary Surgeon, P.S. Falshaw, and his minions conducted onboard inspections of the animals to ensure they passed health requirements. Animals were then off-loaded. Healthy ones were transferred to agents, who sold them to butchers and arranged for their slaughter. Unhealthy animals were taken to pens at a quarantine station on Beach Road, "and there tended until such time as they are thought to be fit for slaughtering." If a dealer tried to pass a sick animal to the abattoir, and was caught, "the hairy portion" of the tail of the ailing beast was clipped to ensure that it was not taken to the other slaughterhouse.[63]

At the abattoir, animals were placed in pens, and inspected again. Once the animal received a chop indicating that it had "passed inspection and fit for slaughter," it was placed in stalls at the rear of the abattoir and then processed. "For cattle, there are two slaughter men, four dressers and a couple of coolies employed." Each cow then was led from the stall to the slaughterhouse. As soon as it passed the entrance to the building,

> it walks into a noose, which secures its near hind leg and near fore leg and, in a twinkling the animal is lying on its side, with its neck stretched across a receptacle sunk in the floor. The slaughterer approaches from behind, slits its throat and the animal quickly bleeds to death. When its last kick is over, the head is severed from the trunk, and the body is turned over and partly stripped of its hide, drawn on a pulley, dressed, and sent to the cooling room. There is then another inspection for indications of any internal complaint, and if the carcase is found free from taint it is chopped on the legs, shoulders and sides ready for removal by the butchers to the various markets.

---

[62] Of the almost 100,000 pigs officially slaughtered in 1906, only 8,500 were imported, mainly from Vietnam and Kedah. By the end of the colonial era, Bali surpassed Siam as the main beef supplier. This was mainly due to disease outbreaks among the cattle in the Thai kingdom. Anonymous, "The Food Supply: Chinese and Their Exclusive Delicacy," *ST*, 27 Apr. 1907, p. 7; Anonymous, "The Food Supply: Preparing Meat for the Local Market," *ST*, 26 Apr. 1907, p. 7; CO275/149: "Report on the Veterinary Department, Malaya, for the Year 1937," p. 877.
[63] Anonymous, "The Food Supply: Preparing Meat for the Local Market."

Prior to its shipment to local markets, inspectors examined the butchered meat once again, and then applied a chop indicating it was suitable for consumption, and the type of meat it was—such as a large "S" or "G" indicating either mutton or goat—to prevent any fraud.[64]

As for pork, farmers in Singapore raised pigs in the outskirts of the municipality, and transported them to the abattoir in the middle of the night. Upon arrival at one of the slaughterhouses, the coolies would grab the porcine tails and lift them from their transport crates and "deposit the squealing pigs in a convenient gully that runs along immediately outside the pens." The slaughtering occurred between 2 a.m. and 6 a.m.[65] Workers in the abattoir would approach the animals slated for slaughter and,

> with heavy long-handled hammers, stun the pigs, which are lifted from the gully by coolies, who carry them in their arms, place them on cemented blocks, where butchers stand with keen-bladed knives. The throats of the unconscious animals are quickly pierced and immediately that death has occurred, the carcases are thrust into scalding water, scraped clean of bristles, dressed, and hung up in the cooling room ready for final inspection. The whole business is expeditiously carried out, it being calculated that, from the time the pig leaves the pen till the moment it sways on the hooks in the cooling chamber, scarcely ten minutes have elapsed.

In the cooling room, dressers would inject water into the veins of the pig carcass using "antiquated wooded pumps." This drove the blood out of the arteries, and made the pork heavier, "though the meat will not keep so long."[66]

No remains of the slaughtered animal were allowed to remain at the abattoir. As the report mentioned, "All refuse and offal is placed in specially constructed carts and removed to the jungle; tails, hides, heads, horns, entrails are at once taken away by contractors." Blood was collected and sent to other suppliers, who converted it into paint. This meant that numerous carts, filled with animal remains, would

---

[64] Anonymous, "The Food Supply: Preparing Meat for the Local Market."
[65] This then allowed for cattle slaughter to occur afterwards, during the morning. Anonymous, "The Food Supply: Preparing Meat for the Local Market." Anonymous, "The Food Supply: Chinese and Their Exclusive Delicacy."
[66] Anonymous, "The Food Supply: Chinese and Their Exclusive Delicacy."

ply the streets of Singapore. Prior to its removal, however, the refuse accumulated outside the slaughterhouses. "Night comes and passes. Still the heap remains. Wait a day, perchance two, till the scavengers in the heat and bustle of the morning or the crowded hour of noon, sweep this rubbish, which we are duly watching, into open carts while the passersby swallow their daily dole of microbe encrusted dirt." These carts smelled, and were covered in flies, "with wings and feet soiled by the refuse—the nursery of tubercular typhoid, beri-beri bacilli,—they nestle on the meat we shall probably enjoy at dinner." Eventually, the development of incinerators superseded the need for disposal of the rotting remains in the forest. After the incinerators were constructed the animal remains were placed on carts, "now full to overflowing," and coolies would push them to the facilities located opposite the abattoirs. These incinerators were large facilities in their own right, with the first one constructed in Singapore along Syed Alwi Road known as "the Destructor."[67]

In 1906 more than 140,000 animals were slaughtered in the public abattoirs of Singapore. Only 599 animals were rejected that year, mainly because they were already dead following their transport on closely packed ships. The abattoirs charged 25 cents per head to process a pig, goat or sheep, while bullocks cost 70 cents and buffaloes 80 cents. If the animals needed to be kept in the government-approved pens near the abattoirs prior to slaughter, the owners were charged 5 cents for every pig for 24 hours, while others animals merited a charge double that amount. "It is impressed upon the butchers that all animals left in the pens are at the risk and under the care of their owners, who must feed, water, and, if necessary, bed them at their own cost." If animals were to be slaughtered for "domestic ceremonies or sacrificial purposes" the fees were tripled, but allowed through licenses.[68]

Falshaw ensured the public that any disease related to livestock was rare in Singapore. In the 14 years since he assumed his responsibilities in 1892, there had been only three cases of tuberculosis among cattle,

---

[67] Anonymous, "The Food Supply: Preparing Meat for the Local Market"; Anonymous, "The Food Supply: Pertinent Criticisms of Correspondents," *ST*, 29 Apr. 1907, p. 7; Woo Pui Leng, *The Urban History of Jalan Besar*, (Singapore: Urban Redevelopment Authority Singapore, 2010).

[68] Anonymous, "The Food Supply: Some Secrets of Singapore's Menu."

and anthrax was totally absent, while parasites in cattle and pigs were so infrequent they were virtually non-existent. This was mainly attributed to the strict system of monitoring, which had reduced the common late 19th-century occurrence of "animals that were destroyed as unfit for use, and the parts of carcasses that had to be cut away as unwholesome." The food supply was "remarkably good and is, moreover, absolutely free from any disease that affects human beings." The desire for continuous reform and modernization of the food supply even resulted in the government abolition of the farm system of operation for all public markets by 1910. This was accomplished swiftly, as the Ellenborough Market was the first market the municipality directly managed in only 1909. This was done in the "interests of public health" as well as "cleanliness and good order."[69]

The realization of a sanitary food supply in Singapore, and the model of modernity that it offered, was reinforced in 1913, when a veterinary officer from Rangoon visited Singapore to observe the work in the Pulau Saigon and Jalan Besar slaughterhouses with the goal of opening a more efficient abattoir system in the Burmese colonial port. The officer visited both abattoirs, as well as the incinerators used for the destruction of carcasses, the veterinary hospital run under the auspices of the Prevention of Cruelty to Animals Department, the quarantine stations for cattle, and the model dairy and bazaar. In his report, he offered praise of the system, although "the abattoirs are small, but compact, having the bullock and pig slaughtering houses in the same compound."[70] British authorities had created a modern food system for delivering meat to an imperial population. A large percentage of this meat was pork, thus filling the needs of the majority of the residents of Singapore. While beef was still processed, access to what was considered a very European protein would undergo a further transformation as developing technologies allowed for the possibility of importing frozen meat, slaughtered far from Singapore, for an interested population.

---

[69] Hallifax, "Municipal Government," p. 334; Anonymous, "The Food Supply: Some Secrets of Singapore's Menu."

[70] This resulted in chambers being used for slaughtering, which was contrary to the accepted practice at the time of having a "Central Hall system." It was necessary, however, "owing to various factions of the Chinese community who create much disturbance if not separated." Anonymous, "Pigs and Pork," *ST*, 1 Aug. 1913, p. 10.

Protein and Slaughterhouses for a Modern City

The official opening of an abattoir in the mid-1890s was an important symbol of modernity, science and sanitation in the imperial port of Singapore. The planning and construction of the slaughterhouse was plagued with delays, with the entire process taking over six years to complete. A factor in these delays had been criticism from a new player in the meat industry in Singapore, the Australian Meat Company (later the Australian Beef Company), which operated ships from Darwin with the goal of establishing "a wholesale and retail butchering business in Singapore." With its entry into the market in 1892, two years prior to the opening of the abattoirs, it was hoped that it could provide "a plentiful supply of really good beef at a reasonable price." To ensure this possibility, the company secured 150 acres (60.7 hectares) in the New Harbor, with processing facilities and storerooms. Officials from the company, however, soon complained that the various proposed locations for a slaughterhouse were "too much out of the way."[71]

The role that the Australian Meat Company played in early negotiations over the development of the abattoirs in the 1890s was one of the primary factors in the selection of Pulau Saigon for the first abattoir, and it was the site where most of their cattle were eventually processed. The compromises enacted to please a foreign, imperial supplier of beef, however, were still problematic because up to 20 percent of the cattle on ships died on the voyage, which led to investigations from the colonial government in the early decades of the century in the name of animal cruelty, and resulted in a virtual monopoly for the Siamese route in the supply of beef, as it was closer to Singapore. A solution to this problem appeared in 1903 with the establishment of the Cold Storage Company in Singapore, which had the specific goal of importing frozen meat, fresh butter and fruits from Australia for the well-to-do of the port. The company purchased land along Borneo Wharf in Keppel Harbor, and had warehouses with insulated rooms constructed with the capacity to store up to 200 tons of frozen meat. This would address what many in the British community considered to be an issue of considerable importance in Singapore, the lack of high-quality beef. An editor of *The Straits Times* wrote of his anticipation at the possibility

---

[71] Anonymous, "A New Food Supply for Singapore," *SFP*, 4 May 1892, p. 3; Anonymous, "Municipal Commission," *The Daily Advertiser*, 5 Jan. 1893, p. 2.

of this trade when he described his desire for "a rumpsteak from an Australian bullock and a pat of fresh butter at breakfast time," which would "freshen up the inner man and make us better fit for the troubles and worries of business hours," and be of particular benefit to "our British soldiers and sailors."[72]

The first shipment of frozen meat for Cold Storage arrived in Singapore in March 1905. Over 75 percent of the first consignment was beef, 225 tons of the meat from over 800 head of cattle, reflecting the importance of this protein to the colonial diet.[73] The arrival of the meat from Australia was proclaimed a triumph of economies of scale and technology, as the prices offered—particularly for mutton—were initially much lower than those found in the markets. Within a month, however, these prices rose to match that slaughtered in Singapore, leading to criticism of the company and the supposed benefits of imported meat. Cold Storage had difficulty overcoming these initial difficulties for the remainder of the first decade of the century, and the company quickly developed a reputation for offering meat that was not competitively priced, and often from substandard cuts. In addition, shipments occasionally became rancid after arrival at Singapore harbor while the service staff was perceived as particularly surly. All of this led to a temporary closure of its retail operation. The company was only able to sustain business during this period due to contractual obligations with the British military and orders from ships in the port. It was not until 1910 that Cold Storage opened a successful retail space on Orchard Road that allowed the elite to gain access to the foodstuffs from Australia in a less wholesale atmosphere.[74]

The highlight of the new store—once again—was beef. It was, after all, the reason the company had been developed, to satisfy the cultural and dietary needs of the British community in an outpost of

---

[72] Goh Chor Boon, *Serving Singapore: A Hundred Years of Cold Storage, 1903–2003* (Singapore: Cold Storage, 2003), pp. 21–4; Goh, *Technology and Entrepôt Colonialism in Singapore*, p. 168–73; Anonymous, "The Singapore Cold Storage Company," *ST*, 20 Jun 1903, p. 4.

[73] The rest of the shipment included mutton, fresh butter, milk and a few sundries. Goh, *Serving Singapore*, p. 26.

[74] The "Orchard Road Depot" had opened in 1905. It was only in 1910, under new management, that it gained support from shoppers. Anonymous, "Wednesday, 22nd March," *ST*, 22 Mar 1905, p. 4; Lewis and Lambert, "Cold Storage Depot," *ST*, 6 Apr. 1905, p. 5; Goh, *Serving Singapore*, pp. 29–31.

empire. While Cold Storage (laughingly) described the Orchard Road outlet as being in a "working-class" area, it served the needs of elite residents from the nearby Emerald Hill, Selegie and River Valley suburban districts. These areas were filled with European residents, and the contents of the store were "essentially Australian, even to the ornamentation," featuring "frozen quarters of beef and refrigerated carcasses of mutton," as well as frozen milk and canned meats.[75]

By 1915, during the Great War, the efficiency of the abattoirs, developments in technology, and pressures due to continuation of the conflict, led other Australian meat exporters to propose a scheme to use the slaughterhouses in Singapore to supply beef to Malaya at a reasonable price. The meat would travel on ships and then hoof to the Pulau Saigon abattoir, and then as processed beef to Kuala Lumpur via the night express train on "properly built meat vans." The key factor in such a proposal was that the meat would be frozen. Following the end of the war, these networks of imperial and global trade remained, creating more work for the abattoir as well as enquiries on how to provide a sanitary and efficient supply of meat to the expanding population of Malaya.[76]

In 1921 a special committee reported to the Municipal Commission on markets and the food supply of Singapore. While much of the report focused on the make-up and functioning of markets on the island—with a report that "certain races," specifically Hokkiens at Clyde Terrace Market and Teochews at Ellenborough Market, were creating unhealthy monopolies and competition influencing prices of fish and other proteins—emphasis was directed toward the question of continued importation of cattle from Australia. The report recommended direct intervention and support of shipping from Western Australia and that the abattoirs differentiate their tasks, with one focusing on locally raised animals while the other be set aside for those imported by sea or rail. Limited space in the wharfs and grazing space for imported

---

[75] Anonymous, "The Industrial Stalls," *ST*, 17 Aug. 1910, p. 10; Goh, *Serving Singapore*, p. 38.

[76] The population of Singapore reached 400,000 in 1920, double the number of 1900. In addition, these networks were to address a situation in which frozen meat cost 50 to 100 percent more in Malaya due to delivery costs from Singapore. Up-Country, "Rd Cold Storage Co., Ltd.," *ST*, 9 Jan 1915, p. 11; Anonymous, "The Frozen Meat Supply," *SFP*, 16 Apr. 1915, p. 4; Anonymous, "Singapore= F.M.S. Fresh Meat Trade," *MT*, 18 May 1915, p. 5.

animals awaiting slaughter was also perceived as problematic. A solution was to construct "a quarantine station and grazing ground; all on one site," on an offshore island.[77]

The report on importation of meat from Australia submitted to the municipal commissioners resulted in a trade delegation visiting Singapore from Western Australia in late 1921. The chairman of the delegation, C.S. Nathan, emphasized the use of ships to import both live animals and frozen meat from Freemantle. He pointed out that the delegation had come with 3,000 sheep, "all reared in Western Australia," in "most excellent condition," with only three lambs dying on the voyage.[78] This was to be the beginning of the development of the next phase of providing access to Australian livestock for residents of Singapore and Malaya, although much of the discussion focused on the importation of beef to please the colonial diet.

To provide an adequate supply of beef and mutton for Singapore in the 1920s, it was argued that the construction of a new abattoir was necessary, with Pasir Panjang being the proposed site.[79] To consider whether this was the best approach, Municipal Engineer H.L. Pearson visited Australia in 1922 to examine their facilities and investigate alternatives to the monopoly "of frozen meat in the hands of an Australian Company and that of live cattle in the hands of a native ring." Pearson considered three possible methods for transporting beef and mutton to Singapore—"(a) On the hoof, (b) Chilled, (c) Frozen." The preferred method in Singapore was importation of live animals, as "all religious prejudices in connection with the act of slaughter can be fully satisfied in the simplest manner." The processing of animals in Australia, however, had advantages due to the loss of weight and muscle tone during the journey to Southeast Asia. Pearson clearly preferred the shipment of frozen meat. He proclaimed that the shipment of live animals left him with "nothing but surprise that the deaths are not far greater and that most of the survivors are fit for human consumption" following their taxing journey. In addition, "setting aside all humanitarian reasons it must be obvious to any one who witnesses the handling of cattle from

---

[77] Anonymous, "Municipal Markets," *ST*, 26 Mar. 1921, p. 11; Anonymous, "Municipal Commission," *ST*, 29 Oct. 1921, p. 9; Anonymous, "Cold Storage," *ST*, 1 Aug. 1922, p. 10; Anonymous, "Singapore Food Supply," *SFP*, 25 Mar. 1921, p. 12.

[78] Anonymous, "Trade Reciprocity," *ST*, 12 Nov. 1921, p. 10.

[79] Francis J.J. Van Cant, "Malaya's Opportunity," *SFP*, 16 May 1922, p. 10.

Australia ... that there is considerable loss in weight and quality in the process." This was also applicable to the shipping of sheep, although they tended to "travel better."[80]

The proposed abattoir at Pasir Panjang, nevertheless, was not ideal as ships would not be able to berth alongside the facility. This left three possibilities, according to Pearson, if live cattle continued to be imported. The first was to land cattle at Keppel Harbor and then drive them over 1.5 kilometers to the current abattoir. This would require cattle drives to take place over several public roads, leading to closures and a variety of other issues. The second and third alternative required the transfer of cattle to trucks or lighters, which would then carry them over land or water to the abattoir. The "double handling" of the animals also would add to logistical issues and costs. To circumvent all three of these possibilities, Pearson recommended the construction of a long pier at the Pulau Saigon abattoir, from which cattle could be funneled directly into the slaughterhouse.[81]

Questions were soon raised about why there was so much focus on a beef and mutton, as they were of little importance to the diet of the majority of the population. As most people—Chinese in Singapore—consumed pork, any changes to the abattoir system and markets needed to bear this in mind, as it was the most important protein in the society, particularly as the number of pigs slaughtered continued to rise, while the numbers for other types of protein consumed remained relatively stable.[82] In light of these circumstances, by early 1923, the Municipal Commission abandoned the proposal to build a new abattoir at Pasir Panjang, as "the importation of live cattle is an artificial trade which cannot possibly last, once the public have been educated up to the

---

[80] Anonymous, "Killing for Food," *SFP*, 10 Aug. 1922, p. 6; Anonymous, "Cold Storage," *ST*, 1 Aug. 1922, p. 10.

[81] All of this was to handle an estimated 82 local cattle and 100 Australian cattle every day. Anonymous, "Cold Storage," *ST*, 1 Aug. 1922, p. 10.

[82] While the majority of pork consumed in Singapore came from locally raised pigs, the growth in population in the early 20th century merited the beginning of importation, mainly from Vietnam and Bali. Upon arrival, however, the pigs often were "not in a fit condition to be killed, and have for several days before being sent to the butcher to be fed up for the purpose." By the late 1920s imported pigs began to receive attention from the SPCA due to charges of cruelty. Anonymous, "Abattoir Agitation," *SFP*, 28 Feb. 1894, p. 3; Anonymous, "Singapore S.P.C.A.," *ST*, 5 Nov. 1929, p. 6.

advantages of cold storage," and began focusing on the development of facilities for the importation of frozen meat.[83]

Table 2: Animals slaughtered in the municipal abattoirs, Singapore, in 1906, 1928 and 1937[84]

Animal	1906	1928	1937
Pigs	99,362	188,785	304,682
Sheep	23,312	32,069	32,572
Goats	6,860	8,250	4,501
Cattle	10,948	18,208	17,584
Buffaloes	174	857	82

Efforts to modernize the delivery of protein to Singapore were also extended into the surrounding seas. This began as early as the first decade of the 20th century, when the *kelong* that dotted the southern shores of Singapore came to be marked as "shipping hazards." New rules and regulations were passed, including Ordinance IX of 1909, which regulated fisheries in these waters and doubled the number of fisheries officers, although most of their work was "solely with a view to the prevention of obstruction to shipping by fishing stakes." This was the beginning of a rapid increase in the amount of fish supplied to the Singapore market, which can be seen in the rise in the number of fishing boats operating out of Singapore from 200 to 490 between 1908 and 1920. Registered *kelong* also grew from 249 to 341 during the same period, although they were less frequently located along the southern shores of the island.[85]

---

[83] Anonymous, "Killing for Food," *SFP*, 10 Aug. 1922, p. 6; Anonymous, "Government Abattoir Scheme," *SFP*, 14 Mar. 1923, p. 6.

[84] Anonymous, "The Food Supply: Some Secrets of Singapore's Menu"; Anonymous, "Eating Houses and Hawkers' Stalls," *MT*, 23 Sep. 1930, p. 10; CO275/149: "Report on the Veterinary Department, Malaya, for the Year 1937," p. 884.

[85] The importance of Singapore in the fish trade can be seen in the town of Bagan Si Api Api on the Rokan River in Sumatra, which exported 26,000 tons of dried fish and 2,700 tons of *belacan* (fish paste) in 1904 alone, with most of it going to the main urban center of the Straits Settlements. Butcher, *The Closing of a Frontier*, p. 82; J.F.D. Hardenberg, "The Fishfauna of the Rokan Mouth," *Treubia* 8, 1 (1931): 81–168; Reeves and Reeves, "Port-City Development and Singapore's Inshore and Culture Fisheries," pp. 126–9; Wright and Cartwright, *Twentieth Century Impressions of British Malaya*, pp. 215–6.

By the early 1920s the colonial government commissioned a report that led to the development of a Department of Fisheries. This new government entity monitored the fleet of ships that drifted across Dutch and British colonial boundaries employing new technologies, such as driftnets, and provided Singapore with fresh fish throughout the colonial era. Steamships with cargos of salted fish from ports in Java and Sumatra supplemented these supplies. Records throughout the colonial era report the vast number of fishing vessels, and even the eventual inclusion of a large Japanese fleet, that regularly stopped in Singapore harbor, and quickly grew to control 40 percent of the commerce in supplying fish to the port by the late colonial era.[86]

In the meantime, back on land, with the abandonment of a possible slaughterhouse in Pasir Panjang, the two aging abattoirs continued to operate, although this resulted in government authorities being the recipients of a seemingly constant grumbling from the public over issues such as odors and disruption to traffic and business throughout the municipality. One of the most persistent complaints at this time focused on the "shrieks of the poor beasts" from 1:30 to 3:30 in the morning, when pigs were slaughtered at the Pulau Saigon abattoir, reportedly from being immersed alive in boiling water. Reflecting how the civilizational discourse had become part of the discussion, the main complainant—E.M. Stephenson—opined, "as long as we feed on beef, mutton, pork etc., we cannot afford to be too squeamish, but surely it is the duty of a British civilized community to see that the conditions under which the animals are slaughtered are as humane as possible." Facing a litany of complaints and suggestions, the authorities soon began considering the closure of the both abattoirs built in the 1890s, and the shift of animal slaughtering to "the edge of town" or the construction of a new facility near one of the current sites.[87]

---

[86] David G. Stead, *General Report upon the Fisheries of British Malaya with Recommendations for Future Development* (Singapore: Government Printing Office, 1923); C.N. Maxwell, *Preliminary Report on the Economic Position of the Fishing Industry of the Straits Settlements and the Federated Malay States* (Singapore: Government Printer, 1921), p. 6; Eric Tagliacozzo, *Secret Trades, Porous Borders: Smuggling and States along a Southeast Asian Frontier, 1865–1915* (New Haven: Yale University Press, 2005).

[87] E.M. Stephenson, "The Nightly Pig Debacle," *SFP*, 19 Oct. 1925, p. 3; Anonymous, "And Still We Wait," *SFP*, 31 Oct. 1925, p. 8; Anonymous, "The Municipality," *MT*, 7 Nov. 1925, p. 8; Anonymous, "Cruelty to Animals and Abattoirs," *MT*, 6 Sep. 1926, p. 6.

The issue of a new abattoir became a subject for debate for several years among the municipal commissioners in the mid-1920s. As the reclamation and construction was going to be a long-term and expensive project, the municipal commissioners decided to allocate $4,000 for repairs to the existing facilities, and renewed the call for the use of an offshore island for grazing and slaughtering purposes in 1925. The most common proposal during this period was a consolidation of the two slaughterhouses at one site, located on a reclaimed "piece of swamp somewhere near Lavender" Street. This reclaimed site theoretically would have "suitable wharfage facilities for landing cattle, sheeps and pigs, and railway transport," thus reflecting the focus on imported animals instead of those reared in Singapore. Over the next two years numerous meetings, reports and inquiries were made about the import of cattle to Singapore. During this period, "some sixty-six communications" passed between "the Colonial Secretary, the Municipality, the Harbour Board, the F.M.S. Railways, etc ... on the subject of a suitable site for landing and slaughtering imported stock." As one observer noted, it was a subject that "was pressing four years ago: it is more than ever pressing now," particularly as the population of Singapore expanded rapidly to some 600,000 by 1930, a doubling of the number of residents in 20 years.[88]

Another key issue, beyond the location of the new abattoir and the growing population, was ensuring that "all slaughtering in Singapore is done by the Mohamedan method, which means cutting the throat of the beast, after certain religious rites are performed, and with no preliminary stunning whatever." This issue had first arisen out of concerns over Muslims refraining from the purchase of frozen meat at Cold Storage, and it soon became conflated with the sale of live poultry in the markets. Traditionally, from the perspective of the government, there was no requirement to slaughter poultry and ducks at the abattoirs. Birds were sold in markets alive, or quickly slaughtered as part of the transaction between seller and buyer. Much of this came to a head

---

[88] Another factor in this proposal was that the only suitable location on shore for a new slaughterhouse had been designated for the Yacht Club. In addition, the abattoir budget was a mere pittance, compared to that for senior officers' quarters ($100,000) or housing for subordinate staff of the Municipal Commission ($200,000). Anonymous, "Ninety to One Against," *SFP*, 6 Nov. 1925, p. 8; Anonymous, "And Still We Wait," *SFP*, 4 Nov. 1925, p. 2; Anonymous, "Municipal Commission," *SFP*, 26 May 1923, p. 12.

following a report of a Muslim butcher causing "unnecessary cruelty to a fowl" when he slaughtered a chicken in the market in Penang was put on trial. Similar cases were cited throughout the Straits Settlements in the late 1920s, with much of it centered on the adherence to halal practices versus the use of methods promoted in British abattoirs, such as stunning the animal prior to slaughter, which the government advocated. The debate would go on for the remainder of the colonial era.[89]

In this context, in 1927, the government appointed a committee to look into a range of these issues, including "the alleged prevalence of cruelty to animals in Singapore." They visited cattle ships, abattoirs, and bird shops. Everything they saw on the cattle ships was "generally in very good condition." The reports suggested that the unloading of the cattle from ships could be improved as it was often at the mercy of tides that influenced the height of the planks. Other methods of transferring the animals ashore were also problematic. Ideally, they were "lifted through hatches by means of the ship's derrick and a canvas belt passed under their middles and they are then swung out and lowered into the well of the 'Shoe Boat.'" While the harnesses were generally fine, the condition of the "Shoe Boats" was also an issue. For pigs, they were lifted in a "pig basket," which ideally used two hooks, one at each end. The common practice, however, was to use one hook, which often resulted in great distress (possibly, even injury) to the pig if there was uneven weight distribution in the harness. The layout of the abattoir was also a problem. Cattle awaiting slaughter were kept very close to the place where they would be killed. "It is wrong that animals awaiting slaughter should be able to witness the actual killing, they should also be far enough away not to be affected by the smell of blood, which as is well-known, affects cattle very much."[90]

The recommendations of the committee focused on how the PCA could become involved in monitoring the system of transporting food animals in Singapore and their subsequent slaughter. Among the primary proposals was the appointment of an assistant inspector from the department to the staff of the veterinary surgeon. His "chief duty would be to ensure that the strict observance of the Port Rule

---

[89] H.W.H. Stevens, "Live Stock Supplies," *SFP*, 19 Mar. 1926, p. 16; Anonymous, "P.C.A. in Singapore," ST, 27 Oct. 1926, p. 8; Anonymous, "Cold Storage," *ST*, 1 Aug. 1922, p. 10; Yahaya, "The Question of Animal Slaughter."
[90] Anonymous, "Alleged Cruelty to Animals," *SFP*, 2 July 1927, p. 3.

and Regulations for the carriage of Livestock and the unloading and landing of the same." He would be provided with a motorboat, which he could use to patrol the harbor and visit random livestock ships. In addition, new standards would be developed for the size of the canvas band that lifted cattle and requirements emphasized related to the use of two hooks in the lifting of pigs. Finally, "as a temporary partial alleviation of the situation at the present Abattoirs, it is recommended that screens be erected between the cattle pens and killing floors."[91]

By the late 1920s the abattoirs were perceived as a municipal service badly in need of renewal as, in the words of one report, there was "considerable misapprehension" with regard to whether the meat was suitable for human consumption. The Pulau Saigon abattoir "was on its last legs, and Jalan Besar abattoir was in anything but a suitable condition, according to modern ideas." Accounts also periodically appeared in the papers reporting mismanagement and "irregularities," often involving disinterested workers or tainted meat. As a stopgap measure, a temporary abattoir was proposed on a budget of $150,000 on reclaimed land in the Jalan Besar area while a new one was constructed, with the goal of replacing the original slaughterhouse and closing the one on Pulau Saigon. Eventually temporary slaughterhouses began operating on Bukit Timah Road and in Kampong Bahru, the latter of which was near the railway station, allowing for greater access to markets in Malaya. These temporary slaughtering sites—"makeshift solutions"—operated for several years, while the Pulau Saigon abattoir also continued to provide meat for the Singaporean and Malayan market.[92]

Construction on a new abattoir at Jalan Besar began in 1928. During its erection, a number of proposals were debated with regard to its layout and amenities. The main consideration was the development of separate facilities dedicated to the slaughtering of pigs, to accommodate its outsized role in the local diet as well as to create distinct spaces for the processing of the meat so as not to offend the Islamic community. There were also proposals for the construction of another slaughterhouse and quarantine station "in the valley of the Singapore

---

[91] Anonymous, "Alleged Cruelty to Animals," *SFP*, 2 July 1927, p. 3.

[92] Anonymous, "Discovery at Abattoirs," *ST*, 9 June 1928, p. 11; Anonymous, "'Iced Pork': The True Position of Affairs," *MT*, 5 July 1930, p. 7; Anonymous, "Municipal Board Meeting," *MT*, 29 Oct. 1927, p. 10; Anonymous, "Singapore Abattoirs," *SFP*, 23 Sep. 1929, p. 6.

River and near Buona Vista Road," which would accommodate imported cattle and sheep from Australia, although much of it was dependent on the possible construction of a spur for the railway to serve the facility.[93] Most of these proposals were for naught, except for a separate facility for the processing of pork.

The new Jalan Besar abattoir was completed in 1932, and it provided one centralized site for the slaughter and processing of animals for meat in Singapore. The facility was divided into three sections, which handled the slaughter of all cattle, sheep, goats and buffaloes, while there was a separate building along French Road to process pigs.[94] In this new complex the entire slaughtering process for animals in Singapore had been modernized even further. Pigs, for example, were initially hit with a jolt from "an electrical stunning apparatus" in hope that it would reduce the number of complaints from nearby residents of noise during the killing process. In addition, the pork was to be stored in a "chiller," which would preclude the need for work throughout the night, a move that had been met initially with "a storm of indignation" from the Chinese community, as "chilled pork was not worth eating." Other modern techniques quickly followed. Within two years, all animals moving through the facilities encountered an "electrothaler," while cattle were funneled through "Weinberg casting pens," a narrow stall that slowly inverts the animal until it is lying on its back, which addressed some of the concerns related to Muslim ritual requirements in the slaughtering process. As one observer proudly concluded, "In the new abattoir, too, it will be possible to exercise much more expert supervision and it will be possible once and for all to put a stop to the many abuses of the present system of slaughtering."[95]

The abattoirs, and how protein was delivered to Singaporean society, represented the ability of the government to implement a rationalization of the entire process of raising and consuming proteins that

---

[93] Anonymous, "Singapore Abattoirs," *SFP*, 23 Sep. 1929, p. 6.

[94] Although the Pulau Saigon facility had officially closed in 1930, it continued to operate for two more years until this specific pig abattoir opened. Anonymous, "Keeping Singapore in Meat," *Morning Tribune*, 7 Mar. 1936, p. 11.

[95] Anonymous, "The Chilled Pork Controversy," *MT*, 6 Dec. 1930, p. 11; Anonymous, "The Health of Singapore," *MT*, 20 July 1932, p. 13; Anonymous, "Municipality's Satisfactory Year," *ST*, 4 Aug. 1934, p. 6; Temple Grandin, "Improving Welfare and Reducing Stress on Animals at Slaughter Plants," in *Livestock Handling and Transport*, ed. Temple Grandin (Boston, MA: CABI, 2014), p. 440.

enhanced its influence over the personal lives of its subjects, including their diet, on a massive scale and based on European standards. As it was reported in the late 1930s, Singapore had "modern Municipal abattoirs, run strictly on the lines recommended by England's Ministry of Health." In these facilities an average of 650 pigs were slaughtered every day, a number that would rise to more than 3,000 as Chinese New Year approached. This meant that under the colonial gaze over 300,000 animals were processed annually in the years leading up to the Japanese invasion of Singapore. This was three times the number of animals handled 30 years earlier at the Pulau Saigon and Jalan Besar abattoirs.[96] These facilities served a population that had expanded from 220,000 in 1900 to almost 800,000 in 1942 on an island that supported less than 1,000 inhabitants a little over a century earlier. The slaughterhouses and markets contributed to rationalizing Singapore into a modern, imperial city, a place filled with human and other animals, some of which they ate.

Beyond the delivery of protein to a growing population, the abattoirs and modern food system in Singapore represented the refinement of the human-animal relationship under imperialism, and the triumph of a sanitary regime. The lives and treatment of these animals were monitored, controlled and regulated, often through governmental departments, ranging from health to transportation. While it was deemed important that animals be treated with concern and care, and that this process take place under hygienic conditions, the ultimate end for these imperial creatures was a violent one so they could provide protein to an expanding population. The disciplining of this relationship ensured that animals remained a commodity to be consumed in colonial Singapore, a thoroughly modern, and model, imperial society.

---

[96] There were also 18 Rural Board licensed slaughterhouses that solely dealt with pigs. Slaughtering took place at night since there "no facilities for chilling or keeping the carcasses." It was illegal to sell the pork from these premises within the Singapore municipality. CO275/149: "Report on the Veterinary Department, Malaya, for the Year 1937," p. 890; Anonymous, "Keeping Singapore in Meat."

The White Monkey

The Japanese Imperial Army captured Singapore in February 1942, bringing an end to one era of colonial rule over the island. The arrival of a new imperial master led to a tremendous amount of consternation among the populace, particularly European residents. One of the concerned and displaced was E.J.H. Corner, the Deputy Director of the Singapore Botanic Gardens. Corner, as described in his post-war account of the period, feared that the invaders would plunder the archives and laboratories of colonial knowledge of the natural world held in various institutions in Singapore. He rushed down to the Town Hall to meet with Japanese officials and demand that they protect the legacy of scientific research that was held at the Raffles Museum and the Botanic Gardens. Japanese officials greeted him with respect and arranged for Corner and many of his colleagues to return to their institutions, where they resumed their work. It was a period of tremendous academic productivity for British scientists in Singapore.[1]

While Corner continued his research on tropical botany under the auspices of Japanese imperial rule, he did so without some of his most famous research assistants, a troop of southern pig-tailed macaques (*Macaca nemestrina*). The botanist had first considered using monkeys on his collecting trips to the forest in November 1929, soon after his arrival in the Straits Settlements. The idea had come to Corner when

---

[1] E.J.H. Corner, *The Marquis; A Tale of Syonan-to* (Singapore: Heinemann Asia, 1981), pp. 23–4; Barnard, *Nature's Colony*, pp. 211–2.

he saw a *berok*, as macaques were known in the region, "climbing the tall coconut palms and twisting off the nuts" while visiting the Malay state of Perlis. He realized that if the monkey "could be trained to pull off twigs, flowers and fruits," it could venture into parts of the forest canopy that were normally off limits to collectors and explorers. Facing ridicule from colleagues, the British colonial botanist did not pursue the possibility any further at the time.[2]

Corner revisited the idea in April 1937 when he stopped at a village near the Thai border while on an expedition to Kelantan and Trengganu. As was usual when conducting research, he began asking about the names of local trees from curious bystanders who had gathered around him. In the midst of these discussions, an elderly villager named Awang bin Salleh walked over with a macaque on a long chain. Corner admired the monkey, although its master bemoaned that it was getting too big to be kept any longer. After some haggling, the botanist purchased the monkey, named Merah ("red" in Malay), and returned to Singapore armed with the advice that it be fed fruit and raw vegetables as well as a raw egg once a week. Insects, spiders, small lizards and birds' eggs that were found while collecting in the canopy would eventually supplement its diet. Corner was also told, the monkey "would never obey me until I had reduced it with a thrashing to tears," to which "he gave no thought to the chastisement." He believed that such an approach was unnecessary, as it had been done to train macaques in their usual task of harvesting coconuts, which was not suitable for their hands and strength. In contrast, Corner wanted Merah and the other botanical monkeys that followed to pursue, "their natural lives among the wild trees, and our task was to make use of this untrammelled enthusiasm."[3]

Merah was a remarkable research assistant, eventually collecting over 300 unique specimens during its two years of service. Unfortunately, the botanical monkey died following a collecting trip to Fraser's Hill in the Malay Peninsula after it consumed an abrasive and possibly toxic fruit. Realizing the potential that had been shown in Merah's ability to scamper in the canopy and collect specimens heretofore out of the reach

[2] E.J.H. Corner, *Botanical Monkeys* (Cambridge: Pentland Press, 1992), p. 1.

[3] Anonymous, "Monkey Helps Botanist," *SFP*, 31 May 1937, p. 6; Anonymous, "Monkey's New Career," *ST* 30 May 1937, p. 15; Corner, *Botanical Monkeys*, pp. 2–5.

of researchers, Corner obtained two more macaques, named Puteh and Jambul from Awang. Puteh (meaning "white") was ultimately "most able, if unruly," while Jambul (meaning a "tuft of hair") was "docile and much less competent," according to Corner. These new assistants moved into a house at 30 Cluny Road with the Deputy Director who, along with his human assistants, oversaw their care and training, which occurred in the nearby Gardens Jungle.[4]

A newspaper article in *The Sunday Tribune* from 1939 featured the exploits of these "first monkeys to be employed by the Government." The "method of manipulation" employed while collecting specimens involved each *berok* being tied to a long cord over 60 meters in length. A human would manipulate the string "on the principle of a fishing rod" and shout out orders in Malay, instructing the simian to move on to a new tree, focus on a particular specimen, or twist it free. Ultimately, Corner claimed that they recognized a number of directions, with one able to distinguish between 24 commands including "*lari*" (run), "*mari*" (come) and "*chari*" (search for).[5]

These botanical monkeys were essential in the research Corner conducted on the trees of Singapore and the Malay Peninsula, which established him as one of the leading tropical botanists in the world. "For the first time," he remembered,

> I was able to botanize freely in the forest. I would take the monkeys in a wooden cage in the back of a car over to the great forest in Johore, which could enter from a road on the eastern side, and we would spend the day collecting specimens off trees and climbers, and we would return time and again to the same place to study the leafing or flowering of the trees, which we had thus learnt without having to destroy them.[6]

The only reward these research assistants received for this labor was a drink of lemonade at the end of a day collecting, which left the

---

[4] These human assistants included a "monkey boy." Corner, *Botanical Monkeys*, pp. 6–9.

[5] Anonymous, "Government Trains Monkeys to Collect Fruits, Twigs," *The Sunday Tribune* (Singapore), 22 Jan. 1939, p. 3; Corner, *Botanical Monkeys*, pp. 17–8; John K. Corner, *My Father in a Suitcase: In Search of E.J.H. Corner, the Relentless Botanist* (Singapore: Landmark Books, 2013), pp. 102–3.

[6] Corner, *Botanical Monkeys*, p. 16.

Image 7.1: E.J.H. Corner with one of his botanical monkeys. Courtesy of the Cambridge University Digital Library.

monkeys contented "and there would be no trouble in the car on the way home."[7]

Over the next few years, several more monkeys joined the troop, becoming part of a larger contingent of primates that were nurtured and trained to serve colonial knowledge. Throughout this period, between 1939 and 1941, the various *berok* became part of the Corner household, even accompanying the Deputy Director on trips about the town. One day the botanist even took Puteh to visit the Punggol Zoo that William Basapa operated, at which—as Corner described—"some animals were resident and on show; others were in transit for their destinations." Puteh strolled through the compound, scrutinizing and even taunting the animals. After a tiger leapt at the bars of its cage in retaliation, the monkey fled to the arms of Corner, its protector. The two visitors to the zoo then proceeded to the enclosures where simians

---

[7] Corner, *Botanical Monkeys*, p. 20.

were kept. Puteh interacted well with his fellow apes, reaching out to a chimpanzee, and then cooing and playing with a black gibbon. Only after an elephant and bullock approached, was the botanical monkey startled back into reality, rushing back to Corner's embrace. "He was and, yet, was not part of that brutish zoo," is how the botanist concluded his description of the encounter.[8]

As the visit to the Punggol Zoo suggests, Corner considered the monkeys under his care to be members of his extended family. He cherished the contributions that they made to his research, and would often relax in the compound of his house while they frolicked during their down time from collecting and training. Most of these monkeys, however, died from a variety of issues, ranging from natural poisons in the specimens they collected to strangling, which a disgruntled coolie in the Gardens administered in an act of "cowardly vengeance." By late 1941 only five macaques remained in the program.[9]

With the imminent arrival of the Japanese forces in Singapore, Corner became concerned over the fate awaiting these unique members of his household. Two days before the British surrender, he freed four of the macaques that had blurred the line between a domestic pet and a utilitarian helper in his research. Three of them "were soon captured and became the pets of Japanese soldiers." The fourth, Merah II, roamed Singapore, mainly living in the Gardens Jungle, although there were reports it wandered as far as Thomson Road in search of food. In late October 1942 Corner was informed that a macaque with a collar had fallen into the Rochor Canal. Suspecting that it was his former assistant, he rushed to the "great open sewer," and found Merah II "clinging with one hand to a shrub overhanging the flooding waters of the canal which swept over his shoulders. It was sodden, dazed, half-drowned, skinny and starving." Corner dragged the monkey out of its predicament, and took it to a friend, T. Balasingham, who cared for the *berok* for the remainder of the Japanese Occupation. Corner last saw Merah II in October 1945. The macaque no longer recognized its former colonial master. As Corner recalled, "he had grown so large and strong that, in his dominion, he no longer acknowledged me."[10]

---

[8] Corner, *Botanical Monkeys*, pp. 21–2.
[9] Corner, *Botanical Monkeys*, pp. 19, 39–48.
[10] Corner, *The Marquis*, pp. 97–8; Corner, *Botanical Monkeys*, p. 49.

While Corner had released four of his botanical monkeys to the forest upon the eve of the invasion, there was one he refused to set free. It was Puteh, the assistant that he considered "the cleverest and my favorite." Despite the care and affection Corner felt for the macaque, this imperial creature had a different fate. In the months prior to the Japanese invasion, Puteh had begun to show signs of belligerence, to the point that it had "become savage." One day, when Corner was playing with two of the younger macaques in the garden of his house, the beast rushed at his colonial master "with open jaws and slobbering fangs." Puteh bit into Corner's forearm, slicing through muscle. Corner rushed to Singapore General Hospital, where the chief surgeon "joined up the pieces" of hanging flesh. He recovered in a hospital ward for a week, suffering from an infection that caused his arm to swell severely, and was told not to use the appendage for four months. In the aftermath, Puteh's fangs were sawn off and it was confined to a cage. As the Japanese entered Singapore, and after releasing Merah II and the other three monkeys to the Gardens Jungle, the botanist walked up to the cage with a gun. Puteh "peered inquisitively into the barrel of the small revolver, just as he used to peer into the holes of tree trunks." E.J.H. Corner shot Puteh. "Death was instantaneous."[11]

---

[11] The date of the execution is up for debate, although the act is not. Corner, *My Father in a Suitcase*, pp. 104, 107; Corner, *Botanical Monkeys*, pp. 50–1; Corner, *The Marquis*, pp. 22, 97–8.

Acknowledgements

While this monograph has a single author, it is the product of numerous people who have influenced my understandings and approaches to the material, and this has been taking place over many decades. The origins of this book began when I was a graduate student, initially in Ohio and then Hawaii, when I was encouraged to explore topics and societies from new perspectives. This continued throughout my academic career, with a continual gathering of accounts and ideas related to animals until I was comfortable writing them down over the three years preceding its publication. In each instance friends, colleagues and fellow researchers have provided comments and feedback that force me to consider the material in new ways.

Much of the work on this book began with specific research in libraries and archives throughout the world, although Singapore and the United Kingdom have been the main centers for such activity. At each institution, there have been librarians and archivists who have provided exceptional and vital access to materials. To all of them, whether cited or not, my sincere thanks is extended. Those who merit particular consideration include Han Ming Guang and Tim Yap Fuan from the National University of Singapore Library, Fiona Tan at the National Archives of Singapore, and Christina Soh at the Singapore Botanic Gardens Library and Archives. In London, Annabel Teh Gallop has always made the British Library a welcome site of research, while the Natural History Museum and Wellcome Trust contain wonderful scientists and scholars who offered access to an astonishing range of materials and openness that make them models for all institutions.

This research also percolated out of work done in the classroom in Singapore. While I have been at the National University of Singapore for 20 years, over the past decade I have led students on a journey through the Singaporean archives and environmental histories in specific classes during their final year of undergraduate study. In our exploration of the sources and approaches, I often have stumbled onto hidden stories from our past, which have led me into some of the studies that are contained in this book. While all of the students enrolled in these courses have helped me understand the material with fresh eyes and new perspectives, some individuals made particularly important contributions, which deserve mention, including Valerie Yip, Justin Clarke, Sandy Yeo, Lock Hui Qi, Sophie Sim, Heleyna Ann Fernandez, Cheryl Lek, and particularly Choo Ruizhi.

Outside of the classroom, all of my colleagues at the National University of Singapore, and particularly those in the Department of History, have influenced my grasp of this material, whether they realize it or not, through their own contributions to the field and comments given to me in the hallway, canteen or sitting around in various offices. Among those whose support have made this possible in a more direct manner are Maitrii Aung-Thwin, Donna Brunero, Brian Farrell, Ian Gordon, Ho Chi Tim, Priya Jaradi, Paul Kratoska, Medha Kudaisya, Kelvin Lawrence, Joey Long, Sharon Low, John Miksic, Jennifer Morris, Oona Parades, Sandeep Ray, Peter Schoppert, John Solomon, and Nurfadzilah Yahaya. All of their help has been greatly appreciated.

Beyond the confines of the university, there are also many friends and colleagues who have shared information and time, which has greatly enhanced this work. I have benefitted from being surrounded by a supportive network at every step of the process of writing this book, as well as in daily life, whose constant encouragement, as well as criticism and mocking of certain topics or the lack of progress, kept me motivated. Among those who deserve particular recognition in this process are Martin Bazylewich, Ryan Bishop, Cynthia Chou, Robert Cribb, Patrick Daly, Will Derks, Mark Emmanuel, Ian Gordon (once again), Alvin Hew, Li Hongyan, Sandra Manickam, Matthew Minarchek, Mok Mei Feng, Miles Powell, Jan van der Putten, Joanna Tan, Nigel Taylor, David Teague, Ted Wong, Jeff Yeo, and finally Belle, Chris, Matilda and Chloe Yong.

Last, but not least, is family, whose constant support and understanding make life so fulfilling and enjoyable. Maureen Danker, Julia Barnard, Jordan Wade, as well as Cheryl Lester, Philip Barnard, and Harry and Wanda Barnard enrich my existence through their mere presence, while Claudia Ting makes every moment a joy. They have been teachers, guides, friends and family on this journey.

Bibliography

Note on Archival Records

Archival Records are identified with their full designation the first time they are cited. Subsequent citations follow the common abbreviation. In this sense, the India Office Records in the British Library becomes "IOR" while the Henry Nicholas Ridley collection at that Royal Botanic Gardens, Kew will be referred to as "HNR" and the "National Archives of Singapore as "NAS."

Newspapers

The Chicago Sunday Tribune
The Daily Advertiser
The Graphic
The Malaya Tribune
The Mid-Day Herald
The Morning Tribune
New Straits Times
Singapore Chronicle and Commercial Advertiser
The Singapore Free Press and Mercantile Advertiser
The Straits Advocate
The Straits Eurasian Advocate
The Straits Observer
The Straits Times
The Straits Times Overland Journal
The Sunday Tribune (Singapore)

Published Sources

Abdullah bin Abdul Kadir. "The Hikayat Abdullah, An Annotated Translation by A.H. Hill", *Journal of the Malayan Branch of the Royal Asiatic Society*, 28, 3 (1955): 1–345.

An Old Resident (W.H.M. Read). *Play and Politics: Reminiscences of Malaya.* London: Wells Gardner, Darton and Company, 1901.

Anderson, Virginia DeJohn. *Creatures of Empire: How Domestic Animals Transformed Early America.* Oxford: Oxford University Press, 2004.

Anonymous. *Catalogue of the Singapore Dog Show.* Kuala Lumpur: Charles Ward-Jackson for the Malayan Kennel Association, 1936.

Anonymous. "A Century of Sport." In *One Hundred Years of Singapore, Being an Account of the Capital of the Straits Settlements from its Foundation by Sir Stamford Raffles on the 6th February 1819 to the 6th February 1919,* vol. II, ed. Walter Makepeace, Gilbert E. Brooke, and Roland St. J. Braddell. London: John Murray, 1921, pp. 320–67.

Anonymous. *Guide to the Malaya-Borneo Exhibition 1922 and Souvenir of Malaya.* Singapore: Malaya-Borneo Exhibition, 1922.

Anonymous. "Horse-Racing." In *Twentieth Century Impressions of British Malaya: Its History, People, Commerce, Industries, and Resources,* ed. Arnold Wright and H.A. Cartwright. London: Lloyd's Greater Britain Publishing Company, 1908, pp. 562–80.

Anonymous. *Horse-Racing: Its History and Early Records of the Principal and Other Race Meetings. With Anecdotes, etc.* London: Saunders, Otley and Co., 1863.

Anonymous. *List of the Specimens of Birds in the Collection of the British Museum, Part III: Gallinae, Grallae, and Anseres.* London: George Woodfall and Son, 1844.

Anonymous. *Natural History Drawings: The Complete William Farquhar Collection.* Singapore: Editions Didier Millet, 2010.

Anonymous. *A Short History of the Port of Singapore, with Particular Reference to the Undertakings of the Singapore Harbour Board.* Singapore: Fraser and Neave, 1922.

Anonymous. *Singapore Racecourse, 1842–2000.* Singapore: Singapore Turf Club, 2000.

Arnold, David. *Colonizing the Body: State Medicine and Epidemic Disease in Nineteenth-Century India.* Berkeley, CA: University of California Press, 1993.

Arnold, David. *The Tropics and the Traveling Gaze: India, Landscape and Science, 1800–1856.* Seattle: University of Washington Press, 2006.

Baker, Nick. "Bats in the Bamboo." *Gardenwise* 43, (2014): 12–3.

Bankoff, Greg. "*Bestia Incognita*: The Horse and Its History in the Philippines, 1880–1930." *Anthrozoös,* 17, 1, 2004: 3–25.

Bankoff, Greg and Sandra Swart (ed.). *Breeds of Empire: The "Invention" of the Horse in Southeast Asia and Africa, 1500–1950.* Copenhagen: NIAS Press, 2007.

Barnard, Timothy P. "Celates, Rayat-Laut, Pirates: The Orang Laut and their Decline in History." *Journal of the Malaysian Branch of the Royal Asiatic Society* 80, 2 (2007): 33–49.

Barnard, Timothy P. *Multiple Centres of Authority: Society and Environment in Siak and Eastern Sumatra, 1674–1827*. Leiden: KITLV, 2003.

Barnard, Timothy P. *Nature's Colony: Empire, Nation, and Environment in the Singapore Botanic Gardens*. Singapore: NUS Press, 2016.

Barnard, Timothy P. (ed.). *Nature Contained: Environmental Histories of Singapore*. Singapore: NUS Press, 2014.

Barnard, Timothy P. "Protecting the Dragon: Dutch Attempts to Limit Access to Komodo Lizards in the 1920s and 1930s." *Indonesia* 92 (2011): 97–123.

Barnard, Timothy P. "The Rafflesia in the Natural and Imperial Imagination of the East India Company in Southeast Asia." In *The East India Company and the Natural World*, ed. Vinita Damoradaran, Anna Winterbottom, and Alan Lester. London: Palgrave Macmillan, 2015, pp. 147–66.

Barnard, Timothy P. *Raja Kecil dan Mitos Pengabsahanya*. Pekanbaru: Pusat Pengajian Melayu, Universitas Islam, 1994.

Barnard, Timothy P. "'Sufficient Dramatic or Adventure Interest': Authenticity, Reality and Violence in Pre-War Animal Documentaries from South-East Asia." In *The Colonial Documentary Film in South and South-East Asia*, ed. Ian Aitken and Camille Deprez. Edinburgh: Edinburgh University Press, 2017, pp. 223–35.

Barnard, Timothy P. and Mark Emmanuel. "Tigers of Colonial Singapore." In *Nature Contained: Environmental Histories of Singapore*, ed. Timothy P. Barnard. Singapore: NUS Press, 2014, pp. 55–80.

Bastin, John (ed.). *Raffles and Hastings: Private Exchanges behind the Founding of Singapore*. Singapore: Marshall Cavendish and National Library Board, Singapore, 2014.

Bastin, John. "Sir Stamford Raffles and the Study of Natural History in Penang, Singapore and Indonesia." *Journal of the Malaysian Branch of the Royal Asiatic Society* 63, 2 (1990): 1–25.

Bastin, John. "William Farquhar: First Resident and Commandant of Singapore." In *Natural History Drawings: The Complete William Farquhar Collection*. Singapore: Editions Didier Millet, 2010, pp. 8–33.

Beinart, William and Lotte Hughes. *Environment and Empire*. Oxford: Oxford University Press, 2007.

"Bengal Civilian" (Charles Walter Kinloch). *Rambles in Java and the Straits in 1852*. Singapore: Oxford University Press, 1987.

Bird, Isabella L. *The Golden Chersonese and the Way Thither*. New York, NY: G.P. Putnam's Sons, 1883.

Blaisdell, John D. "The Rise of Man's Best Friend: The Popularity of Dogs as Companion Animals in Late Eighteenth-Century London as Reflected by the Dog Tax of 1796," *Anthrozoös: A Multidisciplinary Journal of the Interactions of People and Animals* 12 (1999): 76–87.

Boomgaard, Peter. *Frontiers of Fear: Tigers and People in the Malay World, 1600–1950*. New Haven, Conn.: Yale University Press, 2001.

Boomgaard, Peter. "Hunting and Trapping in the Indonesian Archipelago, 1500–1950." In *Paper Landscapes: Explorations in the Environmental History of Indonesia*, ed. Peter Boomgaard, Freek Colombijn, and David Henley. Leiden: KITLV Press, 1997, pp. 185–213.

Boomgaard, Peter. "'Primitive' Tiger Hunting in Indonesia and Malaysia, 1800–1950." In *Wildlife in Asia: Cultural Perspectives*, ed. John Knight. London: RoutledgeCurzon, 2004, pp. 185–206.

Boomgaard, Peter, Freek Colombijn, and David Henley (ed.). *Paper Landscapes: Explorations in the Environmental History of Indonesia*. Leiden: KITLV Press, 1997.

Borschberg, Peter. *The Singapore and Melaka Straits: Violence, Security and Diplomacy in the 17th Century*. Singapore: NUS Press, 2010.

Braddell, Roland. *The Lights of Singapore*. London: Methuen and Co., 1934.

Brassey, Anna. *A Voyage in the "Sunbeam": Our Home on the Ocean for Eleven Months*. New York: John Wurtele Lovell, 1881.

Brook, Barry W., Navjot S. Sodhi and Peter K.L. Ng. "Catastrophic Extinctions Follow Deforestation in Singapore." *Nature*, 424 (24 Jul 2003): 420–3.

Brooke, Gilbert E. "Medical Work and Institutions." In *One Hundred Years of Singapore, Being an Account of the Capital of the Straits Settlements from its Foundation by Sir Stamford Raffles on the 6th February 1819 to the 6th February 1919*, vol. I, ed. Walter Makepeace, Gilbert E. Brooke, and Roland St. J. Braddell. London: John Murray, 1921, pp. 487–519.

Brown, C.C. (trans.). *Sejarah Melayu or Malay Annals*. Singapore: Oxford University Press, 1970.

Bruce, Mary Grant. *A Little Bush Maid*. Melbourne: Ward, Lock and Company, 1910.

Buck, Frank and Edward Anthony. *Bring 'em Back Alive*. New York: Simon and Schuster, 1930.

Buckley, Charles Burton. *An Anecdotal History of Old Times in Singapore: From the Foundation of the Settlement under the Honourable East India Company on February 6th, 1819 to the Transfer to the Colonial Office as Part of the Colonial Possessions of the Crown on April 1st, 1867*. 2 vols. Singapore: Fraser and Neave, 1902.

Bucknill, John A.S. and F.N. Chasen. *The Birds of Singapore Island*. Singapore: Government Printing Office 1927.

Butcher, John G. *The Closing of the Frontier: A History of Maritime Fisheries of Southeast Asia, c. 1850–2000*. Singapore: ISEAS, 2004.

Cameron, John. *Our Tropical Possessions in Malayan India: Being a Descriptive Account of Singapore, Penang, Province Wellesley, and Malacca; Their Peoples, Products, Commerce, and Government*. London: Smith, Elder and Co, 1865.

Cantley, Nathaniel. *Report on the Forests of the Straits Settlements*. Singapore: Singapore and Straits Printing Office, 1883.

Carnegie, Andrew. *Round the World.* New York, NY: Charles Scribner's and Sons, 1884.

Cavenagh, Orfeur. *Reminiscences of an Indian Official.* London: W.H. Allen and Co., 1884.

Chambert-Loir, Henri. "The *Sulalat al-Salatin* as a Political Myth." *Indonesia,* 79 (2005): 131–60.

Chaplin, Joyce E. "Can the Nonhuman Speak?: Breaking the Chain of Being in the Anthropocene." *Journal of the History of Ideas* 78, 4 (2017): 509–29.

Child, Jacob T. *The Pearl of Asia: Reminiscences of the Court of a Supreme Monarch or Five Years in Siam.* Chicago: Donohue, Henneberr and Co, 1892.

Chou, Cynthia. "Agriculture and the End of Farming in Singapore." In *Nature Contained: Environmental Histories of Singapore,* ed. Timothy P. Barnard. Singapore: NUS Press, 2014, pp. 216–40.

Choy Chee Meh née Lum. "History of the Malaysian Branch of the Royal Asiatic Society." *Journal of the Malaysian Branch of the Royal Asiatic Society* 68, 2 (1995): 81–148.

Clarence-Smith, William Gervase. "Southeast Asia and Southern Africa in the Maritime Horse Trade of the Indian Ocean, c. 1800–1914." In *Breeds of Empire: The "Invention" of the Horse in Southeast Asia and Southern Africa, 1500–1950,* ed. Greg Bankoff and Sandra Swart. Copenhagen: NIAS Press, 2007, pp. 21–32.

Cocteau, Jean. *Round the World Again in 80 Days (Mon Premier Voyage),* tr. Stuart Gilbert. London: Tauris Parke, 2000.

Cohen, Matthew Isaac. *The Komedie Stamboel: Popular Theater in Colonial Indonesia, 1891–1903.* Athens, OH: Ohio University Center for International Studies, 2006.

Cohn, Bernard. *Colonialism and Its Form of Knowledge: The British in India.* Princeton: Princeton University Press, 1996.

Corner, E.J.H. *Botanical Monkeys.* Cambridge: Pentland Press, 1992.

Corner, E.J.H. *The Marquis: A Tale of Syonan-to.* Singapore: Heinemann Asia, 1981.

Corner, John K. *My Father in a Suitcase: In Search of E.J.H. Corner, the Relentless Botanist.* Singapore: Landmark Books, 2013.

Corlett, Richard T. "The Ecological Transformation of Singapore, 1819–1990." *Journal of Biogeography* 19, 4 (1992): 411–20.

Crawfurd, John *A Descriptive Dictionary of the Indian Islands and Adjacent Countries.* London: Bradbury and Evans, 1856.

Crawfurd, John. *Journal of an Embassy from the Governor-General of India to the Courts of Siam and Cochin-China: Exhibiting a View of the Actual State of Those Kingdoms.* London: H. Colburn, 1828.

Cribb, Robert "Conservation in Colonial Indonesia." *Interventions* 9, 1 (2007): 49–61.

Cribb, Robert, Helen Gilbert and Helen Tiffin. *Wild Man of Borneo: A Cultural History of the Orangutan*. Honolulu, HI: University of Hawai'i Press, 2014.

Crosby, Alfred. *Ecological Imperialism: The Biological Expansion of Europe, 900–1900*. Cambridge: Cambridge University Press, 1986.

D'Aranjo, B.E. *A Stranger's Guide to Singapore*. Singapore: Sirangoon Press, 1890.

Dammerman, Karel Willem. *Preservation of Wild Life and Nature Reserves in the Netherlands Indies*. Weltevreden: Emmink, 1929.

Dawson, Warren R. "On the History of Gray and Hardwicke's Illustrations of Indian Zoology, and Some Biographical Notes on General Hardwicke." *Journal of the Society for the Bibliography of Natural History* 2, 3 (1946): 55–69.

Dodson, John and Guanghui Dong. "What Do We Know about Domestication in Eastern Asia?" *Quaternary International* 426, (2016): 2–9.

Earl, George Windsor. *The Eastern Seas, or, Voyages and Adventures in the Indian Archipelago, in 1832–33–34: Comprising a Tour of the Island of Java, Visits to Borneo, The Malay Peninsula, Siam and &c.; Also an Account of the Present State of Singapore, with Observations on the Commercial Resources of the Archipelago*. London: Wm. H. Allen and Co, 1837.

Echenberg, Myron. "Pestis Redux: The Initial Years of the Third Bubonic Plague Pandemic, 1894–1901." *Journal of World History* 13, 2 (2002): 429–49.

Fairholme, Edward George and Wellesley Pain. *A Century of Work for Animals: The History of the R.S.P.C.A., 1824–1934*. London: J. Murray, 1934.

Firmstone, H.W. "Chinese Names of Streets and Places in Singapore and the Malay Peninsula (Continued)." *Journal of the Straits Branch of the Royal Asiatic Society* 42, (1905): 53–208.

Fleming, George. *Rabies and Hydrophobia: Their History, Nature, Causes, Symptoms, and Prevention*. London: Chapman and Hall, 1872.

Fox, Walter. *Guide to the Botanical Gardens*. Singapore: Government Printing Office, 1889.

Fudge, Erica. "A Left-Handed Blow: Writing the History of Animals." In *Representing Animals*, ed. Nigel Rothfels. Bloomington, IN: Indiana University Press, 2002, pp. 3–18.

Fudge, Erica. "Milking Other Men's Beasts." *History and Theory* 52, 4 (2013): 13–28.

Ghosh, Durba. "Another Set of Imperial Turns?" *American Historical Review* 117, 3 (2012): 772–93.

Goh Chor Boon. *Serving Singapore: A Hundred Years of Cold Storage, 1903–2003*. Singapore: Cold Storage, 2003.

Goh Chor Boon. *Technology and Entrepôt Colonialism in Singapore, 1819–1940*. Singapore: ISEAS-Yusof Ishak Institute, 2013.

Grandin, Temple. "Improving Welfare and Reducing Stress on Animals at Slaughter Plants." In *Livestock Handling and Transport*, ed. Temple Grandin. Boston, MA: CABI, 2014, pp. 421–50.

Grier, Katherine C. *Pets in America: A History*. Chapel Hill, NC: The University of North Carolina Press, 2006.

Grove, Richard. *Green Imperialism: Colonial Expansion, Tropical Edens, and the Origins of Environmentalism, 1600–1860*. New York: Cambridge University Press, 1995.

Guan Jingwen. "*The Journal of the Indian Archipelago and Eastern Asia*, 1847–1863: A Study in Colonial Knowledge and Context." Unpublished B.A. (Honours) Thesis. Department of History, National University of Singapore, 2011.

Hack, Karl. "Framing Singapore's History." In *Studying Singapore's Past: C.M. Turnbull and the History of Modern Singapore*, ed. Nicholas Tarling. Singapore: NUS Press, 2012, pp. 17–49.

Hardenberg, J.F.D. "The Fishfauna of the Rokan Mouth." *Treubia* 8, 1 (1931): 81–168.

Hails, Christopher. *Birds of Singapore*. Singapore: Times Editions, 1987.

Hallifax, F.J. "Municipal Government." In *One Hundred Years of Singapore, Being an Account of the Capital of the Straits Settlements from its Foundation by Sir Stamford Raffles on the 6th February 1819 to the 6th February 1919*, vol. I, ed. Walter Makepeace, Gilbert E. Brooke, and Roland St. J. Braddell. London: John Murray, 1921, pp. 315–40.

Hanitsch, R. *Guide to the Zoological Collections of the Raffles Museum, Singapore*. Singapore: The Straits Times Press, 1908.

Hanitsch, R. "Raffles Library and Museum, Singapore." In *One Hundred Years of Singapore, Being Some Account of the Capital of the Straits Settlements from Its Foundation by Sir Stamford Raffles on the 6th February 1819 to the 6th February 1919*, vol. I, ed. Walter Makepeace, Gilbert E. Brooke and Roland St. J. Braddell. London: John Murray, 1921, pp. 519–77.

Hardwicke Thomas and J.E. Gray. *Illustrations of Indian Zoology, Chiefly Selected from the Collection of Major-General Hardwicke*. 2 vols. London: Treutell, Wurtz, Treutell Jun. and Richter, 1830–4.

Harrison, Brian. "Animals and the State in Nineteenth-Century England." *The English Historical Review* 88, 3 (1973): 786–820.

Hornaday, William T. *Two Years in the Jungle: The Experiences of a Hunter and Naturalist in India, Ceylon, the Malay Peninsula and Borneo*. New York, NY: C. Scribner's Sons, 1885.

Hughes, Julie E. *Animal Kingdoms: Hunting, the Environment, and Power in Indian Princely States*. Cambridge, MA: Harvard University Press, 2013.

Hunt, Lynn. *The New Cultural History*. Berkeley, CA: University of California Press, 1989.

Huntingford, Felicity A. and Sunil Kadri. "Welfare and Fish." In *Fish Welfare*, ed. Edward J. Branson. Oxford: Blackwell Publishing, 2008, pp. 19–31.

J.E.L., *Ten Days in the Jungle*. Boston: Cupples, Upham and Company, 1885.

Jones, Russell. "George Windsor Earl and 'Indonesia'." *Indonesia Circle* 22, 64 (1994): 279–90.

Kathirithamby-Wells, Jeya. "Human Impact on Large Animal Populations in Peninsular Malaysia from the Nineteenth to the Mid-Twentieth Century." In *Paper Landscapes: Explorations in the Environmental History of Indonesia*, ed. Peter Boomgaard, Freek Colombijn, and David Henley. Leiden: KITLV Press, 1997, pp. 215–41.

Kathirithamby-Wells, Jeyamalar. *Nature and Nation: Forests and Development in Peninsular Malaysia*. Singapore: NUS Press, 2005.

Kathirithamby-Wells, Jeyamalar. "Peninsular Malaysia in the Context of Natural History and Colonial Science." *New Zealand Journal of Asian Studies* 11, 1 (2009): 337–74.

Keane, A.H. *A Geography of the Malay Peninsula, Indo-China, the Eastern Archipelago, The Philippines and New Guinea*. London: E. Stanford, 1892.

Keppel, Henry. *The Expedition to Borneo of H.M.S. Dido for the Suppression of Piracy: with Extracts from the Journal of James Brooke, Esq., of Sarawak*. 2 vols. London: Chapman and Hall, 1846.

Kheraj, Sean. "Animals and Urban Environments: Managing Domestic Animals in Nineteenth-Century Winnipeg." In *Eco-Cultural Networks and the British Empire: New Views on Environmental History*, ed. James Beattie, Edward Melillo and Emily O'Gorman. London: Bloomsbury, 2015, pp. 263–88.

Kloss, C. Boden. "Notes on a Cruise in the Southern China Sea." *Journal of the Straits Branch of the Royal Asiatic Society*, 41 (1904): 53–80.

Knox, Thomas W. *The Boy Travellers in the Far East: Part Second, Adventures of Two Youths in a Journey to Siam and Java, with Descriptions of Cochin-China, Cambodia, Sumatra and the Malay Archipelago*. New York: Harper and Brothers, 1880.

Koh Keng We. "Familiar Strangers and Stranger-Kings: Mobility, Diasporas, and the Foreign in the Eighteenth-Century Malay World." *Journal of Southeast Asian Studies* 48, 3 (2017): 390–413.

Kwa Chong Guan and Peter Borschberg (eds.). *Studying Singapore Before 1800*. Singapore: NUS Press, 2018.

Langdon, Marcus and Kwa Chong Guan. "Notes on 'Sketch of the Land Round Singapore Harbour, 7 February 1819'." *Journal of the Malaysian Branch of the Royal Asiatic Society* 83, 1 (2010): 1–7.

Layton, Lesley. *Songbirds of Singapore: Growth of a Pastime*. Singapore: Oxford University Press, 1991.

Lees, Lynn Hollen. "Discipline and Delegation: Colonial Government in Malayan Towns, 1880–1930." *Urban History* 38, 1 (2011): 48–64.

Lees, Lynn Hollen. *Planting Empire, Cultivating Subjects: British Malaya, 1786–1941*. Cambridge: Cambridge University Press, 2017.

Leong Foke Meng. "Early Land Transactions in Singapore: The Real Estates of William Farquhar (1774–1839), John Crawfurd (1783–1868), and Their Families." *Journal of the Malaysian Branch of the Royal Asiatic Society* 77, 1 (2004): 23–42.

Lim Kim Seng. *Birds: An Illustrated Field Guide to the Birds of Singapore.* Singapore: Sun Tree Publishing, 1997.

Low, James. *A Dissertation on the Soil and Agriculture of Penang or Prince of Wales Island, in the Straits of Malacca: Including Province Wellesley on the Malayan Peninsula. With Brief References to the Settlements of Singapore and Malacca, and Accompanied by Incidental Observations on Various Subjects of Local Interest in these Straits.* Singapore: Singapore Free Press, 1836.

Lye Lin Heng. "Wildlife Protection Laws in Singapore." *Singapore Journal of Legal Studies* (1991): 287–319.

Makepeace, Walter. "The Machinery of Commerce." In *One Hundred Years of Singapore, Being an Account of the Capital of the Straits Settlements from its Foundation by Sir Stamford Raffles on the 6th February 1819 to the 6th February 1919*, vol. II. Ed. Walter Makepeace, Gilbert E. Brooke, and Roland St. J. Braddell. London: John Murray, 1921, pp. 166–234.

MacKenzie, John M. *The Empire of Nature: Hunting, Conservation and British Imperialism.* Manchester: Manchester University Press, 1997.

Maier, Henk. *We Are Playing Relatives: A Survey of Malay Writing.* Leiden: KITLV, 2004.

Maxwell, C.N. *Preliminary Report on the Economic Position of the Fishing Industry of the Straits Settlements and the Federated Malay States.* Singapore: Government Printer, 1921.

Mayer, Charles. *Trapping Wild Animals in Malay Jungles.* Garden City, NY: Garden City Publishing, 1921.

McNair, J.F.A. *Perak and the Malays.* Kuala Lumpur: Oxford University Press, 1972.

McNair, J.F.A., assisted by W.D. Bayliss. *Prisoners Their Own Warders.* London: Archibald Constable and Co., 1899.

Mikhail, Alan. "A Dog-Eat-Dog Empire: Violence and Affection on the Streets of Ottoman Cairo." *Comparative Studies of South Asia, Africa and the Middle East* 35, 1 (2015): 76–95.

Miksic, John N. *Singapore and the Silk Road of the Sea, 1300–1800.* Singapore: NUS Press, 2013.

Miller, Ian Jared. *The Nature of Beasts: Empire and Exhibition at the Tokyo Imperial Zoo.* Berkeley, CA: University of California Press, 2013.

Milner, Anthony. "Colonial Records History: British Malaya." *Kajian Malaysia* 4, 2 (1986): 1–18.

Minarchek, Matthew. "Plantations, Peddlers, and Nature Protection: The Transnational Origins of Indonesia's Orangutan Crisis." *TRaNS: Trans— Regional and—National Studies of Southeast Asia* 6, 1 (2018): 101–29.

Nance, Susan. "Introduction." In *The Historical Animal*, ed. Susan Nance. Syracuse, NY: Syracuse University Press, 2015, pp. 1–17.

Newbold, T.J. *Political and Statistical Account of the British Settlements in the Straits of Malacca, viz. Pinang, Malacca, and Singapore; with a History of the Malayan Atates on the Peninsula of Malacca*. 2 vols. London: John Murray, 1839.

Noltie, H.J. *Raffles' Ark Redrawn: Natural History Drawings from the Collection of Sir Thomas Stamford Raffles*. London: The British Library and Royal Botanic Gardens Edinburgh, 2009.

O'Connor, Terry. *Animals as Neighbors: The Past and Present in Commensal Animals*. East Lansing, MI: Michigan State University Press, 2014.

O'Dempsey, Tony. "Singapore's Changing Landscape since c. 1800." In *Nature Contained: Environmental Histories of Singapore*, ed. Timothy P. Barnard. Singapore: NUS Press, 2014, pp. 17–48.

Osborne, Megan S. "Early Collectors and Their Impact on the Raffles Museum and Library." *The Heritage Journal*, 3 (2008): 1–15.

Otter, Chris. "Civilizing Slaughter: The Development of the British Public Abattoir, 1850–1910." In *Meat, Modernity, and the Rise of the Modern Slaughterhouse*, ed. Paula Young Lee. Durham, NH: University of New Hampshire Press, 2008, pp. 89–106.

Owen, G.P. "Shikar." In *One Hundred Years of Singapore, Being an Account of the Capital of the Straits Settlements from its Foundation by Sir Stamford Raffles on the 6th February 1819 to the 6th February 1919*, vol. II, ed. Walter Makepeace, Gilbert E. Brooke, and Roland St. J. Braddell. London: John Murray, 1921, pp. 367–80.

Oxley, T. "The Zoology of Singapore." *Journal of the Indian Archipelago and Eastern Asia*, 3 (1849): 594–7.

Oxley, Thomas. "Some Account of the Nutmeg and Its Cultivation." *Journal of the Indian Archipelago and Eastern Asia* 2, 10 (1848): 648–50.

Palsetia, Jesse S. "Mad Dogs and Parsis: The Bombay Dog Riots of 1832," *Journal of the Royal Asiatic Society* 11, 1 (2001): 13–30.

Pearson Susan J. and Mary Weismantel. "Does 'The Animal' Exist?: Towards a Theory of Social Life with Animals." In *Beastly Natures: Animals, Humans, and the Study of History*, ed. Dorothee Brantz. Charlottesville, VA: University of Virginia Press, 2010, pp. 17–37.

Pemberton, Neil and Michael Worboys. *Rabies in Britain: Dogs, Disease and Culture, 1800–2000*. Basingstoke: Palgrave Macmillan, 2007.

Peters, W. "Uber den Vespertilio calcaratus Prinz zu Wied und eine neue Gattung der Flederthiere, Tyloncteris." *Königlich Preussicschen Akademie Wissenschaften zu Berlin* (1872): 699–706.

Pfeiffer, Ida. *A Woman's Journey Round the World from Vienna to Brazil, Chili, Tahiti, China, Hindostan, Persia and Asia Minor*. London: Ingram, Cooke, and Co., 1852.

Pieris, Anoma. *Hidden Hands and Divided Landscapes: A Penal History of Singapore's Plural Society*. Honolulu: University of Hawai'i Press, 2009.

Pilon, Maxime and Danièle Weiler. *The French in Singapore: An Illustrated History (1819–Today)*. Singapore: Editions Didier Millet, 2011.

Poon, Shuk-Wah. "Dogs and British Colonialism: The Contested Ban on Eating Dogs in Colonial Hong Kong." *The Journal of Imperial and Commonwealth History* 42, 2 (2014): 308–28.

Powell, Miles Alexander. "People in Peril, Environments at Risk: Coolies, Tigers, and Colonial Singapore's Ecology of Poverty." *Environment and History* 22, 3 (2016): 455–82.

Powell, Miles A. *Vanishing America: Species Extinction, Racial Peril, and the Origins of Conservation*. Cambridge, MA: Harvard University Press, 2016.

Pryor, E.G. "The Great Plague of Hong Kong." *Journal of the Royal Asiatic Society of Great Britain and Ireland-Hong Kong Branch* 15, 69 (1975): 61–70.

Pyenson, Lewis and Susan Sheets-Pyenson. *Servants of Nature: A History of Scientific Institutions, Enterprises and Sensibilities*. New York: W.W. Norton and Company, 1999.

Rai, Rajesh. "The 1857 Panic and the Fabrication of an Indian 'Menace' in Singapore." *Modern Asian Studies* 47, 2 (2013): 365–405.

Rai, Rajesh. *Indians in Singapore, 1819–1945: Diaspora in the Colonial Port City*. New Delhi: Oxford University Press, 2014.

Reeves, Peter and Noelene Reeves. "Port-City Development and Singapore's Inshore and Culture Fisheries." In *Muddied Waters: Historical and Contemporary Perspectives on Management of Forests and Fisheries in Island Southeast Asia*, ed. Peter Boomgaard, David Henley and Manon Osseweijer. Leiden: KITLV, 2005, pp. 121–42.

Reid, Anthony. *Southeast Asia in the Age of Commerce, 1450–1680. Volume One: The Land Below the Winds*. New Haven: Yale University Press, 1988.

Reith, G.M. *Handbook to Singapore, with Map and a Plan of the Botanical Gardens*. Singapore: The Singapore and Straits Printing Office, 1892.

Ridley, H.N. "Bats in the Bamboo." *Journal of the Straits Branch of the Royal Asiatic Society*, 50 (1908): 103–4.

Rimmer, Peter J. "Hackney Carriage Syces and Rikisha Pullers in Singapore: A Colonial Registrar's Perspective on Public Transport, 1892–1923." In *The Underside of Malaysian History: Pullers, Prostitutes, Plantation Workers*, ed. Peter J. Rimmer and Lisa M. Allen. Singapore: Singapore University Press, 1991, pp. 129–60.

Ritvo, Harriet. *The Animal Estate: The English and Other Creatures in the Victorian Age*. Cambridge, Mass: Harvard University Press, 1987.

Ritvo, Harriet. "Animal Planet." *Environmental History* 9, 2 (2004): 204–20.

Ritvo, Harriet. "On the Animal Turn." *Dædalus*, 136 (2007): 118–22.

Ritvo, Harriet. *The Platypus and the Mermaid, and Other Figments of the Classifying Imagination*. Cambridge, Mass.: Harvard University Press, 1997.

Ritvo, Harriet. "Pride and Pedigree: The Evolution of the Victorian Dog Fancy." *Victorian Studies* 29, 2 (1986): 227–53.

Ross, John Dill. *The Capital of a Little Empire: A Descriptive Study of a British Crown Colony in the Far East*. Singapore: Kelly and Walsh, 1898.

Rothfels, Nigel. *Savages and Beasts: The Birth of the Modern Zoo*. Baltimore, MD: Johns Hopkins University Press, 2002.

Saha, Jonathan. "Among the Beasts of Burma: Animals and the Politics of Colonial Sensibilities, c. 1840–1940." *Journal of Social History* 48, 4 (2015): 910–32.

Savage, Victor R. *Western Impressions of Nature and Landscape in Southeast Asia*. Singapore: Singapore University Press, 1984.

Savage, Victor R. and Brenda S.A. Yeoh. *Toponymics: A Study of Singapore Street Names*. Singapore: Eastern Universities Press, 2003.

Scidmore, Eliza Ruhamah. *Java: The Garden of the East*. New York: The Century Co., 1899.

Sim, Sophie. "Fishy Tales: *Singapura Dilanggar Todak* as Myth and History in Singapore's Past." Unpublished Master's Thesis, Department of History, National University of Singapore, 2005.

Skabelund, Aaron. "Animals and Imperialism: Recent Historiographical Trends." *History Compass* 11, 10 (2013): 801–7.

Skabelund, Aaron Herald. *Empire of Dogs: Canines, Japan, and the Making of the Modern World*. Ithaca, NY: Cornell University Press, 2011.

Shadle, Brett L. "Cruelty and Empathy, Animals and Race, in Colonial Kenya." *Journal of Social History* 45, 4 (2012): 1097–116.

Sodhi, Navjot S. and Ilsa Sharp. *Winged Invaders: Pest Birds of the Asia Pacific with Information on Bird Flu and Other Diseases*. Singapore: SNP Reference, 2006.

Solomon, John. *A Subaltern History of the Indian Diaspora in Singapore: Gradual Disappearance of Untouchability, 1872–1965*. New York, NY: Routledge, 2016.

Stead, David G. *General Report upon the Fisheries of British Malaya with Recommendations for Future Development*. Singapore: Government Printing Office, 1923.

Stoddart, Helen. *Rings of Desire: Circus History and Representation*. Manchester: Manchester University Press, 2000.

Stuart, A. "Exports, Imports, and Shipping. Straits Settlements." In *Twentieth Century Impressions of British Malaya: Its History, People, Commerce, Industries, and Resources*, ed. Arnold Wright and H.A. Cartwright. London: Lloyd's Greater Britain Publishing Company, 1908, pp. 162–81.

Sweeney, Amin. "Abdullah bin Abdul Kadir Munshi: A Man of Bananas and Thorns." *Indonesia and the Malay World* 34, 100 (2007): 223–45.

Tagliacozzo, Eric. *Secret Trades, Porous Borders: Smuggling and States along a Southeast Asian Frontier, 1865–1915.* New Haven: Yale University Press, 2005.

Tan, Cedric Kai Wei et al. "Managing Present Day Large-Carnivores in 'Island Habitats': Lessons in Memoriam Learned from Human-Tiger Interactions in Singapore." *Biodiversity and Conservation* 24, 12 (2015): 3109–24.

Tan, Fiona L. P. "The Beastly Business of Regulating the Wildlife Trade in Colonial Singapore." In *Nature Contained: Environmental Histories of Singapore*, ed. Timothy P. Barnard. Singapore: NUS Press, 2014, pp. 145–78.

Tan, Sumiko. *The Winning Connection: 150 Years of Racing in Singapore.* Singapore: Bukit Turf Club, 1992.

Tarling, Nicholas (ed.). *Studying Singapore's Past: C.M. Turnbull and the History of Modern Singapore.* Singapore: NUS Press, 2012.

Tarulevicz, Nicole. *Eating Her Curries and Kway: A Cultural History of Food in Singapore.* Urbana, Ill: University of Illinois Press, 2013.

Tarulevicz, Nicole. "'I Had No Time to Pick Out the Worms': Food Adulteration in Singapore, 1900–1973," *Journal of Colonialism and Colonial History* 16, 3 (2015). *Project MUSE*, doi:10.1353/cch.2015.0037.

Temminck, C.J. *Monographies de Mammalogie, ou description de quelques genres de ammiferes, don't les especes ont ete obersvees dan les differens musees de l'Europe.* Leiden: C.C. Vander Hoek, 1840.

Thomas, Keith. *Man and the Natural World: Changing Attitudes in England, 1500–1800.* London: Allen Lane, 1983.

Thomson, J. *The Straits of Malacca, Indo-China, and China; or Ten Years' Travels, Adventures, and Residence Abroad.* New York: Harper and Brothers, 1875.

Thomson, J.T. *Some Glimpses into Life in the Far East.* London: Richardson and Company, 1864.

Tiew Wai Sin. "History of *Journal of the Malaysian Branch of the Royal Asiatic Society (JMBRAS)* 1878–1997: An Overview." *Malaysian Journal of Library and Information Science* 3, 1 (1998): 43–61.

Tofighian, Nadi. "Mapping 'the Whirligig of Amusements'" in Colonial Southeast Asia." *Journal of Southeast Asian Studies* 49, 2 (2018): 277–96.

Trocki, Carl A. *Prince of Pirates: The Temenggongs and the Development of Johor and Singapore, 1784–1885.* Singapore: NUS Press, 2007.

Tweedie, M.W.F. "The Stone Age in Malaya." *Journal of the Malayan Branch of the Royal Asiatic Society* 26, 2 (1953): 3–90.

Turnbull, C.M. *A History of Modern Singapore, 1819–2005.* Singapore: NUS Press, 2008.

Vincent, Frank. *The Land of the White Elephant: Sights and Scenes in South-Eastern Asia: A Personal Narrative of Travel and Adventure in Farther India, Embracing the Countries of Burma, Siam, Cambodia, and Cochin-China, 1871–2.* London: S. Low, Marston, Low and Searle, 1873.

Wagoner, Phillip B. "Precolonial Intellectuals and the Production of Colonial Knowledge." *Comparative Studies in Society and History* 45, 4 (2003): 783–814.

Walcott, Arthur S. *Java and her Neighbors; A Traveller's Notes in Java, Celebes, the Moluccas, and Sumatra.* New York: G.P. Putnam's Sons, 1914.

Walker, Brett L. "Animals and the Intimacy of History." *History and Theory* 52, 4 (2013): 45–67.

Wallace, Alfred Russel. *The Malay Archipelago: The Land of the Orang-Utan, and the Bird of Paradise. A Narrative of Travel, with Studies of Man and Nature.* London: Macmillan and Co., 1869.

Walley, Thomas. *A Practical Guide to Meat Inspection.* Edinburgh: Young J. Pentland, 1890.

Warren, James Francis. *Ah Ku and Karayuki-san: Prostitution in Singapore, 1870–1940.* Singapore: NUS Press, 2003.

Warren, James Francis. *Rickshaw Coolie: A People's History of Singapore, 1880–1940.* Singapore: NUS Press, 2003.

Warren, James Francis. *The Sulu Zone, 1768–1898: The Dynamics of External Trade, Slavery and Ethnicity in the Transformation of a Southeast Asian Maritime State.* Singapore: Singapore University Press, 1981.

Wasick, Bill and Monica Murphy. *Rabid: A Cultural History of the World's Most Diabolical Virus.* New York: Penguin Books, 2012.

Whyte, James Christie. *History of the British Turf, from the Earliest Period to the Present Day.* 2 volumes. London: Henry Colburn, 1840.

Willis, A.C. *Willis's Singapore Guide.* Singapore: Advertising and Policy Bureau, 1936.

Winstedt, R.O. *A History of Johore (1365–1941).* Kuala Lumpur: Malaysian Branch of the Royal Asiatic Society, 1992.

Wong Lee Min. "Negotiating Colonial Identities: Malaya in the British Empire Exhibition, 1924–1925." Unpublished Master's Thesis, Department of History, National University of Singapore, 2013.

Wong Lin Ken. *The Trade of Singapore, 1819–69.* Kuala Lumpur: MBRAS, 2003.

Woo Pui Leng. *The Urban History of Jalan Besar.* Singapore: Urban Redevelopment Authority Singapore, 2010.

Worsfold, W. Basil. *A Visit to Java with an Account of the Founding of Singapore.* London: R. Bentley, 1893.

Wright, Arnold and H.A. Cartwright. *Twentieth Century Impressions of British Malaya: Its History, People, Commerce, Industries, and Resources.* Singapore: Lloyd's Greater Britain Publishing Company, 1908.

Wyhe, John van. "Wallace in Singapore." In *Nature Contained: Environmental Histories of Singapore,* ed. Timothy P. Barnard. Singapore: NUS Press, 2014, pp. 85–109.

Yahaya, Nurfadzilah. "The Question of Animal Slaughter in the British Straits Settlements during the Early Twentieth Century." *Indonesia and the Malay World* 43, 126 (2015): 173–90.

Yeoh, Brenda S.A. *Contesting Space: Power Relations and the Urban Built Environment in Colonial Singapore*. Kuala Lumpur: Oxford University Press, 1996.

Yeoh Kim Wah. "The Milner Version of British Malayan History: A Rejoinder." *Kajian Malaysia* 5, 1 (1987): 1–28.

Young, Ernest. *The Kingdom of the Yellow Robe. Being Sketches of the Domestic and Religious Rites and Ceremonies of the Siamese*. Westminster: A. Constable, 1898.

Ziegler, Philip. *The Black Death*. Harmondsworth: Penguin, 1970.

Index

abattoirs, 207–35
Abbott, William L., 82, 93
Abdullah bin Abdul Kadir (Munshi), 16–19, 22, 36, 53, 194
Abu Bakar, Maharajah and Sultan of Johor, 55, 72, 79, 92–3, 104, 110, 120
   referred to as "Albert Baker", 104
agriculture, its effects on biodiversity, 24–7
Alexandrovich, Grand Duke Alexei, 103–4
Alsagoff, Omar, 147
animal and bird shops, 67–8, 71, 140, 232
animals and history, 9–13
animal-animal contests, 79–82, 103–6, 123, 145
animal husbandry, 199–218
animal studies, 8–10
Asiatic Society of Bengal, 22
Australian Meat Company, 224

Bankoff, Greg, 11
Basapa, William (also see Ponggol Zoo), 98–101, 145, 239

bats (also see individual species), 26–7, 83–4
beetles, 27n
beef, 111, 193–5, 199–200, 204, 207, 219–21, 224–30
   importance to British identity, 193–4
Bengal, 27, 30, 85, 197n
Bengkulu (Bencoolen), 17fn, 18
Bencoolen Street, 42, 44, 135, 152
biodiversity, 20–35, 49–51, 57–8
Bird, Isabella, 20, 192
birds (also see individual species), 22–4, 26, 34, 50–1, 63–5, 71–2, 94, 100, 140, 145, 193
   song birds, 71–2
Birtwistle, William, 96–7
Blundell, E.A., 30, 43–5
Bonham, Samuel George, 53
Boomgaard, Peter, 11
Brassey, Anna, 63, 72–3, 197
British Museum (Natural History), 82–4
bubonic plague, 183–5
Buck, Frank, 65–6
buffaloes, 111–2
Bugis (ethnic group), 62, 65

bullocks, 106–7, 111–5
  bullock carts, 112–5
Burton, Edward, 127–9

Calcutta, 20, 42n, 45, 59, 78, 87,
  89, 120, 185
Carnegie, Andrew, 63–4
cats, 17, 23, 71, 81, 140n, 142, 143
cattle, 62, 106–7, 111, 118, 120–1,
  139, 194, 200–7, 210–34
  trade in, 62, 203–7
Cavenagh, W. Orfeur, 32, 45n
centipedes, 19–20, 22
Changi, 92
Chasen, F.N., 50–1, 93, 146
Cheah Hong Lim, 55
Cheeseman, A., 161, 171–2, 177,
  179, 182
chickens, 81, 144–5, 193, 197,
  203n, 232
circus, (also see individual circuses),
  65, 66, 74, 76–9, 100
class differences, conflict, 34, 45n,
  46–8, 54–5, 71n, 79, 108–9,
  119–20, 149–50, 162–6, 171,
  186, 188, 192, 206, 208, 226
Clementi, Cecil, 145–6
cockfighting, 79, 116, 121, 122n,
  145
cockroaches, 20, 91
Cocteau, Jean, 99
Cold Storage (store), 71, 224–6, 231
Corner, E.J.H., 236–41
Crawfurd, John, 22, 27, 37, 104,
  195
Cribb, Robert, 11
crocodile, 24, 31, 36, 64, 137n
Crosby, Alfred, 8
cruelty toward animals, 103–47
  as civilizational discourse, 116–47,
    204–6
  history in Britain, 117–20

De Souza, Herbert, 67
deforestation, 24–6, 28–9, 35, 49–51
dogs (also see individual breeds),
  36–48, 117, 148–83, 187–91
  as pets in Singapore, 41–2, 46–8,
    69–71, 148–50, 188–9
  culling of, 38–48, 117, 131–2,
    154–83, 187–91
  feral, 37–9, 45, 48
  licensing of, 44, 158–60
Down, S.V.B., 135–6
Dragon's Tooth, 3
Dunlop, Samuel, 125, 128, 157
Dunman, Thomas, 32, 153

East India Company, 5, 17–21, 39,
  57, 85, 88–9, 114–5, 120–1, 154
  governance, 17–8, 20, 28, 104,
    114–5, 152
  trade, 62
  transfer of sovereignty to the
    Colonial Office, 120–1, 154,
    199
elephants, 11, 64, 66n, 78, 92–3,
  95, 101, 104, 121, 240
Ellenborough Market, 196, 223, 226
Eunos Abdullah, 140–1

Falshaw, F. Scott, 135, 220, 222
Farquhar, William, 18–9, 22, 36, 85,
  87, 96, 194
fish, 1–3, 25–6, 86–7, 91
  as food, 193–7, 202–3, 229–30
  as pets, 72
Fort Canning Hill, 56, 78, 97, 208–9
Fryer Circus, 66

gambier (also see pepper), 5, 13, 18,
  25, 29, 35, 93, 114, 169
Gentle, Alexander, 134, 175

gharries, 107–10
gibbons, 56, 67, 71n, 98, 240
Green, J.L., 129
Grey, J.E., 85–7

Hampshire, F.K., 161, 166–8
Hanitsch, Richard, 83–4, 91, 93, 95
Hardwicke, Thomas, 85–7
Harmston's Circus, 77–9
Hervey, D.F.A., 122–3, 125, 126
Hooper, W.E. 136, 138, 141, 179
Hornaday, Charles, 39–40, 57–8,
    74–5
horses, 60–2, 106–11
    horse racing, 53–6
hunting, 32–5, 50, 52–3, 58, 138n
hydrophobia (also see rabies), 151
    false hydrophobia, 164n, 174
Hydrophobia Committee, 166,
    168–72

Ibrahim, Sultan of Johor, 188
Ilanun (ethnic group), 4
Illustrations of Indian Zoology, 85–7
Indian bullock drivers, 113–4
Indian convicts, 32, 40–4, 114
insects (also see individual species),
    19–21, 26, 79, 88, 237
invasive species, 27–9, 72

jackals, 27–8
Jalan Besar abattoir, 210–4, 217–8,
    223, 233–5
Javan myna, 72
Johor, 4, 26, 44, 55, 67, 78, 92–3,
    104–5, 110, 116, 119, 176, 188,
    238
Journal of the Straits (later Malayan,
    and later Malaysian) Branch of
    the Royal Asiatic Society, 94

Kampong Glam, 18n–19n, 42
Kloss, C. Boden, 82, 93–4

large flying fox, 26–7
legislation
    to protect animals, 50, 125,
        129n, 141–2, 146–7
    to regulate animals, 118–22,
        156, 165, 172, 176–7,
        185–6, 199, 203–4, 215,
        217, 229
Legislative Council, 50, 90, 120,
    138–9, 141, 145–6, 156,
    166–8, 172, 175–6, 204, 209,
    213
lesser bamboo bat, 83–4
Logan, J.R., 88, 90n, 94
    "Logan's Journal", 94
Low, James, 20, 23, 25, 33, 62–3,
    110, 112n,

macaques, 56–7, 74, 94, 236–41
Malayan Kennel Club, 188–9
Marip, Haji, 66–7, 95
markets (also see specific ones),
    62–3, 144, 146, 192–8, 214,
    223, 226
Mayer, Charles, 66–7, 77n, 92, 100
MacRitchie, James, 134, 209, 214
McNair, J.F.A., 40, 104–5
menagerie (see zoos)
menagerie race, 80–1
monkeys (also see individual species),
    23, 50n, 56–7, 64, 66, 68,
    71, 74, 77–8, 94, 80–1, 145,
    236–41
mosquitoes, 20–1
Municipal Commission, 96, 139–42,
    159–61, 170, 175, 178–9, 186,
    209–11, 217–8, 227–8, 231
municipality, 133–4

orangutans, 11, 58, 64, 74
Orchard Road, 66, 142, 153, 162, 165, 225, 196, 200, 214, 226
Orchard Road Market, 196, 214
otters, 23, 24, 72
Owen, G.P., 26, 35, 179–83
Oxley, Thomas, 22–3, 26

Paglar, E.F., 132, 135–6
parakeets, 23, 25, 63
Parameswara, 2
parrots, 63, 71, 75
Pass, Sydney Charles, 46
Pasteur, Louis, 151, 167n
Pasteur Institute, 151, 166–7, 184
pasture, lack of in Singapore, 194, 200
Prevention of Cruelty to Animals (Department, PCA), 138–42, 232–3
pangolin, 50n, 72–3
pepper, 5, 13, 18, 25, 29, 35, 169
pets, 68–73, 148–50, 188–9
pigs (also see wild boar), 9, 29, 121, 129, 139, 195–7, 200, 206, 208, 210, 212–5, 217–8, 220–3, 228–35
police, 158, 170, 182, 200
    as dog killers, 38–40, 43–4, 46, 48, 141, 153–7, 186
    assisting with cruelty cases, 123–8, 135–7, 142, 190n
Ponggol Zoo, 98–102, 239–40
pork, 193, 195–7, 210, 212–4, 217–23, 228–9, 230, 234
port facilities, 58–60
    presence of animal traders at, 62–8
population (numbers), 7
praying mantis insect, 79
Pulau Saigon, 201, 208–13, 218n, 224, 226, 228, 230, 233–5

Pulau Ubin, 88, 180n
pythons, 31, 64, 72n, 75, 101

rabies, 40, 150–83, 187–90, 204
    history of, 148–51
racial conflict, differences, 116–7, 127, 162–3, 178
    between authorities and Chinese residents, 121, 123, 130, 144–5, 171–2, 192, 195, 212–5, 226
    between authorities and Indian residents, 34, 42–3, 113–4, 123, 131–2, 192
    between authorities and Malay residents, 34, 192, 194
Raffles Hotel, 107
Raffles Library and Museum, 50, 75n, 83, 90–5, 98, 101, 146, 236
Raffles Place, 61–2, 148
Raffles, Thomas Stamford, 5, 17–8, 85, 104
    role as a collector of specimens, 21–2, 85, 87
rats, 16–9, 72n, 163, 185–6
Read, W.H.M., 53–4, 125, 194, 200
Reid, Anthony, 104, 194
Reid, Arnot, 164–5, 172, 174
rewards, for killing animals, 18–9, 31–2, 41, 43, 52, 165, 171, 175, 186
Riau, 4, 18, 82, 93–4
rickshaws, 106–7, 109
Ridley, H.N. (Henry Nicholas), 72, 83–4, 92, 94, 137–8, 164n, 174, 177, 180
Ritvo, Harriet, 9n, 10, 87, 149
Robertson, Kenneth B.S., 46–7
Rochor, 43, 67, 98, 101, 133, 139, 196, 210
Rochor River, 36, 240

Royal Society for Prevention of Cruelty to Animals (RSPCA), 119, 124–6, 146

Sang Nila Utama, 2
sanitation, 199–203, 207–8, 214, 217, 219
sanitary regime, 198–9, 235
Scidmore, Eliza, 114
scorpions, 20, 22
Seah Eng Tong, 147
Sejarah Melayu, see Sulalat al-Salatin
shipping (of animals), 110, 148–50, 204–7
shops, wild animal, 67, 71, 101, 139–41, 145–6, 232
Siam, 75, 100n, 104, 113, 203–4, 219–20,
slaughterhouse (see abattoirs)
Singapore Botanic Gardens, 47, 50, 57, 75–6, 83–4, 90–1, 137–8, 152, 236–8
zoo at, 75–6,
Singapore Dog Ordinance of 1891, 176–7
Singapore General Hospital, 161, 173, 241
Singapore River, 5, 17, 115, 196, 201, 209
Singapore Sporting Club, 53–5, 61, 79, 126
Singapore Turf Club, 54, 188
Singaporean historiography, 3–9, 12–5
pre-14th century, 3–4
pre-1819, 3–5
colonial, 4–9
Singapura Dilanggar Todak, 1–3
Smith, Cecil Clementi, 161, 175
snakes, (also see pythons), 21–3, 31, 57, 65, 145
spaniel (dog), 131, 149, 183, 188–9

SPCA (Society for the Prevention of Cruelty to Animals), 122–38, 142–7, 154n, 190, 199, 204, 228n
St. John's Island, 164, 185, 231
Straits Branch of the Royal Asiatic Society, 94
Sulalat al-Salatin, 1–3
Sumatra 2, 4, 18, 22, 59, 61, 67, 93, 98, 100, 110, 203, 229 fn, 230
swordfish, 1–3

Tan Cheng Lock, 146
Tan Tock Seng Hospital, 161, 173, 186
Tanglin, 133, 153, 164–5, 200, 217
Teluk Ayer Market, 196, 214, 216
Temonggong of Singapore, 4, 104
terrier (dog), 46, 70–1, 148–9, 152, 162, 182, 188
Thomson, John Turnbull, 20, 23, 29, 72, 110, 121, 193, 198
Thomson Road, 133, 217, 240
Tiger Club, 52–3
tigers, 11, 23, 28–36, 52–3, 58, 64, 66, 78, 92, 98, 100–1, 104–5, 137, 193, 239
trade, 58–60
animal trade, 60–7
Turnbull, C. Mary, 7–8

Van Kleef, Karl, 95–6
Van Kleef Aquarium, 96–8
Veterinary Surgeon, 142, 170–1, 188, 205n, 215–16, 220, 232

Wallace, Alfred Russel, 27n, 87–8
Warren, James, 8

Whampoa (Ho Ah Kay), 74
    menagerie at compound, 74–5
wild birds and animals protection
    ordinances, 50–1, 100
wild boar, 23, 24, 29, 33, 34, 35

zoos, 73–6, 98–102, 239–40